Economic
Institutional Change in
Tokugawa Japan

Economic Institutional Change in Tokugawa Japan

Ōsaka and the Kinai Cotton Trade

WILLIAM B. HAUSER

Cambridge University Press

Published by the Syndics of the Cambridge University Press
Bentley House, 200 Euston Road, London NW1 2DB
American Branch: 32 East 57th Street, New York, N.Y. 10022

© Cambridge University Press 1974

Library of Congress Catalogue Card Number: 73–80478

ISBN: 0 521 20302 3

First published 1974

Printed in Great Britain
by Cox & Wyman Ltd
London, Fakenham and Reading

To my parents
Philip M. Hauser and Zelda B. Hauser

Contents

Tables

Maps

Acknowledgments

Many persons have contributed to the successful completion of this study. My greatest debts are to John Whitney Hall, A. Whitney Griswold Professor of Far Eastern History at Yale University. He supervised the dissertation phase of this study, offered valuable criticism of the form and content of that early version, and has been a regular source of advice and encouragement since its completion. In Japan, I was privileged to study with Professor Miyamoto Mataji, formerly of the Faculty of Economics, Ōsaka University, and now of Kansai Gakuin University. Professor Miyamoto offered an inexhaustible source of bibliographic assistance and an introduction to the community of Japanese economic historians. Professor Sakudō Yōtarō, of the Faculty of Economics, Ōsaka University, provided assistance with documentary problems during my dissertation research. Professor Uda Tadashi, now of Otemon University, and Mr Takahashi Kyūichi, now at Kōbe University, kindly helped with my study of Tokugawa Japanese. Professor Yasuoka Shigeaki of Dōshisha University was of invaluable assistance with problems of interpretation associated with both the thesis and this monograph. He, and other members of the Miyamoto group, offered encouragement and assistance during my studies at Ōsaka University in 1965–6 and in subsequent visits to Japan in 1969 and 1972.

At the University of Michigan I have benefited from the ideas of Professors Richard K. Beardsley, Robert E. Cole, Gary Saxonhouse, Yoshihara Kunio, Albert Feuerwerker, Ernest P. Young, Roger F. Hackett, and countless others. Professor Cole kindly read drafts of Chapters 6, 7, and 8 and offered helpful suggestions for revision. Professor Bernard Susser, of Northern Illinois University, read the dissertation version of this study and offered useful suggestions for revision. Professor E. S. Crawcour, of Australian National University, provided interpretive and bibliographic insights. His own work on Tokugawa economic history first attracted me to this area of involvement. Many others offered their time and suggestions for this monograph. The officers of Cambridge University Press provided useful critiques of the original manuscript and had the patience and confidence to wait for the present version, and the staff edited and improved the overall presentation.

This, like all long-term undertakings, would never have been completed without financial assistance. My parents provided encouragement and generous support during my years of graduate study. Yale University supported me for several years and the United States Educational Commission in Japan provided a Fulbright Fellowship for two years of study in Japan. The Center for Japanese Studies of the University of Michigan provided several summer fellowships and support for a three-month stay in Japan in 1969. The Horace H. Rackham School of Graduate Studies, University of Michigan, assisted with research grants to cover the cost of typing and other expenses and supported a six-week stay in Japan in 1972. During the academic year 1971–2, the National Endowment for the Humanities awarded a Younger Humanist Fellowship, Grant Number F-71-233, which enabled me to pursue the writing and research of this study full-time. Without this year of uninterrupted work this monograph might never have been completed.

Fundamental to this study was the availability of an excellent Japanese library at the University of Michigan. I owe a great debt to the past and present staff of the Asia Library, University of Michigan, for their development of this remarkable collection. Other collections used in the United States included the Orientalia Division of the Library of Congress, the Asia Library of Yale University, and the Harvard Yenching Library. In Japan, my major research was done at the National Diet Library in Tōkyō. In addition I used the Ōsaka University Library, the Ōsaka Prefectural Library, the Ōsaka Municipal Library, and the library at the Ōsaka Chamber of Commerce and Industry. I also had access to the personal collections of Professor Miyamoto Mataji, Sakudō Yōtarō, Horie Yasuzō, and Yasuoka Shigeaki. I am extremely grateful for the assistance I received from each of the above collections.

The maps included in this study were prepared by Professor Robert D. Robertson of Wittenberg University. The manuscript was typed by Mrs Marguerite Schaible. Proofreading was assisted by Robert Borgen, James McClain, and Susan Lester Hauser.

All those who offered support and encouragement for this study could not possibly be enumerated. I am grateful for their interest, but assume full responsibility for all errors of content and interpretation contained in the final result.

W.B.H.

University of Michigan
May 1973

1 Introduction

The rapid development of Japan into a modern nation, beginning with its forced opening in 1853 and continuing down to the present, has focused considerable attention on the 'miraculous' transformation of this formerly 'feudal' Asian country into a modern industrialized state. The 'economic miracle' of Japan's recovery from the devastation of the Pacific War, like the 'miracle' of her rapid industrial development in the late nineteenth and twentieth centuries, reflects a combination of Western attitudes concerning the potential of Asian peoples and some fundamental misconceptions about the pre-conditions which enabled these developments to come to fruition. Just as economists have reinterpreted modern economic growth to take into consideration factors such as education and social institutions and have placed less emphasis on material resources, so have historians revised their interpretations of the nature of Japanese society during the Tokugawa period (1600–1868) prior to the Meiji era and the 'modernization of Japan'. Both processes of revision contribute to our understanding of why Japan, alone among non-Western nations, was able from the early twentieth century to participate as an equal in the world community. Economists and historians alike have noted the particular social and institutional factors which distinguish the modern Japanese experience from that of other non-Western nations.

Increasingly, revisionist interpretations of the Japanese experience conclude that neither European nor American models of economic development effectively explain the emergence of Japan as a major world power. This has resulted in a broadening of interest in the traditional base from which Japan's industrial and political development began. But, as a consequence, many studies of the Tokugawa period are distorted by their concern with the forces which lay behind the overthrow of Tokugawa 'feudalism and despotism' and resulted in the emergence of what is termed a militaristic, modern, or highly industrialized nation. Many Japanese scholars emphasize the militaristic aspect of the Japanese experience and have searched into the Tokugawa period for the roots of the authoritarian tendencies which they feel inexorably led to the humiliation of Japan in the Pacific War. Western historians, impressed with the remarkable progress of Japan and her transition into a powerful member of the world community, tend instead to emphasize elements of the Tokugawa period which contributed to modernization or industrialization.

The present study focuses on processes of social and institutional change which occurred during the Tokugawa period, but within the Tokugawa context rather than as the basis for subsequent developments. It is not its intention to analyze the causes of Tokugawa decline or point out the underpinnings of modern economic growth. Instead, it is a case study of economic institutional change in Ōsaka and three provinces of the surrounding Kinai region. Incorporating the major cities of Ōsaka and Kyōto and the provinces of Settsu, Kawachi, Izumi, Yamato, and Yamashiro, the Kinai region was the most economically advanced area of Tokugawa Japan and offers an excellent regional focus for this type of study.

This study was motivated by a number of considerations. To begin with, Japanese commercial activity changed significantly during the Tokugawa period. This was associated with increased urbanization and the need to supply the commodity requirements of urban residents and with the shift to a peacetime economy after a century of intermittent warfare. These factors contributed to the rapid expansion of trade during the Tokugawa period. Second, the rapid expansion of commerce resulted in the formation of new kinds of commercial institutions. The cotton trade in Ōsaka and the Kinai region illustrates many of them. Third, the structure of the Tokugawa political order and the concentration of trade in major cities made the urban merchants partially dependent on the goodwill of the government. Close ties developed between commercial groups and local political authorities. This study of the cotton trade indicates how these relationships changed over time. Finally, over the course of the Tokugawa period marketing patterns shifted from small-scale local marketing units to a focus on major urban centers and finally to a national system of commodity distribution with both urban and rural foci of marketing activity. The Kinai cotton trade offers examples of this transformation. By concentrating on the institutions associated with the marketing of cotton in Ōsaka and the Kinai provinces of Settsu, Kawachi, and Izumi, it is possible to analyze in detail changes in Tokugawa commerce.

The selection of the Kinai cotton trade as the focus of this study resulted from several qualifications. To begin with, there is abundant published documentation on Ōsaka and the Kinai region. Second, cotton was a major commercial crop in the provinces of Settsu, Kawachi, and Izumi, and both cotton farming and cotton-related by-employment had a major impact on village life in Kinai. Third, during the Tokugawa period cotton became the primary fiber used in Japanese textiles. With the expansion of cotton cultivation came increased demand for cotton cloth to clothe both urban and rural members of Japanese society. Consequently, cotton became an important staple commodity and was marketed throughout Tokugawa

Japan. Finally, the marketing system for cotton in Ōsaka and the Kinai region changed significantly between the mid-seventeenth and the mid-nineteenth centuries and offers an excellent focal point for a study of monopoly and competitition in Tokugawa commerce.

This study is divided into eight chapters: an introduction, six chapters which view economic institutional change from three perspectives, and a conclusion. Chapters 2 and 3 describe the characteristics of commercial activity during the Tokugawa period. Concentrating on Ōsaka and the Kinai region, and to a lesser extent Edo (modern Tōkyō) and the surrounding Kantō region, it examines the expansion of trade, the growth of marketing systems, and the appearance of functional differentiation in the mercantile community. An effort is made to illustrate the interaction of government policy and institutional changes in the commercial sector of society. These two chapters establish the context, in political, economic, and social terms, in which trade was conducted during the Tokugawa period.

Chapters 4 and 5 are a detailed study of the Ōsaka cotton trade. The growth of Ōsaka as a center for marketing and processing cotton and the development of merchant groups to establish trade rights and business procedures are treated. Interaction between the merchant associations and the Ōsaka city government is shown to pass through several stages of evolution. Finally, the growth of new sources of competition and efforts to preserve the trade rights of the Ōsaka merchants are viewed from the perspective of the Ōsaka commercial community.

Chapters 6 and 7 expand the inquiry into the towns and villages of Settsu, Kawachi, and Izumi. Chapter 6 is concerned with the expansion of cotton cultivation in Kinai, its impact on land utilization and cropping patterns, and the attractions, costs, and risks of cotton farming. The village perspective on cotton cultivation and cotton-related by-employment is presented. Chapter 7 describes the growth of the Kinai cotton trade. The roles played by rural merchants and cotton cultivators are shown to change in the late eighteenth and nineteenth centuries as they increasingly challenged the monopoly rights of the Ōsaka cotton merchants. The process of institutional change described from the Ōsaka perspective in Chapters 4 and 5 is reinterpreted from the viewpoint of the cotton cultivators and rural cotton merchants.

In the final chapter the implications of this study for economic and social change during the Tokugawa period are enumerated, and generalizations suggested by this case study are applied to our understanding of early modern Japan. The dynamics of economic institutional change, as illustrated by the Kinai cotton trade, are viewed as being characteristic of Japanese society during the Tokugawa period. Finally, the impact of these changes on traditional Japan are suggested as are their implications for modern economic growth and industrialization.

THE WESTERN HISTORIOGRAPHIC CONTEXT

This case study of the Kinai cotton trade is an attempt to present a micro-study of economic institutional change in Tokugawa Japan. It combines a synthesis of Japanese scholarship on Tokugawa economic history – particularly commercial history – with detailed examinations of the Ōsaka and Kinai cotton trades. Recent Japanese scholarship and published local histories were used for both the comprehensive discussion of Tokugawa commerce and the case studies. As a result, my findings in the Ōsaka and Kinai examples are shown to be consistent with current Japanese interpretations of Tokugawa economic history.

The need for a study of this kind was recently suggested by Kozo Yamamura in a review article entitled 'Agenda for Asian Economic History.'[1] Professor Yamamura notes that the dramatic increase in Japanese academic interest in Tokugawa economic history has not resulted in similar activity by Western scholars. For example, the major monograph in English on Tokugawa economic history, Charles David Sheldon's *The Rise of the Merchant Class in Tokugawa Japan: 1600–1868*, includes in its bibliography only seven Japanese-language studies published after 1950 – the most recent from 1956 – and most of the works cited were published prior to the Pacific War.[2] Further, this study views the Tokugawa period as a series of conflicts between urban and feudal influences and associates the rise of the merchant class with the decline of the Tokugawa shogunate. This greatly oversimplifies a complex process of economic and social change and is inconsistent with the results of current scholarship. While more recent Japanese studies are reflected in the work of E. S. Crawcour and Kozo Yamamura, neither offers a comprehensive view of recent work on Japanese commercial history.[3]

Evidence of the changing interpretations of Tokugawa economic history in Japan can be found in a bibliographic review article by Susan B. Hanley and Kozo Yamamura.[4] But this offers a guide to recent Japanese publications rather than a review of current interpretations in Japan. Chapters 2 and 3 of this book, based in part on works cited by Professors Hanley and Yamamura, attempt to fill a portion of this gap in the English-language bibliography.

Japanese agricultural history in English is largely dependent on the publications of Thomas C. Smith. His monograph *The Agrarian Origins of Modern Japan* is a comprehensive study of Japanese villages in transition during the Tokugawa period.[5] Professor Smith has also published articles on Japanese villages, the land tax system, and farm family by-employments during the Tokugawa period.[6] In addition are studies by William Jones Chambliss, Chie Nakane, Harumi Befu, and Susan B. Hanley, the last of whom examines demographic changes in a Japanese village.[7] Each of these works has contributed to our knowledge of Japanese rural history. My study differs from them in its concentration on the cultivation, processing, and marketing of a single commodity – cotton – and its concern with the changing nature of these processes.

Other studies of Japanese economic history deal in part with the Tokugawa period. For example, Henry Rosovsky's *Capital Formation in Japan, 1868–1940* includes a section on the traditional sector of the economy and discusses aspects of Tokugawa economic history.[8] Johannes Hirschmeier's study *The Origins of Entrepreneurship in Meiji Japan* also deals in part with the Tokugawa background to modern entrepreneurial activities in Japan.[9] 'The Tokugawa Heritage' which underlay the economic development of Japan is discussed in article by E. S. Crawcour.[10] While this listing is by no means comprehensive, it illustrates the range of English-language scholarship on Tokugawa economic history. In none of these studies is a regional case study integrated into an examination of the institutional transformation of urban and rural trade. This study is an effort to supply an inquiry of this type and expand our knowledge of economic and social change in pre-industrial Japan.

This examination of economic and social change in Tokugawa Japan investigates evidence of institutional change from three perspectives. The first is by means of a discussion of Tokugawa commerce, with emphasis on the growth of urban market centers and the expansion of Ōsaka into the major market city in the Kinai region and western Japan. Second is the analysis of the Ōsaka cotton trade, focusing on the marketing of cotton goods in the city of Ōsaka. Third is the treatment of the expansion of cotton cultivation and the diffusion of cotton processing and marketing activities in the Kinai provinces of Settsu, Kawachi, and Izumi. Each section attempts to discuss the period from the mid-seventeenth century to the mid-nineteenth from a different perspective. Those topics treated from all three viewpoints are particularly important to the overall analysis. The object of covering the entire period from three different angles, with some unavoidable duplication, is to broaden the scope of the inquiry.

Throughout this study, a major concern is the delineation of social change in an historical perspective. Each formalizing of an institution is viewed not as the termination of a process of change but rather as a further step in a continuous process of social change. The transformation of economic and social institutions is seen as an ongoing action in which the form and function of institutions are regularly modified or reinterpreted. This inquiry is viewed as a study of Tokugawa commercial history in particular and of economic and social change in more general terms. I hope that the result offers new insights into the transitional nature of the Japanese tradition.[11]

One stylistic point which may confuse some readers is the use of dates in the text. The pre-modern Japanese calendar is divided into year periods of uneven length and is based on phases of the moon rather than on solar cycles. Consequently, translating Japanese dates involves first determining the proper year in the Gregorian calendar and then translating lunar months and days into solar-based units. This is a time-consuming process, and I believe that the dates referred to in the text are not sufficiently important to justify the effort. Consequently, only the years are translated into the Gregorian calendar. Thus 1841/6/11 refers to the eleventh day of the sixth lunar month of the traditional Japanese calendar of the Gregorian year 1841. In the few cases where the translation is complete, 1841/6/11 reads 28 July 1841. Readers who wish complete translations of dates are advised to use a set of Japanese chronological tables for assistance.[12]

2 Tokugawa Commerce: 1600-1720

ŌSAKA IN THE 'BAKUHAN' SYSTEM

Comprehension of the economic history of Japan during the Tokugawa period requires that the political framework within which all economic activity took place first be described. The consolidation of Tokugawa power and the unification of the country under the Tokugawa shogunate after 1603 were based on a balance of authority between the Tokugawa house including its immediate vassals and that exercised by the daimyo. The country was divided into areas directly controlled by the Tokugawa house (*chokkatsuryō*) and independent domains (*han*) administered by the daimyo. In addition, some areas were assigned to major religious institutions and for the support of the imperial nobility, but the scale of these holdings was sufficiently small to make them of minimal significance. In both the shogunate – the locus of national political power – and the daimyo governments – the locus of local authority within the *han* – fiscal requirements were supplied from tax revenues collected within the directly administered territories. No system by which the shogunate could regularly tax the daimyo was in operation. The shogunate was completely dependent on the revenues produced by Tokugawa lands, the profits from mines, currency debasement, and special exactions for its normal operations and expenditures.

Structurally, the Tokugawa political order is normally referred to as the *bakuhan* system. The term combines the Tokugawa *bakufu* (shogunate) and the daimyo *han* and suggests the division of authority between these two forms of political control. Within their own territories each possessed comparable political authority, the primary differences being *bakufu* control over foreign trade and issues of national significance. In addition, the Tokugawa house had the authority to certify daimyo claims to their domains and legitimate succession within the daimyo houses.[1]

Surveillance of the daimyo was a primary concern of the Tokugawa *bakufu*. To facilitate control a system of alternate attendance, the *sankin kōtai*, was required of all daimyo by the shogunate. Supervision included a requirement that the daimyo maintain permanent residences in the shogunal capital at Edo (modern Tōkyō), that their wives and children be resident in the capital city, and that they and a group of their retainers alternate between the shogunal capital and the castle town of their domains on a

7

fixed schedule. This policy combined political control with fiscal requirements which were designed to prevent the daimyo from amassing excessive funds within their domains, for the costs of the ceremonial processions to and from Edo and the maintenance of families and retainers in the city placed a considerable drain on *han* finances.[2]

In addition to assuring the subservience of the daimyo, the *sankin kōtai* system also tended to have a stimulating effect on the economy as a whole. By requiring the daimyo to spend a large portion of their revenues outside their domains, the fiscal demands of the system indirectly encouraged the growth of a transportation network to ship tax revenues, normally paid in kind, to the central cities where they were sold for cash. The cash acquired was used for the expenses of the *sankin kōtai* system as well as other expenses for which payments in kind were inconvenient.

Ōsaka, located in the heartland of Japanese cultural development, with easy access to water-borne transport and close to the imperial capital at Kyōto, was a natural site for the development of a commercial marketing complex. The city had served as a port of entry for missions from Korea and a port of embarkation for expeditions to Korea and had been the site of a temporary imperial capital prior to the erection of the first permanent capital at Nara in the early eighth century. The modern history of Ōsaka began in 1496 when it was chosen as the location for the Ishiyama Honganji temple by the Buddhist monk Rennyō Shōnin. Surrounded on the north and east by rivers and by the sea to the west and situated on the primary land and water routes leading to Kyōto from western Japan, Ōsaka offered an excellent location for a branch temple for the *Ikkō* (single-minded) sect.[3]

From the time of Rennyō's death in 1499 until 1532 little is known about the Ishiyama temple at Ōsaka. A town grew before the gates of the temple and it expanded dramatically in 1532 when the main Ishiyama temple in Kyōto was overrun by rivals and the survivors fled to Ōsaka. The temple was then heavily fortified and became the new main temple of the *Ikkō* sect. Lying outside of the immediate Kyōto area and occupying a strategic position relative to the imperial capital, the Ishiyama Honganji at Ōsaka expanded rapidly as a temple and fortress between 1533 and 1580. Merchants and artisans migrated to the city and the *Ikkō* leaders expanded their military and political influence in the Kinai region.[4]

In 1580 the *Ikkō* concentration of power at Ōsaka was shattered. Oda Nobunaga, in his quest to pacify and unify the country, managed to overwhelm the *Ikkō* defenders and forced them to abandon their stronghold. The fortress was given over to Ikeda Nobuteru and subsequently given to Toyotomi Hideyoshi after Nobunaga's death in 1582. Utilizing the strategic location as a means of extending his influence in the Kinai area, Hideyoshi built a new and formidable castle on the site of the former Honganji temple.[5]

Under Toyotomi control the city expanded and had a revenue base of approximately 5000 *koku* of rice.[6] Daimyo closely associated with Hideyoshi constructed residences near the castle as a symbol of their loyalty to his authority. As the city increased in size and importance new lands were reclaimed and incorporated and canals dug to improve water-borne transport. By 1615 and the second battle of Ōsaka castle, when the Tokugawa obliterated the Toyotomi house and the last major source of organized opposition to its control, the city was well provided with internal waterways and had developed into an important market center.[7]

During the first quarter of the seventeenth century Ōsaka developed into a central rice market for western Japan. Hideyoshi had shipped rice from Shikoku to Ōsaka prior to his death in 1598. In preparation for the confrontation with the Tokugawa in 1614–15 great quantities of rice were collected from western Japan, Kyūshū, and the Kinai region and stored in the city. There is some question as to whether Ōsaka was already a major rice market by 1615 or whether the collection of vast quantities of rice in the city was singularly related to the impending battle. There is evidence that the quantity of rice received in Ōsaka in 1614–15 was less than normal, the result of a partial blockade set up by Ieyasu to divert rice to nearby Amagasaki.[8] But the establishment of Ōsaka as a major rice market may have followed the transition to Tokugawa control of the city.

Following the fall of Ōsaka castle to the Tokugawa forces it was given over to Matsudaira Tadaaki, a Tokugawa collateral whose domain it remained from 1615 to 1619. He encouraged the former merchant residents of the city to return, initiated a reconstruction program, and invited merchant residents of other cities including Fushimi to settle in Ōsaka.[9] Reconstruction of the city progressed rapidly and new canals were opened to improve internal transport facilities. The canals were financed and constructed by merchant groups who realized their importance to the development of trade.[10]

In 1619 Matsudaira Tadaaki was transferred to a domain at Yamato Koriyama and Ōsaka was made directly administered Tokugawa territory. Reconstruction and development of the city continued and various daimyo governments worked together with the *bakufu* to expand and improve the city. Both Satsuma and Tosa *han* constructed canals in the city which improved the sites of the markets used for sales of *han* goods. Because of Tosa's role in developing the lumber market, Tosa *han* lumber received special priority in subsequent market transactions.[11]

During the three decades following the battles of Ōsaka, the city was reconstructed and expanded as a market center. Although the city was initially developed as a political and military center by Hideyoshi, the Tokugawa encouraged its growth as a major market complex. This was emphasized when in 1634 the third shogun Tokugawa Iemitsu visited

Ōsaka and, as evidence of his satisfaction with the growth of the city as a commercial center, exempted it from all land tax payments to the *bakufu*. This absolved property owners in the city from regular tax obligations to the shogunate and added to their financial flexibility. To symbolize their gratitude the Ōsaka *chōnin* (townsmen) erected a bell tower to sound the time in the city.[12] Many of the merchants in the city assisted the *bakufu* in expanding Ōsaka and were rewarded for their efforts with special privileges of social status and local advisory rights, similar to those enjoyed by the purveyors to the daimyo in the latter half of the sixteenth century.[13]

As the reconstruction of Ōsaka continued, it began to replace other cities in the Kinai region in commercial importance. Under Hideyoshi many of the merchants from the formerly independent city of Sakai had been encouraged to migrate to Ōsaka and Sakai had declined in importance. Under Tokugawa control this process was continued and merchants were also encouraged to move to Ōsaka from the garrison town of Fushimi near Kyōto. In 1619 the *bakufu* razed Fushimi castle and moved the guard to Ōsaka, thus assuring the decline of Fushimi as a major power center and adding further to the expansion of Ōsaka. By the 1640s the position of Ōsaka in Kinai commerce had been greatly expanded and many local market towns which had formerly enjoyed close ties with the rural population had been displaced in importance. Towns like Amagasaki and Sakai decreased in importance as Ōsaka absorbed their function as markets for dried sardines, used for fertilizer, and other commodities.[14]

Internally, Ōsaka was divided into three administrative sections (*kumi*) and subsidiary residential neighborhoods (*machi*). Each of the residential neighborhoods had local officials appointed from among the *chōnin* who presided over the transmission of official notices, kept census records, settled minor law suits, oversaw property transfers, and controlled fires. These officials were appointed from among the property owning residents of the *machi* and were approved by high officials at the *kumi* level of city administration. The administrative hierarchy of Ōsaka included two city magistrates. Serving in alternate months, the eastern and western city magistrates took turns in taking responsibility for the administration of the entire city. A similar situation existed in Edo where administrative control alternated between the northern and southern city magistrates.[15]

Chōnin referred to urban residents who were not members of the samurai class. In the strictest sense it referred to urban property owners. It was the propertied *chōnin* who served as the officials within the *machi*. All others were excluded from administrative participation and from responsibility to the neighborhood offices for local expenses. The non-property owners included individuals who rented land, stores, or houses; often lived in lodging houses; and were the small shopkeepers, employees, service personnel, peddlers, entertainers, artisans, and laborers of the city.[16]

Many *machi* were united by occupational ties as well as by proximity. In many towns including Ōsaka, some of the neighborhoods were named for the merchant or artisan groups concentrated within their boundaries. These included neighborhoods of fish merchants; vegetable merchants; rice dealers; drygoods, paper, oil, lumber, or horse traders; lodging houses; and peddlers. Artisan neighborhoods included those for dyers, carpenters, tile makers, *tatami* mat makers, stone cutters, blacksmiths, coopers, and other craftsmen.[17] In neighborhoods of this kind, the tie of trade or occupation securely bound the *chōnin* together. This enabled the city government to control commerce or handicraft industries through the neighborhood administrative structure. When *chōnin* established their own groupings, they did not normally take the form of community living patterns. This kind of occupational grouping in neighborhoods, particularly for merchants, was more in the interest of the city government than of the traders themselves.[18]

With few exceptions, the major cities of the Tokugawa period were the castle towns of the daimyo and the shogun. Castle town construction concentrated the samurai around the daimyo strongholds and separated them from the rural cultivators.[19] Underlying this process of urban development was the separation of production and consumption, a condition which developed throughout the wars of unification in the sixteenth century and which was predicated on the increased production of the rural cultivators. Before castle towns could be maintained, it was necessary for the agricultural population to be able to supply them with sufficient foodstuffs to provision a large group of non-agricultural warrior-bureaucrats and their associated service personnel.[20]

Castle towns had to satisfy the military requirements of the daimyo and their retainers, the daily living requirements of the samurai class, the financial needs of the ruling class, and the marketing needs of an urban center. Merchants and artisans were collected in the cities to fulfill these needs and were thus separated from the cultivators in the villages and kept apart from the samurai in the cities by being placed in special neighborhoods within the castle towns.[21] Daimyo, in their eagerness to attract merchants and artisans to their castle towns, offered liberal conditions and the attractions of newly developed and expanding markets. The castle towns consequently became the economic centers of the domains and the former market towns tended to be displaced and declined in importance.[22]

ŌSAKA IN THE SEVENTEENTH CENTURY

The growth of Ōsaka as a commercial center was initially related to its function as an exchange market for daimyo tax rice. During the first quarter

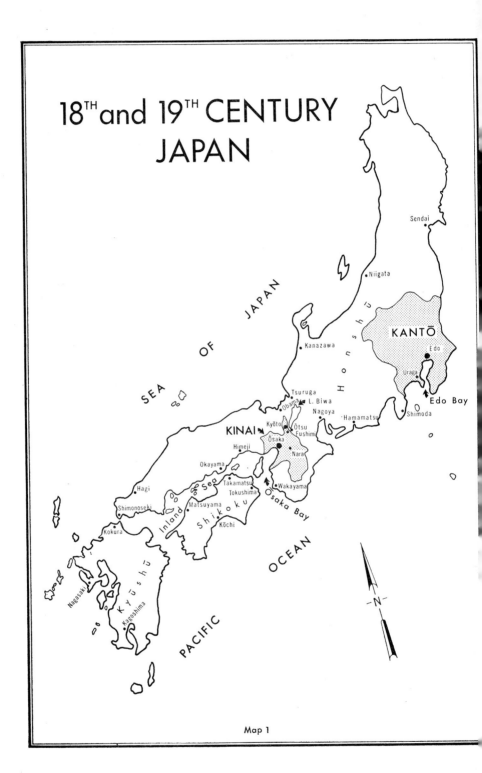

18TH and 19TH CENTURY JAPAN

Sendai

Niigata

SEA OF JAPAN

Kanazawa

Honshū

KANTŌ

Edo

Uraga

Edo Bay

Tsuruga

Obama

L. Biwa

Nagoya

Hamamatsu

Shimoda

Kyōto

Ōtsu

Fushimi

KINAI

Ōsaka

Himeji

Nara

Okayama

Wakayama

Hagi

Takamatsu

Tokushima

Osaka Bay

Shimonoseki

Inland Sea

Matsuyama

Shikoku

Kōchi

Kokura

Kyūshū

PACIFIC

OCEAN

Nagasaki

Kagoshima

N

Map 1

of the seventeenth century Ōsaka became important as a major rice market in western Japan. Daimyo from western Honshū, Kyūshū, and Shikoku shipped large quantities of tax rice to Ōsaka, while those along the Japan Sea coast sent rice to Tsuruga or Obama from which it was transported overland and on Lake Biwa to the rice markets of Ōtsu, Kyōto, and Fushimi. As can be seen in Map 1 there were thus two independent routes to the major population centers in the Kinai region.[23]

The quantity of rice shipped to the Kinai region during the first quarter of the seventeenth century is estimated to have been as high as one million *koku* annually.[24] Total national rice production at the end of the sixteenth century is estimated to have been around eighteen and one-half million *koku*, illustrating the importance of the Kinai rice markets.[25] As the *bakuhan* system was consolidated and Ōsaka came to dominate the Kinai market, both the volume of rice shipped to Kinai and the proportion which was received in Ōsaka increased. The importance of the Ōsaka rice market is illustrated by the construction of 111 daimyo rice warehouses in the city by 1626.[26]

As the role of Ōsaka as a major market for daimyo rice sales expanded, the city also developed as a market center for other commodities. Associated with this process were the appearance of new kinds of specialized merchants within Ōsaka and changes in the institutional structure of the Ōsaka market. Characteristic of the increasing functional differentiation within the Ōsaka market was the appearance of merchants known as *tonya*. *Tonya*, pronounced *toiya* in Ōsaka, were individual merchants or merchant houses. Some served as wholesale merchants, consignment agents, or receiving agents, while others supervised processing industries or served as shipping agents. *Tonya* thus referred to a wide variety of merchant types. It should be kept in mind, however, that *tonya* designated individual traders, for example the ten cotton *tonya*, but did not designate a group of merchants joined in an association. Groups were known as *nakama* or *kumiai*, and groups of *tonya* were often joined in *tonya nakama* or *tonya kumiai*. The lack of precision in Japanese and the fact that nouns can be either singular or plural has led to considerable confusion in the use of *tonya* in the Western bibliography.[27]

During the early seventeenth century, very few merchants in Ōsaka called themselves *tonya*. At this point, there was little need to differentiate between functional levels in the marketing process. Among the earliest recorded *tonya* were the Kyōguchi and Edoguchi oil *tonya*, mentioned in 1616 and 1617 respectively, both of which shipped oil from Ōsaka to Kyōto or Edo. By 1624 *tonya* had appeared for fresh produce and fish, salted fish, carp, lumber, and cotton goods. Thirty-two fresh produce *tonya* moved to the Temma district of Ōsaka in 1652. *Nakagai*, intermediary merchants or jobbers, did not become prevalent in Ōsaka until the 1680s, suggesting that market *tonya* did not yet function as true wholesalers at this stage of development.[28]

Another seventeenth-century development was the organization of some trades into *nakama* associations by the *bakufu* as a means of placing controls over their activities. These included pawnbrokers, second-hand dealers, old gold and copper traders, and the imported silk (*ito wappu*) merchants. Trades which established specialty *tonya* during this period were extremely limited. If occupations concerned with foreign trade or subject to close police surveillance are excluded, all of the trades for which functional differentiation had begun to appear were exclusively related to the production and consumption requirements of Ōsaka and its immediate vicinity. These included food and other daily necessities, agricultural fertilizers such as dried sardines, and lumber consumed in urban construction.[29]

The commercial ties between Ōsaka and other areas of Japan during the first half of the seventeenth century are difficult to describe because of fragmentary documentation and the lack of an institutionalized marketing mechanism. Ōsaka had emerged as a major rice market for western Japan, but the associations between Ōsaka and points east, particularly Edo, are unclear. There is evidence that some goods from Ōsaka were shipped to Edo early in the century, and a document of 1619 asserts that cotton cloth, seed cotton, oil, *sake*, vinegar, and soy sauce were shipped to the shogunal capital by sea.[30] The volume of this trade or its importance for supplying the consumption requirements of Edo cannot presently be estimated. There is evidence that Edo was being supplied with grains, firewood, charcoal, bean paste, fish oil, and salt from the Kantō region and eastern Japan by the first half of the seventeenth century. These commodities did not require the application of complex processing technology and were produced in agricultural or fishing villages. Goods which required sophisticated processing technology such as ginned cotton, cotton cloth, *sake*, and soy sauce were largely supplied to Edo from the Kinai region, the most advanced section of the country in terms of processing industries and commercial agricultural development.[31]

The roles of Ōsaka as a national market center and as a major supplier of Edo are more clearly evident in the second half of the seventeenth century. With the consolidation of Tokugawa control and the regularization of the *sankin kōtai* system, it was increasingly necessary for a major market center to assist in the marketing of not only tax rice revenues but also other goods produced in the *han* of western Japan. Ōsaka emerged as the best location for such a market with the expansion and regularization of shipping facilities to and from the city in the 1660s and 1670s.[32]

The improvement of seagoing transportation to and from Ōsaka was initiated by the *bakufu* under the direction of the ambitious and imaginative merchant Kawamura Zuiken. Under *bakufu* sponsorship Kawamura regularized shipping routes from the Japan Sea around the western end of Honshū and along the Inland Sea to Ōsaka – known as the westward route (*nishi mawari*) – and also along an eastward route (*higashi mawari*) from the Japan Sea coast around the eastern end of Honshū and then down the Pacific coast to Edo. In addition there were improvements in shipments from Ōsaka to Edo. These routes were critical to the emergence of both Ōsaka and Edo as major market centers.[33]

Kawamura was commissioned by the *bakufu* to organize rice shipments from northern Honshū to Edo in 1670. Following the success of this project, he was commissioned to develop longer routes from the Japan Sea coast, as he proved effectively that with good management shipping losses and costs could be greatly reduced.[34] Kawamura proved that if crews were carefully selected, good bottoms employed, harbor taxes waived, and weather restrictions and disaster relief facilities provided, large volumes of rice could be safely shipped at low cost. He also arranged for markets to be constructed along the routes, established a lighthouse and pilot boats in the Strait of Shimonoseki, and arranged for daimyo protection of the shipping routes near their domains.[35] As the result of Kawamura's activities, the water link from the Japan Sea coast to Ōsaka and the one from Ōsaka to Edo improved greatly during the 1670s.[36]

Prior to the development of the westward sea route the ports of Tsuruga and Obama on the Japan Sea had been tied to the Kinai region by a route which went overland to Lake Biwa, down the lake by water to Ōtsu, and from there to Kyōto and Fushimi. Rice was the major commodity transported over this route and during the 1650s and 1660s around one million bags of rice passed through Tsuruga and Obama annually. The success of the westward shipping route greatly diminished the importance of this route from the Japan Sea to Ōtsu as it was far cheaper to take the longer route around the western end of Honshū to Ōsaka than to pay the loading and unloading fees and overland costs of the shorter route to Ōtsu and Kyōto. This led to a decline in rice shipments to Tsuruga from the 1670s through 1690s as daimyo moved their rice warehouses to Ōsaka, and increasingly trade via Tsuruga was limited to goods moving between the provinces of Ōmi and Mino and parts of northern Honshū along the Japan Sea.[37] Even Kyōto declined as a market for agricultural commodities as Ōsaka with its superior transport facilities increased in importance.[38]

Expansion of the Ōsaka market accelerated with the success of the westward shipping route. For example, Kaga and Tsugaru *han* on the Japan Sea greatly increased the volume of rice which they shipped to Ōsaka in the 1670s and Ōsaka became a major rice market not only for western Japan but for the Japan Sea area as well.[39] As Ōsaka increased in importance as a market center the city increased in size as well, so that by the 1670s and 1680s it is estimated that the population of Ōsaka was over 300 000.[40]

Related to the expansion of the Ōsaka market was the improvement in credit and banking facilities within the city. An association of money changers was authorized by the *bakufu* in 1662 and a ten-man group was formed in 1670 to coordinate and oversee banking operations.[41] The lack of a unified currency in the early Tokugawa period, a persistent shortage of currency throughout the period, and the use of a silver standard in the Kinai region and westward while a gold standard was in use in Edo and eastern Japan necessitated the development of relatively sophisticated banking facilities. Credit facilities were also required by the merchant community and the daimyo for loans and transfers of credit from one location to another.[42]

By the 1640s money changers in Ōsaka, Kyōto, and Edo were accepting deposits and making loans. Although no interest was paid on deposits, advances were made at an interest rate of around 15 percent per annum. When the money changers in Ōsaka organized into an authorized *nakama* in 1662, they were well on their way to becoming bankers. Notes in the form of deposit receipts were issued, and by the 1650s they were widely circulating in Ōsaka. The establishment of a ten-man group of bankers in Ōsaka in 1670 regularized banking procedures and coordinated all money changers into a centralized institutional structure.[43]

Characteristic of the latter half of the seventeenth century was the increase in *tonya* merchants and associated commercial institutions in Ōsaka. *Tonya* for rice, vegetables, fish, and lumber had appeared in the first half of the century, oil *tonya* by 1616–17, and a cotton market by the 1640s. Outside of dealers in these commodities, used goods dealers, and pawnbrokers, differentiated market systems with specialized *tonya* and *nakama* were not established until after 1650.[44]

Many of the *tonya* active during the first half of the seventeenth century had been of the receiving *tonya* (*niuke tonya*) type. Receiving *tonya* handled a variety of goods, often produced in the same area, and did not concentrate on specific commodities. During the second half of the century a new type of specialized *tonya* dealing with particular commodities developed alongside the receiving *tonya*. Increasingly, receiving *tonya* for products from the Kinai region were replaced by specialized merchants who handled specific commodities in the Ōsaka market. With this increased functional differentiation, the special position of Ōsaka in the *bakuhan* order was further consolidated. With the increased volume of trade in Ōsaka new institutions formed to handle the increased flow of goods to the city more effectively. Many of them took the form of *nakama* or *kumiai* groups of merchants, and while the government issued repeated edicts against the formation of these unauthorized trade associations – six between 1648 and 1670 – such groups increased in importance in the Ōsaka market.[45]

Nakama or *kabu nakama* (trade associations) appeared in increasing numbers during the second half of the seventeenth century and continued throughout the Tokugawa period to be the major form of commercial organization, particularly in urban areas. Merchants and artisans joined in *nakama* as a means of coordinating their activities, monopolizing specific trades, and reducing the level of intra-group and inter-group competition. While initially antithetical to *bakufu* commercial policies, *nakama* were increasingly seen as a means of regulating trade and were granted varying degrees of government authorization.[46] From the government perspective, *nakama* provided a mechanism for police control, control of foreign trade articles, awarding special trade privileges, controlling prices and supplies of goods, insuring the circulation of new currency, regulating business procedures, protecting specific business enterprises, settling trade disputes, developing new urban areas, or increasing government revenues. Most of the *nakama* proved useful for one or more of these purposes.[47]

For the merchant community, membership in a *kabu nakama* symbolized the ties of an individual merchant or merchant house with a collective group engaged in similar commercial or craft pursuits. The *kabu*, membership shares or licenses, authorized the holder to operate one shop, one potter's wheel or lathe, one scale, or one workshop, but many individuals held multiple *kabu* which enabled them to set up branch stores or employ additional craftsmen or transporters. For those without multiple *kabu*, the *nakama* regulations specified how many apprentices or assistants they might employ.[48]

Two major types of authorized *kabu nakama* developed during the Tokugawa period, those which were set up by the government to police or regulate a trade or insure adequate supplies of specific goods, and those which were authorized at the request of a merchant group and which often required the payment of licensing fees and other assessments. The *kabu* which were issued to the *nakama* membership were usually of wood and bore the branded seal of the association and a written designation as well. *Kabu* were assigned to specific individuals or houses and could be used as security for loans and mortgages and could be inherited or sold only with the permission of the association. The name on the *kabu* designated the individual holder and in many merchant houses each successive household took this name when he assumed control of the family enterprise. Records for some houses thus utilize the same names from one generation to the next, a cause of some confusion for subsequent historians.[49]

Within each *kabu nakama* the number of *kabu* was fixed and any additions had to be approved by both the government and the officers of the association. Retirement of *kabu* or abandonment of *kabu* could occur when a suitable heir was not available or a house went bankrupt or discontinued in a trade. The *nakama* could also confiscate *kabu* and expel members when they were convicted of breaking the regulations of the association, and they could be suspended for non-payment of fees. Whenever *kabu* were transferred fees were collected by the association and various entertainments were required of the new possessor. Distribution of *kabu* was carefully controlled to bind the *nakama* together and assure conformity to *nakama* trading or production procedures.[50]

Each of the *kabu nakama* maintained a book of regulations and a list of all members. When changes were made in *nakama* rules or membership, the corrections were pasted into the recordbooks kept by the *nakama* officials. Meetings of the associations were held at regular intervals with some groups meeting several times monthly and others only two or three times each year. Attendance was required and fines levied on those who failed to appear or send a deputy. Meetings discussed business problems, initiated new members, or served as social gatherings, as for example when members joined on an outing, for a party, or for a religious observance.[51]

Each *nakama* had officers who served monthly or yearly terms and were elected or appointed from among the membership. In most associations officials came from the more respected and successful houses, but in some organizations official duties were rotated among the entire membership. Within many *nakama*, subordinate groups known as *kumi* or *kō* elected officers who then served in a body representing each of the associated subgroups. *Nakama* officials represented the membership in dealings with the *bakufu*, with daimyo governments, or with other merchant organizations. They conducted the business of the *nakama*, kept and distributed information, and collected whatever fees were assessed on members. They also adjudicated internal disputes, administered changes in membership and *kabu* possession, and upheld the regulations of the association. All official documents of the *nakama* were required to bear the seal of the appropriate *nakama* official. The officials also conducted the ceremonial obligations of the *nakama* including the semiannual presentations to the city magistrates office in Ōsaka. These yearly or monthly officials held wide powers over the *nakama* and were responsible for insuring the honesty and propriety of the associations' membership. In compensation for the responsibilities of office, they were normally given exemptions from *nakama* assessments, as well as gifts and the respect of all *nakama* members. The burdens of office were severe and in many instances the acceptance of a *nakama* office compromised the business of the individual involved. As a consequence, efforts to avoid the honor were not uncommon.[52]

Many of the *nakama* had strong religious ties with patron saints, Shintō shrines, or Buddhist temples. Money or lanterns were donated to religious institutions, religious ceremonies were commissioned and supported, and religious symbols were used to add to the prestige and solidarity of the commercial associations. In many respects the *nakama* were highly conservative institutions. Regulations required adherence to established procedures and discouraged new processes or trading methods. Membership was usually exclusive and spheres of influence were carefully defined to avoid conflict within the *nakama* or with other associations. Rigid conceptions of propriety controlled many aspects of the personal lives of the membership; social hierarchy within the merchant community was stressed; and life styles and terms of service of subordinates were carefully regulated.[53] Overall, the *nakama* were often restrictive and repressive institutions which discouraged initiative and competition and stifled many of the innovative ideas of their membership.

During the 1660s and 1670s the application of *bakufu* commercial policies to the Ōsaka market changed. The city magistrate Ishimaru Sadatsugu inaugurated a new approach when in 1662 he authorized the money changers' *nakama* mentioned above. Subsequently, *nakama* were authorized for the Ōsaka seed and ginned cotton trades and the Kyōto and Edo oil shipping *tonya*, and the government indicated its willingness to support the monopoly rights granted to these groups. The reception of official status protected the interests of the cotton and oil merchants and added to their status in the Ōsaka commercial community.[54]

Nakama authorization reflected the growing realization by *bakufu* officials that commercial controls could be achieved through the merchant associations. Concern with the expansion of commercial activity led to increased interest in means for directing the course of this growth. Encouraging limited-membership *nakama* was one method for limiting the proliferation of mercantile activity as well as establishing an institutional structure for imposing government controls on the commercial sector.[55] *Nakama* were also useful for limiting commercial expansion. When a competitive market for fresh produce threatened the monopoly of the Temma vegetable market in Ōsaka, the *bakufu* closed it for violating the monopoly rights of the authorized market and localized the produce trade in Temma.[56] The necessity for the *bakufu* to close the rival vegetable market suggests that there was a demand among the consumers for additional sources of fresh produce. Thus, while the *bakufu* could legitimate its action by reference to the monopoly rights of the Temma market, it may well have been against the interests of the Ōsaka *chōnin* in supplementary outlets for wholesale produce.

By the 1660s, a differentiated marketing system had been established for several commodities in Ōsaka. Among them was oil, whose merchants had been dividied into receiving *tonya*, Kyōto and Edo shipping *tonya*, oil pressing *tonya*, and oil *nakagai* (jobbers). *Nakama* had been established for these traders as well as for those active in the cotton trade.[57] The existence of these *nakama* enabled the *bakufu* to direct supplies of cotton and oil to the major cities where they were in demand by the samurai, as well as to limit the expansion of trade. The *nakama* also served to concentrate

Economic Institutional Change in Tokugawa Japan

marketing within the city of Ōsaka and exclude the agricultural population from participation in the marketing process.[58] *Nakama* were also utilized as a source of statistical data on prices and trade volume as a means of providing information to government policy makers. The increasing volume of trade made these data more important, for it was only with access to this kind of information that the government could effectively deal with the economic problems with which it was faced.[59]

The Kinai region, including the five provinces (*kuni*) Settsu, Kawachi, Izumi, Yamato, and Yamashiro, developed commercial agriculture from a rather early date because it included the cities of Kyōto and Ōsaka. Following the consolidation of Tokugawa control and the establishment of the shogunate, the Kinai region was broken up into a complex of directly held *bakufu* territories, including the cities of Kyōto, Ōsaka, and Sakai, lands assigned to the imperial nobility and the imperial house, temple and shrine lands, and small parcels of territory assigned to daimyo in the Kinai region and elsewhere. For example, in the late Tokugawa period, the province of Kawachi was split up among a total of seventy-five separate proprietors. They included eighteen daimyo, three imperial princes, thirty-two Tokugawa vassals, seven Tokugawa administrative officials, five Shintō shrines, and ten temples. In neighboring Settsu, seven of the twelve *gun* (districts) were divided among a total of eighty-eight proprietors. This kind of fragmented holding made control in Settsu and Kawachi extremely difficult and made it relatively easy for the farmers to get into commercial agricultural production.[60]

From around 1660 to 1680, commercial agricultural production in Kinai increased considerably. Associated with the rise in output of market oriented crops was the expansion of marketing facilities in Ōsaka. As *tonya* increased in number in the Ōsaka market, the circulation of commodities to the city improved.[61] It was only after around 1680 that the Ōsaka *tonya* merchants began to be able to control commercial agricultural production in the Kinai region. Commercial leadership in Kinai shifted to the *tonya* merchants from the earlier type of privileged merchants during the last four decades of the seventeenth century. The privileged merchants had maintained their position of power only because of their ties with local political authorities. Gradually they were displaced by *tonya* who used their commercial skills and their economic power to gain control of Kinai commerce.[62]

The varieties of *tonya* active in the Ōsaka market are visible in table 1. The recorded presence of 382 *tonya* in Ōsaka by 1679 illustrates the importance of Ōsaka as a market for the Kinai region. Because earlier figures on *tonya* are lacking, a direct comparison with the first half of the seventeenth century is impossible. However, the existence of both regional and specialized *tonya* indicates the increasing functional differentiation of

20

TABLE 1. Ōsaka *tonya* by type and number, 1679

Kyōto bagged goods buying *tonya*	10	Vegetable *tonya*	20
Nagasaki *tonya*	21	Bingo *tonya*	2
Edo buying *tonya*	17	Hirado whale oil *tonya*	1
Edo shipping *tonya*	3	Sword *tonya*	1
Edo barrel shipping *tonya*	4	Indigo ball *tonya*	3
Paper *tonya*	24	Rare foreign wood *tonya*	2
Cotton cloth *tonya*	8	Owari lumber *tonya*	4
Cloth *tonya*	11	Tosa lumber *tonya*	6
Seed cotton *tonya*	17	Kii lumber *tonya*	6
Tobacco *tonya*	11	North Japan lumber *tonya*	2
Salt *tonya*	7	Awa lumber *tonya*	2
Green tea *tonya*	15	Ship-building lumber *tonya*	7
Iron *tonya*	7	Ship lumber dealers	8
Vegetable wax *tonya*	9	Oar *tonya*	9
Shark *tonya*	1	Plain wood *tonya*	2
Kyōto firewood *tonya*	9	Hizen Ifu pottery *tonya*	6
Firewood *tonya*	27	Bizen pottery *tonya*	2
Charcoal *tonya*	7	Satsuma *tonya*	8
Kumano charcoal *tonya*	3	Kii provincial *tonya*	2
Copper smelters	3	Compass *tonya*	2
Dried sardine *tonya*	2	Dried fruit *tonya*	3
Fresh fish *tonya*	16	Coal *tonya*	3
North Japan fish *tonya*	6	Kitchen knife and short sword *nakagai*	2
Salted and dried fish *tonya*	19	Edo shipping *sake* dealers	1
Fowl *tonya*	3	Edo shipping soy dealers	7
Gift label (*noshi awabi*) *tonya*	3	West Japan soy shippers	1
Dried bonito *tonya*	4	Kyōto soy shippers	3

Total (54 types) 382

SOURCE: Takenaka Yasukazu and Kawakami Tadashi, *Nihon shōgyōshi* [History of Japanese commerce] (Kyōto, 1965), p. 164.

the Ōsaka market. The presence of specialty *tonya* for tobacco, tea, iron, firewood, charcoal, pottery, dried bonito, and so forth shows how individual merchants had begun to specialize in particular commodities. Regional *tonya* like those for Nagasaki, Satsuma, and Kii handled a variety of goods originating in the region on which they focused, with the focus of the Nagasaki *tonya* being imported goods received at this *bakufu*-controlled port with a monopoly on foreign trade.

The increasing specialization of the Ōsaka merchants and the consolidation of the dominant role of Ōsaka as the market center of the Kinai region resulted in the displacement of many other market centers as noted above. By the 1680s this process was well under way.[63] By the end of the seventeenth century Ōsaka was not only a major rice market but was the primary commodity market for western Japan. The last two decades of the century saw the flowering of Ōsaka as a commercial center and as the focal point for the new popular culture of the *chōnin*. This period was one of thriving commercial activity and saw a proliferation of popular cultural developments as well. The Genroku period (1688–1703) is often viewed as a high point in the development of the artistic and literary elements of the new urban life style of the *chōnin*. It is also seen as heralding a decline in the ability of the *bakufu* to effectively regulate the increasingly important activities of the merchant class.[64]

The course of the seventeenth century had brought many changes to the commercial sector of Tokugawa society. Dramatic examples of rapid upward and downward mobility within the merchant class are related at length in the novels of Ihara Saikaku, the great writer of popular fiction of the late seventeenth century. His *Nippon eitai gura* contains numerous examples of how fortunes, built by diligence and self-denial by one generation, were squandered by the next.[65] Other examples of large merchant houses which went bankrupt are discussed in Mitsui Takafusa's *Chōnin kōken roku*. Written as an eyewitness account of the financial and commercial life of Kyōto in the late seventeenth and early eighteenth centuries, the book was intended as a guidebook for business success and a warning against the pitfalls which might lead to ruin for the Mitsui house.[66] Both sources offer ample evidence of the extravagant lives of the most successful merchants and of the dangers of social excess and large loans to daimyo and members of the samurai class.[67]

From an institutional perspective the Genroku period, rather than standing out as a major transitional period, is instead one portion of a longer period of commercial development and institutional change which extended from the 1660s into the eighteenth century. During the last decades of the seventeenth century, many economic problems which were to plague the *bakufu* and the samurai class until the end of the Tokugawa era first came to light. Here were revealed striking manifestations of tendencies which had begun to appear earlier in the century and which did not reach maturity until the first quarter of the eighteenth century. Yet because the cultural florescence of the late seventeenth century is usually referred to as Genroku culture, this term is often used in commercial history as well to designate not just the fifteen calendar years of the Genroku era, but the last decades of the seventeenth century and the beginning of the following century as well.

It is useful to bear in mind that the merchant class, which underlay the rise of urban culture in Tokugawa Japan, was by no means a monolithic social group. *Chōnin* included wealthy merchant property owners, smaller merchants who lived in rented shops or rooms, and itinerant peddlers who purchased goods daily and hawked them on the streets of the city. In addition were service personnel, entertainers, artisans, employees, and day laborers. Life styles varied dramatically as did the scale of their business ventures. Consequently, any discussion of the merchant class has to be qualified to take into account the variance included within this group.

During the second half of the seventeenth century, the institutional composition of the Ōsaka market increased in complexity and there is evidence of specialization and of new forms of functional differentiation within the marketing process. Ōsaka emerged as the major market for the agricultural commodities of the Kinai region and western Japan, and the development of new water routes to the city played a major role in this development. Complementing the growth of Ōsaka as a market center was the growth of processing and handicraft industries within the city, for example, those associated with cotton and copper.

Kabu nakama authorization indicated the growing involvement of the government in attempts to regulate the commercial life of the city. Residential grouping as a mechanism for social control was replaced in the commercial sector by organization of *kabu nakama* by occupational type, a process evident in Ōsaka as well as in many of the castle towns of the daimyo. Associated with this was the emergence of new social distinctions within the merchant class. The property distinctions of the neighborhood associations were displaced in importance by status distinctions associated with occupational groups in which all members were not necessarily of the same propertied class.[68] This resulted in the appearance of status criteria in the merchant community which were independent of *bakufu* authority. Economic status displaced other factors as the principal determinant of social status within the commercial sector of society.

ŌSAKA IN THE EARLY EIGHTEENTH CENTURY

The early eighteenth century saw a continuation of the patterns of commercial expansion and institutional change which had been characteristic of the years after around 1660. A major study of the trade structure of Ōsaka during the mid-Tokugawa period by Yasuoka Shigeaki describes the nature of the mercantile expansion which occurred in Ōsaka during the eighteenth century. Yasuoka lists 5538 *tonya* as actively engaged in commerce in Ōsaka between 1711 and 1715. Dividing them into two groups, Group A including *tonya* with indicated specialization and Group B including *tonya* with regional designations who handled a variety of goods as well as those for whom occupational categories are not available, he placed 3525 or 64 percent in Group A and 2013 or 36 percent in Group B.[69] Table 2 compares the data for the years from 1711 to 1715 with comparable data from 1673–80 and divides the *tonya* by categories into groups A and B. The most obvious change from the earlier to the later period is the dramatic increase in *tonya* merchants. Some of this increase must be attributed to more complete data

TABLE 2. Ōsaka *tonya* for the periods 1673–80 and 1711–15[a]

Tonya type	1673–80	1711–15
Group A		
Shipping	7	18
Money changers	10	1154
Rice	–	40
Cotton yarn and cloth	36	294
Oil and rapeseed	–	340
Agricultural processed goods	34	178
Processing	2	151
Paper	24	67
Sake	1	653
Mining and manufacture	29	149
Lumber	14	32
Firewood, charcoal, and bamboo	37	38
Marine products	56	103
Chinese and Japanese medicine	–	308
Group B		
Regional *tonya*	6	1727
Regional shipping agents	–	286
Total	256	5538[b]

SOURCE: Yasuoka, 'Torihiki soshiki,' II, pp. 590–1.
[a] These dates designate the Empō (1673–80) and Shōtoku (1711–15) year periods from the traditional Japanese calendar.
[b] Corrected from Yasuoka's 5655.

for the later period, but a significant increase in the number of *tonya* is consistent with other indicators related to the growth of the Ōsaka market. Including *tonya* in both classifications, the figures illustrate that the increase was not limited to specialty *tonya*. Thus increased differentiation within the Ōsaka market included the older style regional *tonya* and the more recent specialized *tonya*.

Examination of the *tonya* by type indicates significant increases from the late seventeenth to the early eighteenth century. While only ten money changers are listed for the first period, this category had increased to 1154 in the data for the second. Other evidence suggests that new types of money changers are included in the data for the second period, and these data also appear to be far more comprehensive, as the increase in number is of such a magnitude as to be difficult to accept uncritically. Data on cotton cloth and yarn *tonya* illustrate a significant increase in specialization for these goods. The same can be said for oil and rapeseed *tonya*, those for agricultural processed goods, those engaged in processing, mining, and manufacture, and *tonya* for marine products and medicine, all of which showed significant increases. One of the most impressive changes was that for *sake tonya*, but here, as with the other statistics, a note of caution should be introduced. These are pre-modern data, collected without the kinds of precision and consistency with which modern statistics are collected. Consequently, any conclusions drawn from them have to assume a high degree of omission, inaccuracy, and inconsistency in the figures available. Some of the data may well be misleading, but this does not invalidate the overall conclusion of increased specialization in the Ōsaka market. There is no question that between the first and second periods in table 2, both the degree of functional differentiation and the volume of trade in the Ōsaka market expanded significantly. However, the rate of increase suggested by the data is extremely unlikely and it must be assumed that the data for the period 1711–15 are far more comprehensive than those for 1673–80. Given the inconsistencies of the current data, it is impossible to utilize the statistics with any confidence.

Similar problems exist in interpreting the data on regional *tonya* and regional shipping agents in table 2. The increase in regional *tonya* from 6 to 1727 seems improbable, and significant omissions in the earlier data must be assumed. Likewise, in the data for regional shipping agents, either this was a new category of transport merchant or incomplete data must be assumed. Table 1 lists for the year 1679, lying within Yasuoka's first period, 31 regional *tonya* and 7 Edo buying and shipping *tonya* who fit into Yasuoka's Group B. Both sets of data for the early period may well be greatly in error, but, this notwithstanding, a dramatic increase in this category of regional merchants is suggested.

To assist his analysis of changes in regional trade during the mid-Tokugawa period, Yasuoka has compared the statistics for the years from 1711 to 1715 with similar data from the 1770s. From this comparison he is able to generalize about the changing roles of regional *tonya* and regional shipping agents during the eighteenth century.[70] Table 3 gives these data on regional *tonya* and regional shipping agents.

Table 3 illustrates that there were significant variations among regions in Japan during the eighteenth century. Between the two periods the number of regional *tonya* decreased by around 35 percent. During this same interval, the number of shipping agents increased by around 12 percent. The decline of regional *tonya* was sharpest in areas closely tied to the Ōsaka market, including Kinai, Nankai, and Saikai, and in Tōkai, which was closely tied to Edo. San-yō was also tied to the Ōsaka market and the lack of a sharp decline in regional *tonya* from San-yō reflected in part the increase in *tonya* from Harima and Suō and a low rate of decline in other provinces. But other factors must also have contributed to this apparent inconsistency, and they deserve further inquiry. The decline in

TABLE 3. Regional *tonya* and shipping agents for the periods 1711–15 and 1772–80[a]

| | 1711–15 | | 1772–80 | |
Region	*Tonya*	Shipping agents	*Tonya*	Shipping agents
Kinai[b]	153	52	49	53
Tōkai	262	3	150	20
Tōzan	51	5	31	–
Hokkai	8	–	5	–
Hokuriku	48	4	80	9
San-in	51	10	49	9
San-yō	323	57	285	76
Nankai	483	111	258	102
Saikai	348	44	219	52
Total	1727	286	1126	321

SOURCE: Yasuoka, 'Torihiki soshiki,' II, p. 595.

[a] These dates designate the Shōtoku (1711–15) and An-ei (1772–80) year periods in the traditional Japanese calendar.

[b] The provincial composition of the regions cited in the table is:
   Kinai: Settsu, Kawachi, Izumi, Yamato, Yamashiro
   Tōkai: Iga, Shima, Ise, Owari, Mikawa, Tōtōmi, Suruga, Izu, Kai, Sagami, Musashi, Awa, Kazusa, Shimōsa, Hitachi, Kantō tsuji, Edo
   Tōzan: Ōmi, Mino, Hida, Shinano, Kōzuke, Shimotsuke, Mutsu, Dewa
   Hokkai: Matsumae
   Hokuriku: Wakasa, Inaba, Echizen, Kaga, Noto, Etchū, Echigo, Sado
   San-in: Tamba, Tango, Tajima, Inaba, Hōki, Izumo, Iwami, Oki
   San-yō: Harima, Mimasaka, Bizen, Bitchū, Bingo, Aki, Suō, Suō Iwakuni, Nagato
   Nankai: Kii, Awaji, Awa, Sanuki, Iyo, Tosa
   Saikai: Chikuzen, Chikugo, Hizen, Higo, Buzen, Bungo, Hyūga, Ōsumi, Satsuma, Iki, Tsushima, Nagasaki
Within each province there were not necessarily either *tonya* or shipping agents. See Yasuoka for a further breakdown.

regional *tonya*, rather than indicating a drop in overall trade from these regions, suggests instead that they were being displaced by more specialized merchants of the A type *tonya* discussed above. The increase in regional shipping agents is seen as indicating an increase in mercantile activity in the regions concerned.[71]

Areas which are at variance with the tendencies suggested by the totals in table 3 are Hokuriku, Hokkai and San-in. Each of these regions was distant from a major market center and had a relatively late development of market oriented agricultural production. This explains the increase in regional *tonya* from Hokuriku, the northern end of Honshū, while this kind of *tonya* was declining in all other regions, though not in all provinces. Hokkai, composed of Matsumae *han* on the southern tip of the island of Hokkaidō, was only peripherally included in Tokugawa Japan and was mainly a source of seaweed and other marine products. San-in saw the least change of any region, reflecting its 'back-country' status and relatively low level of commercial development. For each of these regions, geographical conditions and lack of easy access to markets were major factors which distinguished them economically from other areas of Tokugawa Japan.

Import and export statistics for Ōsaka collected in 1714 by the *bakufu* offer useful insights into the scale and nature of the Ōsaka market. Several features of the data are striking, even assuming that they are imprecise. First of all, the value of imports exceeded that of exports by a considerable margin. Second, by and large, exports consisted of processed goods or products of handicraft industry.[72] Imports to Ōsaka in 1714, excluding the tax rice shipments of the daimyo, were valued at 286 560 *kan* silver. About 6 percent of this total by value were foreign trade goods such as cloth and dyestuffs imported via Nagasaki. Exports for 1714 were valued at 95 799 *kan* silver, and of this about 7 percent, including 6587 *kan* worth of copper, was destined to be sent abroad from Nagasaki. Total rice shipments to Ōsaka, including both daimyo- and merchant-shipped rice, were valued at 202 535 *kan* and constituted around 40 percent of the value of all imports to the Ōsaka market. Rice and other grains combined did not exceed 50 percent of the total value of imports.[73]

Designated by commodity types, the 1714 imports to Ōsaka, less grains, are shown in table 4. Table 4 illustrates the commercial agricultural development of commodities other than grains. Oil seeds, including rapeseed and cotton seeds, composed 15.8 percent of imports less grains. Much of this seed was processed in Ōsaka and made into hair and lamp oil for consumption in the city and shipment to other areas. Vegetables, tea, tobacco, salt fish, and seaweed were largely consumed within Ōsaka or nearby areas. Together they composed over 10 percent of imports less grains. Other major imports like lumber, clothing or such clothing-related goods as raw materials and indigo for dyeing, and mining products were consumed within the city or further processed. Dried sardines were largely utilized as agricultural fertilizer and were widely marketed in the Kinai region. 'Others' included medicines, luxury items, and commodities which did not fall into the named categories.

The data from table 4 do not include information on place of origin for the commodities listed. To approximate the geographical origins of major commodities imported to Ōsaka it is necessary to utilize more complete data collected in 1736 by the *bakufu*.[74] The 1736 statistics show that only the Kinai and Inland Sea regions sent multiple products to Ōsaka at this

TABLE 4. Ōsaka imports, less grains, by percent of total value, 1714

Commodity	%	Commodity	%
Agricultural products and processed goods		Marine products and processed goods	
vegetables	1.3	dried sardines	7.8
tea, tobacco	2.8	salt	2.3
oil seeds	15.8	fish	3.9
indigo	0.6	seaweed	0.1
clothing: raw materials	4.5		
clothing: processed goods	13.1	Sub-total	14.1
Tatami mats	2.8		
Sub-total	40.9		
Forestry products and processed goods		Mining products	8.9
		Others	11.7
lumber	16.2		
charcoal	1.1		
wax	0.9		
paper	6.2		
Sub-total	24.4	Total	100.0

SOURCE: Nakai, 'Toshi,' p. 46

time. All told, forty-five out of sixty-six provinces are listed as having sent one or more commodities to Ōsaka. Settsu and Kawachi which surrounded Ōsaka sent the largest number of commodities, followed by Yamashiro, Yamato, and Izumi. Each sent five or more goods to the Ōsaka market.[75] From along the Inland Sea the province of Bungo sent six commodities to Ōsaka, Bizen sent five, Bitchū, Aki, Awa, and Iyo sent four each. Harima, Tamba, and Kii – all of which bordered on the Kinai region – sent four commodities each, but other provinces sent one, two, or at most three commodities to Ōsaka in 1736.[76]

Imports to Kyōto, the other major market in the Kinai region, followed a similar pattern. Twenty-four provinces shipped goods to this center of handicraft production. Nearby Yamashiro, Ōmi, and Tamba sent seven products each to Kyōto and were the major suppliers of the city. They were followed by Settsu with four commodities. The other twenty provinces shipped largely marine, forestry, or cloth-related goods and were limited to one or two commodities each. No goods were shipped directly to Kyōto from along the Inland Sea. All commodities originating from this area first passed through the Ōsaka market prior to arriving in the imperial capital city.[77]

28

Conclusions about the imports and exports of Kyōto are difficult to substantiate because of its inland location. Goods were shipped to and from Kyōto by river boats and overland and there were no centralized facilities for keeping records. Because Kyōto was a center for art and craft production as well as for luxury goods, the *bakufu* was less concerned with regulating market activities there and did not collect the kinds of commercial data available for the Ōsaka market. Consequently, while Kyōto was a major consumption center and one of the three largest cities in Japan during the Tokugawa period, studies of Kyōto commercial life are far less developed than those for Ōsaka and Edo.[78]

Returning our focus to Ōsaka, exports from Ōsaka for 1714, by percentage of total value, are shown in table 5. Products which were imported in

TABLE 5. Ōsaka exports by percent of total value, 1714

Commodity	%	%
Agricultural products and processed goods		72.8
cotton goods	22.2	
seed cotton	5.0	
oil	36.2	
oil wastes (fertilizer)	3.4	
foodstuffs	6.0	
Forestry products and processed goods		5.3
furniture	0.7	
utensils	4.6	
Mining products and processed goods		12.6
iron goods	5.5	
copper goods	0.2	
Nagasaki export copper	6.9	
Others		9.3
	Total	100.0

SOURCE: Nakai, 'Toshi,' p. 80

large quantities and not exported to any appreciable extent included rice, grains, paper, dried sardines, salt, sugar, and lumber. Taking into consideration that some portion of these goods was marketed in the region surrounding Ōsaka, it is still apparent that the bulk of these imported goods were consumed in the city itself. Considering that the combined population of Ōsaka, Kyōto, and Sakai was approaching one million in the early eighteenth century, it is not surprising that large quantities of foodstuffs and other goods were consumed in this area. By 1714, Ōsaka was more important as a consumption center than as a market for the collection and distribution of goods to other areas of Japan.[79]

29

The 1714 import and export statistics for Ōsaka, omissions and errors notwithstanding, show conclusively that the majority of goods imported into the city were consumed locally and not reexported. This differs from the traditional view in which Ōsaka was seen as the 'kitchen of Japan,' a view which assumed that Ōsaka was the source of the major provisions consumed in the shogunal capital of Edo. Agricultural processed goods were the largest single type of exports, but foodstuffs composed only 6 percent of total exports by value and would not have been adequate for supplying the consumption requirements of Edo. Further, if rice is included, total exports were less than one-fifth the value of imports to Ōsaka, emphasizing that the city functioned more as a consumption center than as a distribution and forwarding point.[80]

Processing complemented consumption as a major activity in the Ōsaka commercial complex. Estimates of the artisan population of Ōsaka for the period 1711–14 give an approximation of the importance of this segment of the total city population. Yasuoka estimates that artisans and handicraft industrial workers numbered around 20 000. If copper smelters are included and apprentices, laborers, and *nakagai* are added the total would approach 30 000 to 40 000 workers. Assuming that each worker had on the average two dependents, Yasuoka concludes that the population of Ōsaka dependent on handicraft industry composed 30 to 40 percent of the total population, which in 1714 is estimated to have been around 380 000.[81]

Among imports to Ōsaka, about 60 percent by value were in primary form or semi-finished goods. Exports, in contrast, included only around 12 percent raw materials or semi-finished goods and 88 percent finished goods. Oil and oil wastes, used as fertilizer, composed almost 40 percent of the total value of exports. No oil was imported in 1714, but rapeseed and cotton seed from which pressed oil were produced constituted 16 percent of total imports, indicating that oil pressing was a major processing industry in the city. Oil was exported from Ōsaka in the early seventeenth century and the Edo and Kyōto oil *tonya* shipped oil to these two cities. By 1710, there were 6 *tonya* shipping oil to Edo and 3 shipping to Kyōto as well as 306 rapeseed *tonya*, 25 *tonya* for oil wastes, and 250 *nakagai* who mixed rapeseed and cotton seed oil into lamp oil and sold it to retailers as well as shipping it to western and northern Japan.[82]

After oil and oil wastes, cotton goods were the largest single export. Imports and exports of cotton varied from the normal pattern as processed goods were both imported and exported and even unprocessed seed cotton was exported from the city. Table 6 shows the nature of cotton imports and exports for 1714. Most of the seed cotton was processed in Ōsaka and exported as ginned cotton or cloth. Only around 10 percent of the seed cotton was exported in unprocessed form. White cloth imports were nearly three times the value of exports, while striped cloth exports were over twice

TABLE 6. Cotton imports and exports for Ōsaka, 1714

	Quantity	Value (*kan* silver)
Cotton imports		
Seed cotton	1 722 000 *kin*[a]	6 700
Reeled yarn	116 000 *kin*	3 430
White cloth	2 061 000 *tan*[b]	15 700
Striped cloth	237 000 *tan*	2 800
Cotton exports		
Seed cotton	192 000 *kin*	500
Ginned cotton	108 000 *kan*[c]	300
White cloth	739 000 *tan*	6 200
Striped cloth	698 000 *tan*	7 000
Used cotton	409 000 *kan*	6 000

SOURCE: Nakai, 'Toshi,' p. 82
[a] 1 *kin* equals 1.32 lb.
[b] 1 *tan* equals approximately 12 yd.
[c] 1 *kan* equals 8.72 lb.

the value of imports, indicating that striped cloth was produced in Ōsaka or nearby areas. Production of white cotton cloth was centered in cotton production regions, where weaving was a major form of by-employment in the off-season, and also in market towns scattered in the cotton growing areas of Kinai and western Japan.

While forestry products and related processed goods totalled 24.4 percent of imports to the city, they composed only 5.3 percent of exports, and all were finished goods. Mining products constituted 8.9 percent of imports and 12.6 percent of the value of exports, with over half of the exports being destined for foreign export from the port of Nagasaki. Marine products which made up 14.1 percent of imports were relegated to the composite group of 'others' in the export statistics. The overwhelming majority of export goods were processed goods, substantiating the role of Ōsaka as a processing center.

Many of the processed goods exported from Ōsaka were sent to Edo. By 1724, Edo is estimated to have had a population of close to one million, approximately equally divided between *chōnin* and samurai. The *bakufu*, concerned about supplying the consumption requirements of the shogunal capital city, in 1668 inventoried goods stocked by Edo merchants including rice, wheat, beans, sesame seeds, fuel, rapeseed, pressed oils, whale oil, and fish oil. Thereafter, records were ordered kept for all imports and exports of these commodities in Edo as well as imports from and exports to the various daimyo domains.[83]

Various goods were shipped to Edo directly from the Tōkai and Kantō

31

regions and Pacific coast areas as well as from villages close to the city. Goods of major importance shipped from Ōsaka and Kyōto to Edo in 1694 included oil, cotton cloth, ginned cotton, silk, lacquer ware, copper goods, *tatami* covers, matting, paper, candles, and medicine. Edo also served as a transshipment point for silk, utensils, cotton cloth, and ginned cotton sent from Ōsaka to towns in the Kantō and Tōhoku regions. By 1690, at least nineteen types of *tonya* were active in Edo with both regional and specialized *tonya* represented. Markets for fruit, vegetables, and fish were established in the city and the Edo and Tone rivers used for transporting foodstuffs. Limited handicraft industrial development was under way in Edo, but most was directed towards satisfying the military equipment needs of the samurai. Like Ōsaka, Edo was emerging as a commercial complex by the end of the seventeenth century, but was retarded in development relative to the great Kinai market city.[84]

By the first decades of the eighteenth century a marketing system focused on Ōsaka in the Kinai region had been established and consolidated. The limits of economic expansion had not yet been reached, but some of the limitations of the *bakuhan* order were beginning to appear in the form of social and economic problems. After around 1720, the government was forced to reconsider some of its economic policies in order to reinforce the economic position of the samurai class, stabilize its own economic base, and regulate the expanding commercial sector of society. The increasingly urban character of Tokugawa Japan introduced a whole series of problems which the founders of the Tokugawa *bakuhan* order had failed to anticipate. Beginning in the early eighteenth century and continuing into the nineteenth century the *bakufu* attempted to ameliorate the limitations of the *bakuhan* system. In the mid-nineteenth century internal pressures for change increased to the extent that more dramatic steps were required. These efforts will be discussed in the following chapter.[85]

3 Tokugawa Commerce: 1720–1868

From the first quarter of the eighteenth century the rapid expansion and transformation of Tokugawa commerce slowed perceptibly and a new phase of stability and maturity was initiated. Trade continued to increase during the eighteenth and early nineteenth centuries, but the market systems centered on the major cities dominated this trade and the institutional structure underlying this domination was increasingly consolidated and reinforced. Compared to the first century of Tokugawa rule, the second was less dynamic, less innovative, as both the *bakufu* and the urban merchants worked at regularizing the supply networks and marketing processes for commodities in the major urban centers.

Associated with this stabilization of trade were government efforts to increase its control over the economy. These efforts were generated by economic problems in the form of fiscal crises for the government and a growing imbalance between samurai incomes and their material expectations. To cope with these problems the *bakufu* worked to increase government revenues through land reclamation to expand the tax base; tried retrenchment and sumptuary legislation to reduce expenditures; and initiated commercial controls to reduce commodity prices. The so-called reforms of the Kyōhō (1716–35) and Kansei (1787–93) periods each were designed to increase government revenues and alleviate the financial problems faced by the samurai. Both programs included measures designed to expand government control over the commercial sector. These programs illustrate the changing relationships between the government and the urban merchant associations as well as changes which were occurring within the mercantile sector of Tokugawa society. These and other developments in the eighteenth and early nineteenth centuries will be the focus of this chapter.

THE KYŌHŌ REFORMS

The Kyōhō period (1716–35) was notable for the introduction of a series of new *bakufu* policies which indicated increasing governmental concern with the expansion of commerce and handicraft production and the increasing inability of the samurai class to maintain its economic position in society. Symptomatic of the growing problems faced by the samurai was a rise in commodity price levels which was accompanied by a decline

33

in the price of rice. With samurai salaries computed in units of rice and paid in kind from the rice lands of the shogun and the daimyo, the market price of rice determined the cash value of their incomes. Consequently, the eighth Tokugawa shogun, Yoshimune, ruling from 1716 to 1745, conducted a series of inquiries and initiated new policies – the so-called reforms – which were aimed at determining the nature of and correcting the major economic problems of the day.

The primary components of the reforms were increased diligence in land tax collection, sumptuary regulations and retrenchment directives for the samurai class, and attempts to expand government controls over commodity marketing and the activities of the mercantile sector of Tokugawa society. Because the first two types of reforms are outside the concern of the present study, it is the effort at commercial controls on which we will focus our attention.

The initial reform programs were directed at restoring the financial position of the *bakufu*. The fifth shogun, Tsunayoshi (ruled 1680–1709), had increased the level of *bakufu* expenditures and used up the reserves accumulated by the Tokugawa house. In the early eighteenth century, the shogunal advisor Arai Hakuseki had implemented coinage reforms and import and export regulations designed to improve the quality of circulating coinage and reduce the outflow of specie and metals in foreign trade.[1] In 1721/7, the production and sale of new commodities and creation of new enterprises were prohibited and price reductions were ordered for sundry goods. The following month, the earlier ban on new commodities and new enterprises was repeated and an inquiry was begun into artisan and merchant associations. This resulted in an order for *nakama* formation in ninety-six specific trades to assist the government in applying controls to the commercial sector in Edo. Initially, these groups were to be composed of fifty to seventy members and organized by commodity type, irrespective of previously established groupings. This resulted in considerable opposition from the merchants and artisans and as a result the government backed off and authorized organization along established lines. This initiated a process of *kabu nakama* formation from above by governmental directive in Edo.[2]

This round of *kabu nakama* formation was aimed at control of luxury items and new enterprises and did not include merchants who traded daily necessities such as rice, bean paste, *sake*, firewood, salt, and so forth. Clothing dealers were included, but those specializing in foodstuffs, oil, and other commodities used daily in urban homes were not organized at this time.[3] Reforms initiated prior to 1722/5 varied from those implemented later in the Kyōhō period. Ōishi Shinsaburō has noted that those preceding 1722/5 were ad hoc efforts without any central concept to integrate them into a coordinated program, while those after 1722/5 were part

34

of a coordinated program united in both theory and practice. The dividing point 1722/5 signifies a change in the advisors who were directing policy formation under the shogun Yoshimune. It is after this date that Yoshimune was able to begin his own programs without the interference of senior officials who tried to direct his efforts. It is this shift in direction which caused Ōishi to select 1722/5 as the beginning of the Kyōhō reforms under Yoshimune.[4]

Within the commercial sector, a change in the direction of *bakufu* policy is evident after 1724. In 1724/2 all merchants, both *tonya* and *nakagai*, dealing in ginned cotton, cotton cloth, bleached cotton, silk pongee, textiles, paper, tea, tobacco, bean paste, soy, rice, salt, *sake*, lamp oil, and other goods, all together twenty-three commodities, were ordered to register with the Edo city magistrates' office. Few of these merchants had been included in the *kabu nakama* organized in 1721, indicating that a new approach to commercial control had been initiated. A second order called for price reductions for bean paste, soy, and *sake*. Each of these commodities used rice as a major ingredient in production and yet they had increased in price with other consumer goods while the price of rice had declined. The price reduction order was designed to equalize price levels for rice and rice-related goods. A more general order for price reduction was issued in 1724/3 and this was followed in 1724/5 by *kabu nakama* formation for dealers trading in twenty-one commodities. Associated with *kabu nakama* formation was a request by the government for explanations of the price increases which had occurred for consumer goods other than rice.[5]

Price control policies introduced in 1724 attempted to lower the price of commodities which utilized rice in their production as well as forcing price reductions for other goods which were major consumption items for the samurai class. These included bamboo, charcoal, wood, firewood, salt, oil, cloth, and other merchandise. Both groups of goods had to be made more responsive to changes in the price of rice, rather than being subject to independent price determination, if the financial problems of the samurai were to be alleviated. The government was anxious to lower commodity price levels and raise the price of rice so that a balance could be established between samurai incomes and their material requirements.[6]

Official concern with price controls and increasing the value of the rice-based salaries of the samurai was a new development under Yoshimune. During the seventeenth century, *bakufu* policy had tended to depress the price of rice and guard against what was regarded as excessive consumption. Rice utilization in *sake* manufacture was limited by government order and this proved to be a barrier to the development of rice as a commercial crop. Trade in rice futures which had developed during the first half of the seventeenth century was discouraged in Ōsaka after 1654 when both rice promissory notes and buying rice futures were prohibited. The government hoped to prevent speculation and rapid price fluctuations by controlling the market for rice.[7] Throughout the latter half of the seventeenth century attempts were made to freeze the price of rice in order to stabilize the economic foundation of the *bakuhan* order. Despite these policies speculation in rice futures flourished and the price rose. Then, in the 1720s when Yoshimune moved to control these price increases, the bottom dropped out of the market as the result of increased production and monetary factors and the government was forced to work at raising the price of rice instead.

After 1724 *bakufu* officials in Ōsaka and Kyōto were ordered to reverse their policy on rice futures, assuming that this would have a favorable impact on the price of rice. This was a change of policy by the shogunate and was followed in 1728 by the authorization of futures transactions for rice and in 1730 by the establishment of a central rice market at Dojima in Ōsaka. Limitations on the consumption of rice in *sake* brewing were eliminated as were official price controls, and large rice purchases from the private sector were encouraged. To prevent dumping by daimyo, limits were set on the volume of rice which could be shipped by the various *han* to the major rice markets of Ōsaka, Kyōto, and Edo. This avoided both oversupply and attendant price declines.[8]

The imbalance in commodity prices had caused considerable concern within the *bakufu* and in 1723 inquiries were sent to the city magistrates of Edo, Kyōto, and Ōsaka asking for advice on price control. The two Edo city magistrates in their reply of 1723/10 made the following recommendations:

(1) Merchants dealing in daily necessities should be organized into *tonya, nakagai,* and retailers, for these are the three stages of commodity marketing. They should further be organized into *nakama* and *kumiai*.

(2) Through the *nakama* and *kumiai* dishonest merchants who corner the market and sell at inflated prices could be eliminated and excessive prices controlled.

(3) Prices have risen because of competition between traders, shippers, and producers. If producers were authorized to sell only to officially licensed *tonya,* monopoly profits could be controlled.

(4) The lowering of prices could be assured by investigating commodity circulation at Uraga, the port for Edo, and Ōsaka. Investigation of eleven commodities shipped from Ōsaka to Edo including rice, oil, *sake,* soy, vinegar, firewood, fish oil, salt, bean paste, ginned cotton, and cotton cloth, supplemented by monthly reports from Ōsaka to the Edo city magistrates, could be used to enforce price controls.[9]

The Edo city magistrates advocated the adoption of established merchant categories as the basis for *bakufu* policies toward commerce. The distinctions between *tonya, nakagai,* and retailers were well advanced in trades which had attained a high degree of functional differentiation. This was symbolic of regularized commerce, and the adoption of similar designations by the government made good sense. The formation of *nakama* and *kumiai* was a logical step for the regulation of commerce in Edo. Similar policies of *nakama* authorization had previously been applied in Ōsaka with good results and it was quite natural to apply these policies to Edo as a means of expanding the number of trades incorporated into an institutionalized framework. The *nakama* could then be used as a mechanism for implementing government commercial controls.

Government commercial policies differed in Edo and Ōsaka during the Kyōhō reforms. No policy of *kabu nakama* formation was implemented in Ōsaka in either 1721 or 1724 as these institutions had been authorized in Ōsaka in the late seventeenth century. With official concern largely directed toward improving the economic conditions of the samurai in Edo, reform policy in Ōsaka concentrated on collecting data on shipments from Ōsaka to the shogunal capital. These inquiries in Ōsaka complemented *nakama* formation in Edo and were continuous between 1724 and 1730.[10] Between 1724 and 1726, the *bakufu* investigated importing *tonya*, import volumes, sources of goods, shippers, and so forth. In 1727 shippers were ordered to report the owner, captain, capacity, and port of origin for all vessels of over 200 *koku* burden which entered Ōsaka and also whether or not the vessel was going on to Edo. Both shipping agents and *tonya* were ordered to reveal their regional affiliations and all arrivals in Ōsaka were to be reported to the city shipping office within ten days after landing.[11]

One of the results of the *bakufu* shipping surveys of the Kyōhō period was the emergence of a better picture of the ties between Ōsaka and Edo. With Ōsaka as the major market in Kinai and western Japan, much of the trade in these regions was with Ōsaka. The development of marketing facilities within the city encouraged this process and was in turn enhanced by the expansion of trade with Ōsaka. Largely as the result of the development of an Ōsaka-centered marketing system, many historians of the Tokugawa period have claimed that *bakufu* regulations which required trade between daimyo domains to pass through the city were a major factor in the successful growth of the Ōsaka market. Yasuoka Shigeaki, who has done extensive work on the development of Ōsaka as a commercial center, has been unable to find any evidence to corroborate this theory. No government regulations directing trade from the *han* through Ōsaka have been found, adding weight to the notion that the development of Ōsaka was the result of a favorable geographical location, good transportation facilities by the westward sea route, and the availability of a major consumption area in the Kinai region surrounding the city. This position is further substantiated by the successful challenges to the dominance of the Ōsaka market in the nineteenth century and by studies which have shown the independence of the Edo market with respect to many kinds of goods.[12]

SUPPLYING THE EDO MARKET

The interaction between Ōsaka and Edo during the Tokugawa period has been a subject of controversy in Japanese economic history. The development of Ōsaka into a major commercial center in the seventeenth century and the later development of Edo suggested to many that throughout the Tokugawa period it was the Ōsaka merchants who controlled trade throughout major portions of Tokugawa Japan and who also supplied the major requirements of the shogunal capital. A number of factors contributed to this belief. To begin with, until rather recently studies of the Ōsaka market have been far more extensive than those of Edo. One reason for this has been the availability of more easily accessible documentation on Ōsaka. Much of the documentation for Edo was lost in fires in the city during the Tokugawa period and a large portion of the remainder was lost in the disastrous Kantō earthquake of 1923. Many of the recent studies of commerce in Edo have utilized private collections of family documentation which previously had not been utilized. A second factor was the dominant cultural image of Ōsaka at the end of the seventeenth century. This implied a complementary domination of the economic life of Tokugawa Japan by Ōsaka, and while it was true to an extent it has been greatly overemphasized. Third, many interpretations of the 'rise of the merchant class' and the 'fall of the Tokugawa *bakufu*' assumed a conflict between urban merchants centered in Ōsaka and the 'feudal' authority of the shogunate centered in Edo. This too has contributed to the distorted impression of the role of the Ōsaka merchants.[13]

Recent studies of Tokugawa economic history have discovered that, while there was considerable trade between Ōsaka and Edo, Edo was the center of an independent marketing system as well. These studies have shown that to a large degree the consumption requirements of Edo were supplied directly and were independent of the Ōsaka market. Among the major students of the Edo market have been Ōishi Shinsaburō and Hayashi Reiko.[14] Ōishi has compared the export statistics from Ōsaka for the years from 1724 to 1730 with import statistics for the port of Uraga – port of entry for Edo – for 1726 and has shown that Edo was independent of Ōsaka for many goods and dependent on it for various processed goods.[15]

Hayashi Reiko has compared Ōsaka exports and Edo imports for eleven commodities for the years 1726 and 1856, illustrating the changing nature of the Ōsaka-Edo trade. Table 7 gives her data. It should be noted that her data for 1726 are identical with those used by Ōishi in his study. The statistics in table 7 illustrate the dependence of Edo in 1726 on imports from Ōsaka for such goods as ginned cotton, cotton cloth, oil, soy, and *sake*, but also show how supplies of rice, charcoal, firewood, salt, fish oil, and

TABLE 7. Ōsaka exports and Edo imports for 1726 and 1856

Commodity	Edo imports 1726 (A)	Ōsaka exports 1726 (B)	B/A %	Edo imports 1856 (C)	Ōsaka exports 1856 (D)	D/C %
Ginned cotton (bales)	82 019	98 119	119.6	29 676	9 989[a]	(33.7)
Cotton cloth (100 *tan* bales)	36 135	12 171	33.7	80 168	14 505[a]	(18.1)
Oil (barrels)	90 811	69 172	76.2	100 000	60 000	60.0
Sake (barrels)	795 856	117 687	22.3	1 156 000	1 000 000	86.5
Soy (barrels)	132 829	101 457	76.4	1 565 000	90 000	5.8
Rice (bags)	861 893	3	0.0	3 010 000	—	0
Charcoal (bags)	809 790	764	0.0	2 475 000	—	0
Fish oil (barrels)	50 501	—	0	30 000	—	0
Salt (bags)	1 670 880	—	0	1 600 000 (171 000[b])	1 600 000	—
Firewood (bundles)	18 209 687	—	0	18 370 900 (7 499 300[c])	—	0
Bean paste (barrels)	2 898	—	0	274 320	—	0

SOURCE: Hayashi R., 'Kinsei chūkōki no shōgyō,' p. 192.
[a] Data constructed from data for 1858–9.
[b] The unit used is baskets.
[c] The unit counter used is *hon* which could mean either logs or bundles of firewood.

bean paste appear to have originated elsewhere. Thus it was processed goods which were the primary components of the daily necessities shipped from Ōsaka to the shogunal capital. It should, however, be kept in mind that these are pre-modern statistics, are highly questionable in terms of accuracy, and have to be interpreted with great caution. This qualification notwithstanding, even taking the obvious inconsistencies in the data into consideration, it is apparent that processed goods such as oil, *sake*, and soy were produced in the Kinai region and shipped from Ōsaka to Edo in quantity in the early eighteenth century. Similarly, goods which required less in the way of processing technology, such as charcoal, fish oil, salt, firewood, bean paste, and rice, were clearly supplied to Edo from sources other than Ōsaka. While the export statistics are far from precise, it is highly unlikely that this kind of bulky item would have been shipped from Ōsaka by other than waterborne transport. Thus the absence of significant quantities of these goods in the Ōsaka export data – data which focused on coastal shipping records – confirm the direct supply of charcoal, fish oil, salt, firewood, bean paste, and rice from coastal areas between Ōsaka and Edo, from the Kantō region, or from northeastern Honshū.[16]

Table 7 suggests that rice shipped from Ōsaka was insignificant in supplying the requirements of Edo. By the mid-eighteenth century the population of Edo was around one million and a vast quantity of rice and other foodstuffs was required to sustain it. Rice was shipped to Edo from the Kantō and Tōhoku (northeast) regions beginning in the seventeenth century. Sendai, Nambu, Tsugaru, Akita, and Yonezawa *han* were major suppliers of the Edo rice market and rice crops in these areas had a major impact on the price of rice in the Edo market. Between 1660 and 1700 a rice market was institutionalized in Edo and one of the objectives of the eastward shipping route was to assure that regular supplies of rice would reach the capital by water.[17] Supplementing the rice available on the Edo rice market was that directly imported into Edo by the various daimyo from their domains. This satisfied much of the demand for rice from their households and retainers and as part of their personal baggage was not included in trade statistics for the city. This rice together with that marketed in Edo supplied the needs of the shogunal capital and supported an independent rice marketing system in eastern Japan.[18]

The independence of the Edo market for many commodities in the early eighteenth century is further substantiated by the 1856 data in table 7. These data, like those for 1726, are of questionable accuracy, but they too illustrate the role of Ōsaka as a supplier of processed goods for the Edo market. The importance of Kinai cotton for Edo appears to be much reduced from its role in 1726. This is consistent with the expansion of cotton cultivation and cloth production in the Kantō region and elsewhere in the late eighteenth and early nineteenth centuries.[19] Similarly, the importance of oil shipments from Ōsaka to Edo appears to have been reduced in the nineteenth century, reflecting the expansion of oil pressing outside Ōsaka and the failure of *bakufu* attempts to control both the production and marketing of pressed oils.[20] *Sake* shipped from Ōsaka appears to have increased in importance in the Edo market in the 1856 data while soy, which was being produced in all parts of Japan, appears to have declined dramatically. Since *sake* production was concentrated in Kinai, but also occurred elsewhere, the significance of the *sake* statistics is at present unclear. In any case, the dependence of Edo on exports from Ōsaka seems significantly reduced, indicating the increased independence of the Edo market. This is consistent with the growth of commercial agriculture and processing in the Kantō region and eastern Japan.[21]

LATE EIGHTEENTH CENTURY CHANGES IN THE ŌSAKA MARKET

During the latter half of the eighteenth century changes began to occur in the structure and function of the Ōsaka commodity market. One of the evidences of this change was an increase in the number of *kabu nakama* authorized by the *bakufu* in Ōsaka. Most of the *kabu nakama* had been in existence since the late seventeenth century as either authorized or unofficial merchant associations, but from between around 1760 and the late 1780s they received a new kind of status from the government.[22] Two developments of the second half of the eighteenth century created the incentive for closer ties to the government and new supports for the Ōsaka merchant associations. The first was the growth of new markets in the vicinity of Ōsaka, which was accompanied by a growing independence on the part of the cultivators in the Kinai region. The second was the development of new trade routes which increasingly bypassed Ōsaka and seriously threatened the dominant position of the Ōsaka merchants in the marketing of goods from Kinai.[23]

Complementing the desire for increased government protection of the Ōsaka merchant community was the need for new revenue sources by the *bakufu*. Beginning in the 1750s the *bakufu* began to search for means of cutting back government expenditures and this led to orders for budget economies in 1759, 1763, and 1764. As the result of these measures, the budget was reduced by 30 percent between 1755 and 1771. The reasons for the curtailment are not immediately apparent, for *bakufu* rice revenues were increasing through the 1750s and did not begin to decline until somewhat later. The monetary value of *bakufu* rice revenues was not keeping pace with the rise in tax revenues, however, so the increase in tax receipts was deceptive.[24]

Income from licensing fees was thus one justification for increased *kabu nakama* authorization by the *bakufu* in Ōsaka. However, while the fees from many of the associations were significant, this was not true of all the merchant groups. For example, the twenty-four-*kumi* Edo shipping *tonya nakama* paid 300 *ryō* in gold when it was authorized in 1784 and 100 *ryō* annually thereafter. The pressed rapeseed oil dealers paid 500 *ryō* the first year and 7 *kan* silver thereafter. Other groups paid far smaller fees, for example the straw ash *kabu nakama* which paid 5 *momme* silver per year in licensing fees.[25]

The assessment of licensing fees (*myōga kin*) on the *kabu nakama* by the *bakufu* after 1760 added a new source of government income. Prior to this time there was no regular mechanism for taxing the wealth of the commercial sector. Trade was regarded as morally impure and antithetical to the martial spirit of the samurai and therefore had not been exploited as a source of regular government revenue. With the implementation of licensing fees, the *bakufu* acknowledged the financial power of the merchants and agreed to increase its efforts to protect the urban merchant associations against the growing competition from new markets and new marketing routes. This was a new approach to supplementing the finances of the Tokugawa shogunate.[26]

While tapping the merchant sector for new sources of government revenue was one reason for *kabu nakama* authorization in the late eighteenth

41

century the protection of monopoly rights was another. Not all of the new *kabu nakama* were exclusive, limited membership groups. Some, such as those of oil pressers using water-wheels, pawnbrokers, medicine dealers, and coolies, extended their jurisdiction outside the city of Ōsaka to incorporate competitors in the provinces of Settsu and Kawachi. Others, like the seed cotton and cotton cloth traders, attempted to organize all rural traders in Settsu and Kawachi into a *kabu nakama*, although unsuccessfully.[27] Thus new forms of commercial control were also an objective of *kabu nakama* authorization between 1760 and the 1780s. Expansion of the network of trade associations could preserve the leadership of the Ōsaka merchants and retard the development of new marketing systems in the countryside.

One of the changes which occurred in agricultural production in the Kinai region during the eighteenth century was an increase in rice cultivation. The elimination of restrictions on rice sales and the encouragement of consumption by the commercial sector had made rice a more profitable crop and many cultivators expanded their involvement with rice farming as a result. Commercial rice farming was also encouraged by the liberalization of daimyo controls over rice sales and the expansion of the *sake* brewing industry in the Kinai region. Associated with the growth of *sake* brewing was the appearance of rural rice merchants who collected rice in the villages and sold it directly to the brewers rather than directing it toward satisfying urban food needs. Tax rice was also included in commercial transactions as an increasing proportion of land taxes were paid in cash rather than in kind.[28]

In the early eighteenth century commercially produced rice was usually sold through the urban markets, but as production increased a rural market mechanism developed in competition with the central rice market in Ōsaka. Rural merchants, many of whom had formerly been rural buyers for Ōsaka rice merchants, competed for rice in the villages.[29] In 1756 a rice market was established in Fushimi and the following year a market for buying and selling rice futures was opened in Izumi. By 1772 a rice market was operating in Nishinomiya.[30] In addition was a market which had been operating in Hyōgo for merchant rice since around the 1760s.[31] Each of these markets operated in competition with the Dojima rice market in Ōsaka.

As the demand for rice increased in areas outside the major market cities new trading patterns evolved which took a more direct route from the producers to the consumers, and eliminated the intermediary role of the Ōsaka rice market in Kinai. The Ōsaka rice merchants attempted to preserve their monopoly over rice sales by requesting several times between 1762 and 1783 an extension of their trade rights in the area surrounding Ōsaka. The *bakufu* failed to respond to these requests and it was not until the early nineteenth century when daimyo rice shipments to Ōsaka also declined that the *bakufu* tried to deal with the problem of the new marketing systems for rice.[32]

Competitive marketing systems also developed in the cotton and rape-seed trades in the Kinai region. As processing technology was diffused into Kinai villages the cultivators began to increase their involvement in processing as a form of by-employment. The Ōsaka *tonya* attempted to preserve their monopoly in processing as well as their control over the marketing of processed goods by requesting additional commercial guarantees from the *bakufu*. In the cotton trade this resulted in the reinforcement of existing merchant associations and an effort to extend the jurisdiction of several of them into Settsu and Kawachi. For example in 1773 an effort was made to establish a *kabu nakama* with 1500 *kabu* to incorporate all rural traders in seed cotton and cotton cloth in Settsu and Kawachi. Opposition from rural merchants blocked this effort but the *nakama* was able to extend its jurisdiction to villages bordering on Ōsaka.[33]

Similarly, a *kabu nakama* was organized in 1759 for lamp oil traders in an effort to lower the price of oil. This was a continuation of policies initiated in 1741 which attempted to direct all shipments of oil from Ōsaka to Edo through an authorized network of licensed *tonya*. Efforts were made to localize oil pressing in Ōsaka by directing that all oil seeds, including rapeseed and cotton seed, be sent to Ōsaka for processing. Competition from producers in Hyōgo and Nishinomiya as well as shipments to Edo from these cities and from central and western Japan had undermined government controls over the oil trade. Amagasaki *han* took an independent position on local oil production and as a result was in 1769 ordered to turn over to the government the towns of Hyōgo and Nishinomiya as well as coastal villages located in the *han* where oil was being produced. These areas were assessed at 14 000 *koku* and they were replaced by *bakufu* lands assessed at 19 000 *koku*. In addition, other villages located along the coast were also confiscated in the effort to control the production and sale of pressed oil in Kinai.[34] Despite these efforts, government controls over the marketing of cotton and pressed oils failed and rural competition continued to increase. The objective of the government actions was to preserve the traditional mechanism for commodity marketing centered on Ōsaka and ensure the continued domination of Kinai regional trade by Ōsaka merchants. It was hoped that through the new *kabu nakama* the rural merchants and processors could be made dependent on the Ōsaka merchants, but while the associations did serve to retard the development of rural competition, they had only short-term success.[35]

Competitive marketing systems also developed for goods coming to Ōsaka from outside the Kinai region. For example, the trade route for marketing Tosa firewood was disrupted when a dispute developed among the producers, shippers, and Ōsaka firewood *tonya*. In 1775 Tosa *han* attempted to establish a new trade route and set up its own firewood *tonya* in Ōsaka. The dispute escalated into a confrontation between the *han,* acting to increase its profits from firewood sales, and the *bakufu,* working to preserve the monopoly position of the Ōsaka firewood *tonya nakama.* The interests of Tosa *han* were brought into conflict with *bakufu* policies for preserving and strengthening the established marketing system.[36]

With the growth of specialized markets and the expansion of commercial agricultural production the cultivators began to demand higher prices for their crops. Until the late eighteenth century, the Ōsaka *tonya* could guarantee delivery of crops through a system of advanced payments which provided to the farmers much of the capital required in the productive process. This advance-payment system made the cultivators financially dependent on the Ōsaka merchants and their rural purchasing agents, but the payment had to be maintained at a sufficiently high level to both cover production costs and offer an incentive to the villagers to cultivate the crops which the buyers sought. With the expansion of rural trade came new sources of investment capital which offered competitive resources to the producers and began to undermine the effectiveness of the advanced payment system. In instances when the Ōsaka *tonya* or their agents failed to make a competitive offer, the cultivators were increasingly able to find alternative sources of financing.[37]

Further, the expansion of commercial agricultural output was not effectively absorbed through increased taxation by the daimyo, leading to an increased availability of capital within the villages. For many cultivators it resulted in greater independence and flexibility in their choice of crops and enabled them in some cases to increase their own share of the investment capital for tools and fertilizers required for future production. This together with the increased involvement in various forms of agricultural by-employment decreased the dependence of many farmers on the capital resources of the urban *tonya.*[38]

Further complicating the position of the Ōsaka merchants was the increasing involvement of *han* governments in commercial pursuits, like that of Tosa *han* discussed above. *Han* governments expanded their involvement in commercial agricultural production to maximize the financial returns to the daimyo. Cultivation of cash crops was encouraged and monopoly buying offices were established so that government monopsonies would be able to monopolize the profits from sales of domain goods. Thus in the late eighteenth and early nineteenth centuries the *han* began to compete with the Ōsaka merchants for a large share of the returns derived from sales of *han* goods.[39]

One mechanism for encouraging production within the *han* was importing technology. Kumamoto *han* encouraged silkworm culture and imported techniques from the Kyōto Nishijin silk industry. Yonezawa *han* imported silkworms and skilled technicians from Date and Fukushima *han*, sent the technicians on teaching tours throughout the domain, and then published a book on silkworm and mulberry cultivation for distribution in the *han*. Tsugaru *han* also promoted silkworm culture, imported two experts from the Kinai region, and loaned capital to cultivators to encourage production.[40]

A second means of promoting commercial agricultural production was distributing raw materials or capital for fertilizer and tools, or lending subsistence money to the producers until they received an income from their productive efforts. For example, in Kumamoto *han* wax tree cultivation was encouraged by interest-free loans for fertilizer, tools, and household expenses and many farmers were given as much as one year's food rations to assist them in the first year of cultivation. Those already engaged in production were given low-interest loans to encourage expansion of their involvement. Yonezawa *han* encouraged mulberry production for silkworm culture by establishing seedling parks for mulberry trees and distributing the trees to cultivators for no payment. Fukuyama *han* encouraged *tatami* cover production by giving interest-free loans to cultivators for growing the *igusa* reed necessary as a raw material and making loans to mat weavers as well. Other *han* used tax exemptions, promotion money, and prizes to encourage commercial agricultural production.[41]

A third approach to encourage commercial agriculture was the establishment of buying offices within the *han* which loaned capital and raw materials, spread technology, investigated production problems, and set up marketing systems for the distribution and sale of crops. Many *han* used capital from wealthy merchants or printed special *han* notes to finance these ventures or employed merchants to develop market networks or serve in supervisory positions for a share of the profits. For example the Tokugawa collateral house at Mito had a *konnyaku* (devil's tongue) buying office and used the profits from *konnyaku* sales to repay loans to Edo and Ōsaka merchants. The Matsudaira house of Takamatsu had a sugar monopoly operated through a buying office in the domain which also served to make loans and otherwise encourage sugar production.[42]

A fourth approach to increasing *han* output of commercial agricultural commodities was banning imports of competitive goods. For example, Himeji *han* banned imports of indigo in 1820 to encourage indigo production within the domain. Similarly, the Satake of Akita *han* banned imports of cotton and silk cloth as a means of encouraging local production.[43] Each of the methods discussed above interfered with the established marketing systems centered on Ōsaka or other urban centers. All of them, when combined with the growing competition of rural traders and processing industries, posed serious problems for the preservation of urban domination over the commercial life of Tokugawa Japan.

While competition for market control increased in the late eighteenth century, there is considerable evidence that the volume of commercial agricultural production also increased. One index of this growth was the expansion of processing industries in Ōsaka, the Kinai region, and elsewhere in Japan. From the early eighteenth century until the 1760s, the position of handicraft industry in Ōsaka improved considerably. At the beginning of the century the value of exports from Ōsaka was only around 20 percent of the value of imports to the city. By the 1760s exports had increased to approximately 40 percent of the value of imports. Changes in the financial operation of the Ōsaka market contributed to the improvement of the balance of trade, but there is considerable evidence to justify the conclusion that handicraft industrial goods and agricultural finished goods were produced in greater volume over the course of the eighteenth century.[44]

After around 1760, the volume of raw materials for handicraft industrial production imported into Ōsaka began to decline. This reflected an increase in rural processing activities in the Kinai region and elsewhere, rather than a reduction in agricultural output.[45] Metal industries were not affected by this trend and efforts to increase the role of Ōsaka in the production of iron and brass goods proved successful.[46] In other industries, for example oil and cotton processing in Ōsaka and the silk industry in Kyōto, the predominant position of urban processors was giving way in the face of increased production in the agricultural villages.[47]

Typical of the growing *bakufu* concern with the inroads made by rural processing industries were edicts issued by the Kyōto city magistrate between 1751 and 1788. They discussed prices and the need to strengthen marketing systems, as well as prohibiting direct purchases from unauthorized merchants, and suggested that outsiders could be controlled most effectively by incorporating them into *nakama* where they would be forced to conform with established business procedures. This official encouragement notwithstanding, the admission of rival merchants into the various silk processing *nakama* failed to eliminate the competition from outsiders. Within the *nakama* disputes occurred between old and new members and the expansion of new market forces and rural processors continued. The development of *kabu nakama* to protect Ōsaka and Kyōto merchants from outside competition was not a complete failure, however. Rural competitors were suppressed to some degree and it was not until the nineteenth century that the dominance of the urban merchants was really broken.[48]

The last decades of the eighteenth century marked the beginning of the decline of the marketing system centered on Ōsaka in western Japan. The growth of new markets, the increase in rural merchants, the development of new trade routes, and the growing inability of the Ōsaka merchants and processors to maintain their domination over the Kinai region heralded the increased importance of rural merchants and localized marketing systems. During the 1760s and 1770s the first serious inroads began to be made into the dominant position of the Ōsaka merchants and this was met with a system of reinforced *kabu nakama*. The *nakama* retarded the process of institutional change, but by the first quarter of the nineteenth century the Ōsaka merchant community was being seriously challenged for control over commodity marketing in the Kinai region. While the payment of licensing fees to the *bakufu* increased government support of the urban merchant monopolies, the success of this policy was transient at best. In the nineteenth century the position of the Ōsaka merchants would be further undermined and the willingness of the government to come to their support would diminish dramatically.

THE KANSEI REFORMS

With the death of the tenth shogun in 1786 came a shake-up in government policy-making circles. Tanuma Okitsugu, a leading figure in many of the new commercial policies initiated in the 1760s and 1770s, was quickly removed from *bakufu* office and replaced as senior advisor to the shogun by Matsudaira Sadanobu. Sadanobu, a grandson of the eighth Tokugawa shogun, Yoshimune, was determined to restore the *bakufu* in the image of the 'golden years' under his grandfather. His efforts along these lines constituted the so-called Kansei reforms of 1787 to 1793.

Characteristic of Sadanobu's reforms were attempts to restore the moral fervor of Tokugawa society via retrenchment policies and sumptuary laws, and condemnation of prostitution, bribery, expensive clothing, elaborate hair styles, and lewd literature. Efforts were made to turn back the clock to the beginning of the eighteenth century and negate the changes which had occurred in Japanese society.[49]

Matsudaira Sadanobu and his advisors had developed their reputations as reformers in their own domains. All had instituted policies which had placed the prosperity of their *han* and their personal financial security above all other considerations. Sadanobu instituted a purge of Tanuma's supporters in the *bakufu* and removed the restrictions imposed under Tanuma on the commercial prerogative of the daimyo.[50] The economic orientation of the Kansei reforms resulted in official encouragement of *han* monopolies as a means of improving *han* finances as well as efforts to improve the financial position of the *bakufu*. However, it was no longer possible to improve *bakufu* revenues significantly by improved tax collection and extensive land reclamation projects as had been done by Yoshimune during the Kyōhō reforms.[51]

Various examples of *kabu nakama* abolition during the Kansei reforms illustrate government concern with conflicts between the institutionalized market system and new forces active in commodity marketing. The extension of *kabu nakama* during the 1760s and 1770s indicated the growing instability of urban merchant control over commodity marketing. Many within the *bakufu* were increasingly uneasy with the problems which arose because of restrictive commercial policies. On the one hand, control seemed to be facilitated by the *nakama*, but on the other, the growing opposition to the *nakama* from both cultivators and rural traders indicated that this institutionalized structure was not a universal prescription for regulating commerce.[52]

In 1787 *kabu nakama* for firewood and charcoal *tonya* were abolished as were those for various transporters as a means of expanding trade and transport routes. In 1790 the *kabu nakama* for Kyōto rice shippers was abolished to improve the circulation of this essential commodity. In Edo the *kabu nakama* for rapeseed buying *tonya* and forwarding agents were eliminated as were those for cotton seed *tonya* and *nakagai*. Two objectives underlay these actions. The first was a desire to reverse the process of institutionalization in the commercial sector. The second, at times contradictory, response was a desire to eliminate specific bottlenecks to the smooth flow of goods to the major consumption centers.[53]

Price control was another objective of Matsudaira Sadanobu's reform policies. Low rice output in 1783 sent prices soaring for rice and related goods such as *sake* and bean paste. In 1784 a bumper crop reduced the price of rice, but other commodities failed to follow suit. Price levels remained high until 1790 when the government took the position that excess profits and merchant greed were the cause of the inflated prices. In 1790/2 a national order for price reduction was issued by the *bakufu*. A survey of price levels from 1783 to 1790 was initiated to determine price movements for rice and other goods from their place of origin in the *han* or other areas through the marketing system to the urban retailers. The city magistrates of Edo, Kyōto, and Ōsaka were made responsible for price controls and for marketing studies of consumer goods. In 1790/3 an inquiry was begun in Ōsaka on the marketing of fourteen commodities: soy, salt, bean paste, charcoal, firewood, vinegar, tea, *tatami* covers, dried sardines, groceries, lacquer ware and furniture, pottery, sulphur, and paper. In 1790/4 cotton and cotton cloth were included in the survey. Data were collected on the origin, trade volume, purchase price, buyers, sale price, and *nakama* fees including profits for each of the goods surveyed. A similar inquiry was made in Kyōto and for shipments bound for Edo. These data were then studied and price reductions ordered in Ōsaka beginning in 1790/8. Similar orders were issued in Edo after 1790/9.[54] There is, however, little evidence that these efforts at price control had any real impact on commodity price levels.

Another aspect of the Kansei reforms was the effort to strengthen the position of Edo relative to Ōsaka as a commercial center. The *bakufu* tried to develop sources for emergency loans within the community of Edo merchants as well as set up a group of Edo merchants to assist in the implementation of government commercial policies. This included an effort to reduce the influence of merchant houses which had branches in Edo and their main stores elsewhere in Japan. Control over the Edo market was to be shifted to merchant houses which were primarily concerned with trade in the shogunal capital and maintained their primary outlets there. As part of this program a group of merchants in Edo were designated as purveyors to the *bakufu*.[55] Membership in this special group of Edo merchants varied over time, but all were important Edo merchant houses which had begun their rise to prominence during the early eighteenth century and grown powerful during the 1760s and 1770s. While of some importance to the shogunate during the 1790s, they were of particular assistance as economic advisors to the *bakufu* in the first half of the nineteenth century.[56]

The impact of the Kansei reforms is difficult to assess as they came to a sudden end in 1793 when Matsudaira Sadanobu was removed from *bakufu* office. Some short-term gains had been achieved and *bakufu* finances had been temporarily bolstered, but the negative policies solved none of the problems which underlay the financial weakness of the Tokugawa economic order. The reforms can be viewed as a temporary aberration and portent of the growing confusion and frustration which would characterize government economic policies in the nineteenth century. The gap between economic policy and economic realities – as seen in the changes occurring in commodity marketing and commercial agricultural production – was growing ever wider. Until the end of the Tokugawa shogunate, the position of the urban merchants would be increasingly challenged by the activities of rural merchants and processors. The success of this challenge is evident in the decline of the Ōsaka market and the growth of new trade patterns in the major production areas of the country.

THE DECLINE OF THE ŌSAKA MARKET

The first four decades of the nineteenth century were characterized by changes in marketing patterns in the Kinai area. Associated with these changes was the decline of the dominant role of the Ōsaka market. Illustrative of this decline was the reduction in the volume of goods which were imported into the port of Ōsaka. Increased agricultural output resulted in dramatic increases in imports to Ōsaka until the 1820s and thereafter they fell rapidly as rural competition increased in intensity.[57] The decline in shipments to Ōsaka was not the result of drops in productivity and bad harvests in the 1830s. While no national surveys of agricultural production exist for this period, there are fragmentary data which indicate significant increases in specific crops in various areas of the country. For example, sugar production in Sanuki on the island of Shikoku is said to have increased by as much as 300 percent between 1830 and 1858, while rapeseed production in Okayama *han* is said to have risen six or seven times in the fifty years before 1877. Both rates of increase are improbable, but significant increases in sugar and rapeseed production can be assumed to have occurred. Rapeseed production in Tottori *han* also increased sharply during the nineteenth century. Similar increases are visible for cotton in western Japan.[58]

Table 8 gives the data available on Ōsaka imports for 1736, the 1804 to

TABLE 8. Ōsaka imports for 1736, the 1804–30 average, and 1840

Commodity	Units 10 000	1736	1804–30 average	1840	1736 index	1804–30 average index = 100	1840 index
Daimyo rice	*Koku*	112.0	150	108.5	75	100	72
Salt	Bags	46.3	120	98.6	–[a]	100	82
Charcoal	Bags	69.8	250	181.8	28	100	73
Cotton cloth	*Tan*	121.1	800	300.0	15	100	38
Ginned cotton	*Kan*	4.8	200	134.3	2	100	67
Seed cotton	*Kan*	35.3	150	97.7	24	100	65
Wax	Rolls	9.4[b]	10	6.0	–	100	60
Paper	Rolls	–	13	8.3	–	100	64
Indigo	Bags	2.1	4	4.2	53	100	105
Pottery	Bags	–	1	0.3	–	100	30
Copper	*Kin*	305.0	100	49.0	305	100	49
Animal hides	Pieces	–	10	7.2	–	100	72

SOURCE: Hayashi R., 'Kinsei chūkōki no shōgyō,' p. 226.
[a] The unit used is *koku* rather than bags.
[b] The unit used is *kan* rather than rolls.

1830 average, and 1840.[59] Even granting that the data in table 8 are not reliable, it appears that for most of the commodities listed, imports to Ōsaka hit a peak in the years between 1804 and 1830 and then declined sharply thereafter. The only commodity which did not decline by 1840 was indigo, suggesting that the monopoly market system for indigo was more effectively protected from outside competition than marketing systems for other goods. This was at least partially related to the Tokushima *han* monopoly on Awa indigo which dominated the Ōsaka indigo market.[60]

All other goods included in table 8 declined on the Ōsaka market after around 1830. With the exception of copper, all of the goods for which data are extant showed increases in the volume imported into Ōsaka from 1736 to the first quarter of the nineteenth century, suggesting increases in output. Yet Ōsaka imports for many of these commodities, including daimyo rice, charcoal, ginned cotton, seed cotton, wax, paper, and animal hides, declined by as much as 30 to 40 percent, and cotton cloth and pottery imports declined by almost 70 percent after 1804–30. While the data are not sufficiently reliable to justify acceptance of the figures on rate of decline with any confidence, they do indicate that significant changes had occurred in the trade structure of the Ōsaka market. The trends are unmistakable. If drops in output do not effectively explain these declines, and I am convinced that they do not, significant transitions occurred in the nature of commodity marketing in the Kinai region during the first four decades of the nineteenth century.

Several factors underlay these declines in imports to Ōsaka. One was the extension of *han* monopolies which interrupted shipments of salt, cotton goods, paper, pottery, and hides – among the items covered in table 8 – to Ōsaka.[61] The growth of these monopolies continued in the early nineteenth century and increased in vigor as the strains on the Tokugawa economy intensified in the middle decades of the nineteenth century. The *bakufu* was not ignorant of this problem. During the 1830s the Ōsaka city magistrate Uchiyama Hikojirō advocated that the *han* monopolies be abolished as a means of restoring the marketing position of the Ōsaka merchants.[62] In 1842/3 this theme was raised in a report on commodities and their prices submitted by the city magistrate Abe Masazō. Abe felt the abolition of *han* monopolies was required to curtail the continuing increases in commodity prices.[63]

A second factor was the increased participation of both the cultivators and rural processors and the rural merchants in the marketing process. Between 1804 and 1830 there are many indications of a breakdown in urban-centered marketing networks. These changes were visible in the Kinai region and along the Inland Sea in the late eighteenth century, and were factors in the increase in *kabu nakama* organization after around 1760. Similar changes occurred in the Kantō region and other parts of Japan during and after the first quarter of the nineteenth century.[64] Other factors including new trade routes, the growth of subsidiary markets outside the three major cities, and the increasing inability of the *bakufu* to control the growth of commercial agriculture and rural trade also contributed to the decline of Ōsaka. All of these factors will be discussed in detail with respect to the Kinai cotton trade in Chapters 5 and 7.

One of the indications of the changing role of the producers and rural merchants was the increase in legal disputes between villages in Settsu, Kawachi, and Izumi and the Ōsaka *kabu nakama*. Legal disputes between 1740 and 1797 were largely concerned with fertilizer prices and monopoly practices. Lawsuits brought before the *bakufu* or its representatives in Kinai during the period from 1805 to 1865 were overwhelmingly concerned with the restrictive practices of the monopoly merchants in the pressed oil trade. Other suits were directed at the Ōsaka merchants who dominated the cotton trade, and the number of fertilizer suits dropped precipitously. One study of this pattern of legal disputes suggests that the lack of disputes prior to 1740 illustrates a lack of repressive controls by Ōsaka merchants rather than a lack of documentation. It was only after this period that efforts were made to regulate trade in the Kinai region more effectively. The scale of these suits also increased in the nineteenth century. For example in 1823, 1007 villages of cotton cultivators complained against the restrictive monopoly enjoyed by the Ōsaka cotton merchants. The largest of the nineteenth century disputes involved 1460 villages which joined in a complaint against low oil seed prices and high oil prices in 1824. During the nineteenth century, there were at least seven complaints from groups of over 500 villages from Settsu, Kawachi, and Izumi.[65]

Market controls over rapeseed and cotton were designed to reinforce the deteriorating monopoly rights of the Ōsaka pressed oil and cotton merchants. The opposition generated from the rapeseed and cotton cultivating villages was aimed not at the *bakufu* or the Tokugawa *bakuhan* order, as has been claimed in some interpretations, but rather at removing the restrictions on direct trade in Settsu, Kawachi, and Izumi. Unrest in Kinai villages was symptomatic of the growing interest in a more open market structure, rather than an expression of political dissent. The confrontation was not between the cultivators and the *bakufu*. The *bakufu* was involved as the locus of authority to which the cultivators could turn to voice their grievances. While economic changes played a role in undermining the foundations of the *bakufu*, developments in Kinai were directed at improving the position of the cultivators and rural merchants and were not an organized expression of political opposition to Tokugawa authority.[66]

The lawsuits illustrate the increasingly aggressive efforts by cultivators, often in league with rural merchants, to break the restrictions on direct sales of their goods. Reinforcement of the *kabu nakama* worked to retard the growth of rural marketing systems, but by the nineteenth century rural trade had made significant inroads in the Kinai region. For example, in the oil trade rural merchants increasingly displaced urban oil traders. While temporarily blocked in *bakufu*-controlled villages, they were very successful in nearby daimyo-controlled areas.[67] The *bakufu* found it extremely difficult to deal with this kind of competition with the Ōsaka merchants, although in the oil trade the annexation of parts of Amagasaki *han*, discussed above, enabled it to extend its jurisdiction. This was not so easily done for other commodities, however, although an unsuccessful effort was made to expand *bakufu* control in the Ōsaka area in the 1840s.

In eastern Japan, particularly the Kantō region surrounding Edo, substantial increases in commercial agricultural production were achieved by the late eighteenth century. Although this region lagged behind in rate of commercialization as compared with the Kinai region, it emerged as a major producer of market-oriented commercial crops. With *bakufu* encouragement processing industries such as *sake* brewing were expanded as a means of reducing the dependence of Edo on Kinai *sake* production. Kantō cotton production increased dramatically after the 1760s and 1770s and while the product was inferior to goods from Kinai, it began to make inroads into the Edo market.[68]

Until the early nineteenth century control over both Kantō cotton production and cotton goods imported from Kinai was maintained by the Edo cotton *tonya* associations. Disruption of their control began to be apparent in the last decades of the eighteenth century and became acute in the following century. In 1804 and 1805 the Edo cotton merchants asked that the city magistrates take steps to control the competitive activities of outsiders. Much of the disruption was related to breakdowns in the marketing system from Ōsaka to Edo, but increasingly the Edo cotton merchants attempted to establish institutionalized controls over the Kantō cotton trade as well.[69]

Lawsuits were filed in the nineteenth century by Edo *tonya nakama* to block competitive activities by outsiders in the silk trade, and suits were filed against Edo merchant groups to open up the marketing system for Shizuoka tea, soy, and lamp oil. The *bakufu* attempted to strengthen the Edo merchants by organizing them into reinforced *kabu nakama* and charging licensing fees for their invigorated protection.[70] This tied the Edo *tonya* more closely to the *bakufu*, but, as the increase in complaints from the licensed merchants in the 1830s suggests, it was not effective in suppressing the development of alternative marketing patterns and new merchant groups in the countryside. This is particularly evident with respect to Edo merchant control over Kantō cotton production and distribution.[71]

The difficulties experienced by the Edo merchants were in many ways similar to those experienced by the Ōsaka merchant community in the late eighteenth century. The development of new marketing patterns and the diffusion of processing technology in the villages of the Kantō region and elsewhere undermined established mechanisms for controlling trade. Incursions into urban trade perquisites were greeted with merchant requests for additional government protection, resulting in the formation of new *kabu nakama*. But the *bakufu*, anxious to preserve the urban domination of commerce, did not have the direct authority to control competition which emanated from non-*bakufu* lands. Thus the government was increasingly frustrated by its efforts to control the growth of rural trade and rural processing industries. By the 1840s it was apparent that *bakufu* efforts at commercial control had failed and the government attempted to implement a new approach. These policies were included in the so-called Tempō reforms in which an effort was made to reassert the authority of the shogunate, repair the fiscal condition of the Tokugawa house and its retainers, and restructure commercial controls by abolishing the increasingly ineffective *kabu nakama* system.

THE TEMPŌ REFORMS

The so-called Tempō reforms of 1841 to 1843 combined elements from the earlier reforms of the Kyōhō and Kansei periods with some radical departures oriented towards strengthening the position of the shogun relative to the daimyo. Analysis of the Tempō reforms is complicated by the introduction of a new factor into domestic policy considerations in the form of increased Japanese awareness of a foreign presence in Japanese waters and by historical interpretations of the reforms which link them with both the Meiji restoration of 1868 and the modernization of Japan. The incursions of foreign vessels into Japanese waters in the nineteenth century and the Russian expansion into the northern islands and Hokkaidō placed new pressures on the *bakufu* to assert its authority and take steps to insure the development of defensive fortifications to keep out the foreign menace. This was one factor in the Tempō period which encouraged the assertion of Tokugawa authority over the daimyo. Among historians concerned with modern Japanese history, many have viewed the Tempō reforms as the beginning of Meiji 'authoritarianism' or as an initial step in the 'modernization' of the Japanese economy. Both views have served to distort the role of the Tempō reforms in the context of the Tokugawa *bakuhan* order.

Enacted under the leadership of the senior councillor Mizuno Tadakuni, the Tempō reforms included traditional elements such as moral reform, the encouragement of frugality and retrenchment, recoinage, forced loans from wealthy merchant houses, and the cancellation of samurai debts. More radical elements included were a reassertion of Tokugawa authority by forcing land transfers on some of the daimyo and the abolition of the *kabu nakama* and the *han* monopolies.[72]

Bakufu efforts to reassert the political power of the Tokugawa house over the daimyo came to a head in 1843 when the government ordered that parcels of daimyo and *hatamoto* (Tokugawa retainer) lands which lay within a twenty-mile radius of Edo castle or within a ten-mile radius of Ōsaka castle be transferred to the Tokugawa house in exchange for territory in other areas. The objectives of this move were varied. First, the *bakufu* wished to add these highly fertile areas to its own revenue base. Second, it wished to reaffirm Tokugawa authority over all daimyo and *hatamoto* land holdings. Third, it attempted to improve *bakufu* defenses in Edo and Ōsaka by unifying its control in the countryside surrounding these two major urban centers.[73] Opposition from both daimyo and *hatamoto* to these land transfers was immediate. Even more embarrassing was the hostile reaction from the cultivators who would have been most directly affected. Fearing tax increases and restrictive *bakufu* controls they petitioned to have the

54

order reversed. Faced with outspoken opposition from concerned daimyo, *hatamoto*, and villagers the *bakufu* reversed its position and withdrew its demands. This dealt a telling blow to the prestige of the shogunate, resulted in the ouster of Mizuno Tadakuni, and was a major factor in bringing the Tempō reforms to a rapid end.[74]

In the commercial sphere, Tempō reform policies were not unprecedented. Several *kabu nakama* were abolished during the Kansei reforms of 1787 to 1793. Although less than ten in number, they did set an example for future actions. The decision to terminate the *kabu nakama* was based on several considerations. To begin with, the *bakufu* wished to reassert its authority over commerce. Second, alternative marketing systems had severely compromised the effectiveness of the *kabu nakama* and they had become more of a liability than a source of assistance to the government. Abolition of the *kabu nakama* would eliminate the conflict between urban and rural traders, and, if complemented by the elimination of the *han* monopolies, would serve to reduce prices as well. Consequently, in 1841/12 the *kabu nakama* were abolished and this was followed by a second order of 1842/3 which extended the initial abolition order and consolidated anti-*nakama* policy.[75]

The elimination of the *kabu nakama* resulted in the dislocation of major urban marketing systems and price increases rather than improved circulation of goods and reduced prices as anticipated by the government.[76] The *bakufu* responded with orders for a 20 percent reduction of both prices and wages in Edo and Ōsaka. This was then bolstered in 1842/10 by a government order to eliminate all *han* monopolies to remove their impact on commodity marketing.[77] Faced with shortages of consumer goods in Edo and Ōsaka and attendant price increases the *bakufu* responded with directives which ignored the underlying economic factors. *Kabu nakama* abolition initially dislocated both transport and credit systems, but many of the urban merchant associations continued to function, despite their loss of official protection and support.

The impact of the Tempō reform commercial policies varied considerably. In the Kinai region, competitive market systems were already highly developed by the 1840s and the abolition of *kabu nakama* served to modify government policy and take this process into account. In the Kantō region and Edo, *kabu nakama* abolition had a more immediate impact as communications were disrupted and barriers to rural merchant inroads into the Edo market suddenly disappeared. Yet in both Edo and Ōsaka the *nakama* continued to play a role in the market and new organizations were formed to restore supply routes from Ōsaka to Edo. Once the initial shock of the reform policies had subsided, many groups were able to effectively avoid the intent of the abolition orders.[78]

By 1845 it was obvious that most of the reform policies had failed. Urban groups reorganized and rural trade continued to increase in volume and actively compete with urban merchants. By 1851, the government was anxious to reestablish controls over commerce and construct a mechanism which would incorporate both urban and rural merchants. Not only had *kabu nakama* abolition proved a failure, but the attempt to abolish the *han* monopolies had been largely ignored. In an effort to reassert authority over commercial activities in the major cities, in 1851/3 an order was issued to restore the *kabu nakama* as the basis for regulating trade.[79]

The revised merchant associations after 1851 varied in many respects from those prior to 1841. To begin with, all licensing fees and group payments were eliminated in an effort to reduce commodity prices. Second, all *nakama* were established with open membership policies, with some exemptions for trades which could justify restrictive membership. Both former *nakama* members and outsiders were included in the new associations, although subgroups of new and old members developed within many of the *nakama* for organizational reasons. Thus, while returning to the *nakama* format for control purposes, the *bakufu* indicated its awareness of the growth of competitive merchants and marketing systems. In 1852 the jurisdiction of the *nakama* was expanded and all merchants were ordered to join the new associations. By 1857 official policy had shifted and membership certificates were issued for both new and old members. Finally, in 1858 licensing fees were reinstituted as a means of increasing *bakufu* revenues. For all practical purposes official policy had returned to its position prior to 1841.[80]

The effectiveness of the restored *nakama* after 1851 is very difficult to judge, but there is considerable evidence that they fared no better than their predecessors. *Bakufu* jurisdiction extended no further than before and the incorporation of rural merchants could not be implemented in a comprehensive manner. Antagonism from rural merchants and cultivators to the domination of urban merchant groups continued and many were able to successfully challenge the monopoly rights which were granted the *nakama* by the *bakufu*. The successful continuation of *han* monopolies undermined the urban *nakama* from still another angle, further frustrating *bakufu* efforts at commercial controls. There is thus little to suggest that the post-1851 commercial policies of the shogunate met with any degree of success.[81]

Overall, the Tempō reforms were a dramatic failure for the *bakufu*. Both the efforts at reasserting national political authority and at regulating trade had been frustrated and resulted instead in a lowering of the authority and prestige of the Tokugawa house. The weakness of the government had been revealed on all sides as had its inability to contend effectively with matters of national importance. Although some analysts see the Tempō reforms and the subsequent restoration of the *nakama* as a consistent program for bringing all commercial activity under Tokugawa control, there is little evidence to substantiate this conclusion. It is extremely unlikely that the *bakufu*, incapable of comprehending the impact of the reforms, would consciously have followed a path which was so detrimental to its power and prestige.[82]

CONCLUSIONS

During the eighteenth and the first half of the nineteenth centuries, significant changes occurred in Japanese commerce. The volume of trade increased, hit a peak in Ōsaka around 1820 and probably around 1850 in Edo, and then decreased in both cities as the result of new marketing systems and the emergence of secondary market centers. In the Kinai region, most commodities were marketed via Ōsaka-centered trade routes until the late eighteenth century. Thereafter, alternative marketing patterns increased in importance with the growth of direct trade by rural producers, the expansion of rural commerce, and the augmentation of *han* monopoly systems. In the nineteenth century the dependent role of rural or secondary market towns on the Ōsaka market was gradually replaced by a more direct involvement of these centers in trade with other regions. This was true of both castle towns and of other towns and villages in the Kinai region, as will be discussed in Chapter 7.

Underlying this shift in marketing patterns was the diffusion of both commercial agricultural production and processing technology. In the early eighteenth century Kinai villages exported largely unfinished goods which were then processed in Ōsaka or other urban centers. By the late eighteenth century processing activities were a major source of by-employment in the villages of Kinai and the producers were in a better position to play a direct role in the marketing of their goods. This was particularly visible in the marketing of pressed oils and cotton goods as oil pressing and the ginning, spinning, and weaving of cotton developed in various sections of the Kinai region. Similar tendencies developed for other commodities and in each case the capacity of the urban merchants to control marketing and processing was adversely affected.

Economic change was also related to efforts by the daimyo to assert their control over their domains. *Han* monopolies were a manifestation of the need for new revenue sources by the *han*. When it became apparent that they were having a disruptive impact on trade in Ōsaka and Edo the daimyo in many cases elected to pursue their own interests, even if they conflicted with *bakufu* objectives for regulating commerce. The *han* monopolies worked to encourage the development of new trade routes and secondary market centers and were a factor in breaking down the monopolies of the urban *kabu nakama*. With its limited jurisdiction and inability

57

to interfere directly in *han* affairs – increasingly obvious after the 1840s – the *bakufu* was incapable of suppressing the development of rural trade and its impact on merchants in Ōsaka and Edo.

In the nineteenth century the *bakufu* was in an increasingly difficult situation. It was faced with severe economic problems, saw the position of its samurai retainers progressively undermined, and yet was unable to deal effectively with the underlying causal factors. Significant changes had occurred in Tokugawa society and many of the premises on which the *bakuhan* order had been created no longer held. Urbanization, the expansion of commercial agriculture, and increased trade both in the major cities and in the countryside all were factors which complicated and frustrated Tokugawa efforts to preserve their dominant position in Japanese society. The failure of the Tempō reforms and the increasing pressure from foreign incursions into Japanese affairs placed the *bakufu* on the defensive. When in 1867 a coalition of daimyo raised their standards against the Tokugawa house they confronted a disillusioned and disorganized adversary which was swept aside in the Meiji Restoration.

4 The Ōsaka Cotton Trade: Establishment and Consolidation

HISTORICAL BACKGROUND

Cotton production in Japan began around the sixteenth century.[1] Cotton was introduced to Japan from China as early as the thirteenth century and was initially regarded as a novelty cloth and a luxury item. During the fifteenth century, quantities of cotton cloth were imported from Korea and cotton sales are reported to have been made in the Yamato region. By the early sixteenth century cotton cloth was available in the Nara market in Yamato as well as in Satsuma in southern Kyūshū, but the cloth is thought to have been imported and not domestically produced.

The most reliable date for the introduction of cotton cultivation to Japan is generally regarded as the second quarter of the sixteenth century. While little information is available, it can be assumed that it was brought to Japan either directly from China or from China via Korea. From around this period cotton cultivation and cloth production increased and began to spread to various regions of the country. By the early seventeenth century cotton was being cultivated in Yamato Koriyama, Musashi, Ōmi, Ise, Owari, Mino, Hida, Tamba, Tajima, Settsu, and Kawachi. It was from this time that cotton cultivation and cotton cloth began to have a significant impact on Japanese agriculture and the Japanese life style.

The introduction and development of cotton cultivation in Japan had a profound influence on the nature of Japanese clothing. Prior to the development of large-scale cotton production, the non-aristocratic members of Japanese society had been clothed in garments of rough linen. As cotton cultivation increased and cotton cloth became more widely available, it rapidly replaced linen as the primary component of everyday dress. It had the advantage of being warmer, cheaper to produce, and more flexible than linen and was quickly adapted to suit popular requirements. Initially, cloth production was directed at local needs, but with the proliferation of castle towns and urban residents the demand for cotton cloth increased. On the village level this resulted in an increase in cotton cultivation and an associated increase in cotton processing activities in the market towns which were scattered in the cotton production areas. Because of climatic factors, soil characteristics, and the uneven diffusion of processing technology, the quality of cotton goods varied from region to region. By 1713 it was stated that the highest quality cloth came from the Ise Matsuzaka area, followed by Settsu and Kawachi. Middle grade cloth was produced in Mikawa, Owari, Kii, and Izumi, and goods which originated in Awaji and Harima were regarded as lower grade.

Production of cotton cloth involved several separate operations. First the seed cotton had to be ginned and the seeds removed, often to be used later in the production of cotton seed oil. Then the ginned cotton was willowed and made into *shinomaki* (combed fibers). From this, yarn was spun and finally the cotton cloth woven on a loom.[2] In the production of white cloth, weaving was followed by bleaching. This cloth could then be dyed in a variety of ways or printed with the use of large wooden pattern blocks. When patterns were to be woven the production process was interrupted mid-way and the yarn dyed before it was woven into cloth. This resulted in an unlimited number of patterns and color combinations. Each region or weaving village had its own varieties of colors and designs. Records in the form of pattern books were kept and passed down from one generation to the next and included small pieces of cloth from the patterns which had been designed in the village.[3]

The Kinai region, with its temperate climate and long growing season, rapidly developed into a major cotton production area. With a long tradition of commercial agricultural production for the imperial capital at Kyōto, this region was particularly well suited to the development of large-scale cotton production for the growing urban market. With the growth of Ōsaka as a major market city, cotton goods were directed into the city and it became a center for cotton processing and sales. Until the end of the seventeenth century cotton processing in the Kinai region was largely limited to market towns and Ōsaka, with of course the exception of goods produced for household consumption. The cotton cultivating villages usually sold their excess cotton in the form of harvested seed cotton and all further processing was conducted by specialists. In the early eighteenth century this began to change as more efficient cotton ginning technology spread to the villages and goods were partially processed by the cultivators before sale.

In the Kinai area, Hirano-gō in Settsu became one of the primary market centers for cotton sales and cotton ginning activity. By the early eighteenth century a regular route for the marketing of cotton from the producers to the Ōsaka market had developed with Hirano-gō as an important intermediary point in the network. Variant patterns existed, but in general the accompanying chart suggests the route for seed and ginned cotton in progress from the cultivators to the Ōsaka market.[4] In the left pattern, the cultivator sold his seed and ginned cotton to a sales *tonya* who arranged for the ginning of the seed cotton and then sold his entire stock of ginned cotton to a buying *tonya*. In the right pattern the cultivator sold his ginned cotton directly to a buying *tonya* and his seed cotton to a cotton ginner who

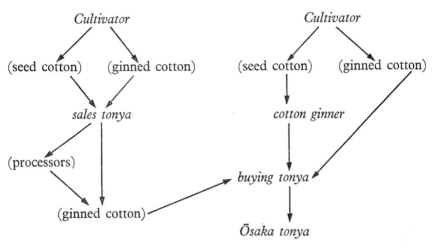

Cultivator *Cultivator*

(seed cotton) (ginned cotton) (seed cotton) (ginned cotton)

sales tonya *cotton ginner*

(processors)

buying tonya

(ginned cotton)

Ōsaka tonya

after processing the goods would then sell them to a buying *tonya*. In both cases, the buying *tonya* sold his accumulated stock of ginned cotton to an Ōsaka cotton *tonya*. As might be expected, with the increase in processing activities in the villages, the buying *tonya* increased the volume of direct purchases from the cultivators. By the 1720s the sales *tonya* in the Kinai region had been largely driven out and either forced to act as agents for the buying *tonya* or direct their efforts elsewhere.[5] By this time the marketing network leading from the cultivator to the Ōsaka market had been effectively consolidated.

Within the city of Ōsaka, a hierarchy of merchant organizations was established to receive, process, sell, and ship the cotton goods which had originated in Hirano-*gō* or elsewhere in the Kinai region. This chapter and the next will be devoted to these merchants and the commercial institutions which they established in the cotton trade.

EARLY INSTITUTIONAL FORMATION

The emergence of Ōsaka as a center for cotton sales and processing in the seventeenth century is understood only in very general terms. The first mention of a cotton market in the city comes from the second quarter of the seventeenth century. Located alongside the vegetable and fresh-water fish markets, the cotton market received seed and ginned cotton produced in the Kinai region and Ōmi. The market operators initiated their transactions by making down payments to the shippers and completed payments only after the goods had been sold. Although little information has survived, it appears that early in its history a fixed commission rate of 1.3 percent of the sale price had been established for all cotton goods sold in the market.[6]

Despite the lack of references to a cotton market in Ōsaka prior to 1625, shipments of cotton goods from Ōsaka to Edo were a regular feature of trade from the beginning of the century. Orders came from Edo and other regions, suggesting that some sort of market mechanism was in operation. During this period we see the first evidence of merchant groups which were formed to regularize and structure the operations of the cotton trade. In the 1640s the seed and ginned cotton *tonya nakama* (*wata-ichi tonya nakama*) was established by merchants active in the market as a means of defining their activities and protecting themselves from outside competition.

Apart from that above, little material remains on the cotton trade during the first half of the seventeenth century. For the second half of the century more data are available, but only the outlines of the growing differentiation within the cotton market are discernible. During the 1670s and 1680s the documentation increases significantly as the result of the official status conferred on several groups in the Ōsaka cotton trade by the Ōsaka city magistrate (*machi bugyō*) Ishimaru Sadatsugu.[7] Designed to introduce a mechanism for government control into the cotton trade, the granting of official recognition to the cotton merchants resulted in the compiling of official documents on their activities.[8]

Among the merchant groups affected by Ishimaru's recognition of commercial institutions was the seed and ginned cotton *tonya nakama*. After its reception of official status, the name of the association was changed to 'the three districts cotton *tonya nakama*' (*sansho wata-ichi tonya nakama*) to symbolize the monopoly rights it was granted for the entire city of Ōsaka.[9] The seventeen members of the previously private and unauthorized association were all included in the cotton *tonya nakama*. The advantage of official status was that protection from outside interference in their commercial activities was included as a means of implementing government controls. Non-*nakama* members were prohibited from competing with the cotton *tonya nakama*. The enforcement power of the Ōsaka city government stood behind the prohibition.

Cotton production during the second half of the seventeenth century was concentrated in the Kinai region which surrounded Ōsaka. The harvested cotton was shipped to Ōsaka and some shipped from there to other regions of the country. Output during the mid-seventeenth century increased as the area devoted to cotton cultivation expanded and large-scale shipments to other parts of the country became common. Between 1658 and 1660 the Ōsaka cotton shippers organized the cotton buying and shipping *tonya nakama* (*wata kaitsugi tsumi tonya nakama*) to consolidate their shipments to Edo and other areas of Japan.[10] During the 1670s, the cotton shipping *nakama* also received official recognition from the Ōsaka city government.

In 1666, a third group, the cotton dealers' and processing *nakama* (*wataya nakama*) was authorized by the Ōsaka city magistrate to function as *nakagai* (jobbers) for the seed and ginned cotton which was received in Ōsaka. This placed it in an intermediary position between the cotton *tonya nakama* and the local retail merchants and also authorized it to purchase cotton from the production regions and engage in various types of cotton processing.[11] Thus the *wataya nakama* or its agents engaged in cotton ginning, dyeing, and various types of weaving within the Ōsaka cotton trade.[12] The *wataya nakama* was divided into subsidiary groups (*kumi*) and was responsible for reporting daily price fluctuations for ginned cotton to the Ōsaka city magistrates' office. During the eighteenth century the functional orientation of the component groups is more apparent but the internal structure at this time is unclear.

The market operations conducted by the *wataya nakama* were characterized by the care taken to ensure that all transactions were conducted in a legitimate fashion. The name, address, and reputation of all clients were investigated and all intermediaries to a sale were examined to determine their past associations with the *nakama* as well as their financial status. Those with outstanding debts were not dealt with until they had settled their accounts. Caution, inquiry into the integrity and character of their potential customers, and honesty underlay the business activity of the *wataya nakama* membership.

Recognition of *nakama* active in the Ōsaka cotton trade by the city government suggests a shift in the official policy relating to commerce. By and large this policy was still directed against the development of privileged groups within the commercial sector. As described in Chapter 2, the *bakufu* continued to issue edicts against private associations during the mid-seventeenth century. Six such edicts were issued in Ōsaka between 1648 and 1670.[13] Even while actively engaged in *nakama* authorization and granting monopoly privileges to specific merchant groups, the government continued to decry private efforts to consolidate monopoly positions. Three prohibitions against such actions were issued in Ōsaka in 1666, 1671, and 1681.[14] Thus while in general an anti-*nakama* policy was adhered to, in the case of the cotton trade specific exceptions were made. What was it about the cotton trade that brought about this indulgent treatment?

Several factors have to be examined in any effort to answer this question. To begin with, the *nakama* authorized within the cotton trade in the 1660s and 1670s were established and functioning as private associations at the time they received official status. Faced with an operating marketing mechanism for cotton, the government found it prudent to grant this mechanism official status as a means of introducing official control. At the same time, by limiting the access of outsiders to the trade it could place restraints on both the organization and to a lesser extent the scale of the operation. Official status and protection transformed a potentially disruptive commercial operation into well defined groups of interacting institutions which could be utilized for official purposes.

Complementing government interest in limiting the proliferation of commercial activities was the desire to maintain the separation of commercial and agricultural pursuits. Fearing that the cultivators would involve themselves in the marketing of their crops, the government was anxious to take steps to prevent deviations from accepted agricultural concerns. While trying to keep the farmers out of commercial activity the government was also anxious to keep the supply of consumer goods to the city at a high level. Thus while discouraging rural sales of cotton, vegetable oil, silk, tobacco, and so on, it was also necessary to satisfy the demands for these goods from the urban centers. E. S. Crawcour in his discussion of this problem has suggested that this was the basic 'contradiction' of the Tokugawa system.

In the light of this difficulty the authorization of *kabu nakama* takes on new meaning. The trades organized as *kabu nakama* were precisely those concerned with the reception in Ōsaka and the forwarding to Edo of goods required by the *bakufu* and the samurai class. The privileges accorded the various *kabu nakama* in the cotton trade ensured the flow of supplies to the cities and prevented sales to other areas. Sales outside the system – called *wakini* or 'under the counter sales' – were strictly forbidden. The *kabu nakama* system was thus the backbone of *bakufu* policy for supplying the cities and the samurai class.[15] The authorization of *kabu nakama* in the cotton trade was a part of this policy. The cotton *tonya nakama*, cotton shipping *nakama*, and *wataya nakama* can be viewed as institutions within the cotton trade which were granted official status as a means of ensuring that the demands for cotton in the Ōsaka and, to a lesser extent, the Edo market were satisfied.

THE KYŌHŌ REFORMS

The early eighteenth century witnessed a major effort on the part of the Tokugawa *bakufu* to rectify a series of financial problems which were plaguing the samurai class and to extend its control over commercial activity. The Kyōhō reforms of the 1720s, discussed in Chapter 2, were a consolidated endeavor to ameliorate serious economic difficulties. One aspect of this effort was the authorization of *kabu nakama* in Edo, but the results of the reforms in Ōsaka were of a rather different nature. No immediate impact upon commercial activity in Ōsaka is apparent as the result of the Kyōhō reforms. However, several aspects of the reform effort are of interest to this study. First was the restructuring of administrative jurisdiction in the Kinai region. Second was the collection of statistics on trade between Ōsaka and Edo. Both are significant for our study of the Ōsaka cotton trade.

The restructuring of administrative jurisdictions in the Kinai region during the Kyōhō reforms extended the administrative authority of the Ōsaka city magistrates. On the surface this would seem to be of little relevance to our inquiry. The effect, however, was to make the Ōsaka city government responsible for public suits which occurred in Settsu, Kawachi, Harima, and Izumi – all of which were primary cotton producing areas. Before 1722, these areas had been administered under the Kyōto city magistrate and the status of Ōsaka as a commercial center was not recognized by extending its administrative jurisdiction. After 1722, the importance of the city and its extensive involvement in the activities of the surrounding Kinai region were acknowledged and this will be of considerable importance when we discuss the disputes which arose between the cotton cultivators and the Ōsaka cotton merchants in the early nineteenth century.

As noted earlier, in Chapter 2, the large-scale authorization of *kabu nakama* in Edo in 1721 and 1724 was not reproduced in Ōsaka. Ōsaka commerce had been organized into official associations by the end of the seventeenth century and similar action was unnecessary. In the case of the cotton trade, *nakama* had been authorized in the 1660s and 1670s and they were by now well established. Associated with the reform policies was an attempt to control the price levels of commodities sold on the Edo and Ōsaka markets. Ōsaka, with its institutionalized trade structure, was looked to as a source of statistical information. Between 1724 and 1730 an investigation was conducted into eleven commodities exported from Ōsaka to Edo and among these were ginned cotton and cotton cloth.

The statistics collected between 1724 and 1730 give an indication of the scale of cotton exports from Ōsaka to Edo.[16] Significant fluctuations are indicated from one year to the next. While ginned cotton and cotton cloth fluctuated together, the magnitude of the fluctuations differed for the two commodities. This suggests that factors other than the size of the cotton crop were involved in the fluctuations and that supply and demand may have varied considerably from year to year. It is difficult to ascertain what influence the Ōsaka cotton merchants had on the volume of cotton which was shipped to Edo. But it is quite possible that they manipulated the volume of goods as a means of maximizing their profits. Because profits were dependent upon the commissions received on completed transactions, the maintenance of high price levels may have been utilized as a mechanism for assuring that income levels would remain high while trade volumes varied. Dependence on market price as the basis of profits encouraged withholding goods in years when over-production threatened price declines, and stockpiling them in anticipation of higher price levels in subsequent years.

Bakufu collection of export statistics for the Ōsaka-Edo trade continued

65

for a considerable period of time after the initial inquiry under the Kyōhō reforms. The first request was made in 1724/5.[17] This was followed by a similar document in 1729/5.[18] In 1730 data for shipments for the eighth through tenth lunar months were requested.[19] Following this came an appeal for price statistics for eleven commodities for the period from 1681 through 1730 in ten-year intervals. This directive dated 1730/11 stated:

Concerning price statistics in ten-year intervals for eleven commodities sold from 1681 to the present.
  Commodities to be included:
    Rice: price per *koku* unit of high, middle, and low grade;
    Bean paste: price per 10 *kamme* unit by weight;
    Charcoal: price per bag in three grades;
    Firewood: price per bundle;
    Salt: price per bag (size dependent on source);
    Sake: price per *koku* in three grades;
    Soy: price per *koku* in three grades;
    Rapeseed oil: price per *koku*;
    Fish oil: price per *koku*;
    Cotton cloth: price per roll;
    Ginned cotton: price per unit of 1 *kamme* by weight.
Statistics for the above goods are to be reported for the years 1681, [1691], 1701, 1711, and 1721 with all prices to be those for the eleventh lunar month. Details on all sales during this period are to be included after careful investigation. The five groups of data are to be assembled independently and transmitted under the seal of the responsible elder by 1730/11/20. Compound prices are to be interpreted so that they will be comprehensible to the authorities. All reports should be sealed by the responsible elder.[20]

Subsequently in 1739/2 a request for data on goods shipped from Ōsaka to Edo was made to the Ōsaka merchant associations.[21] Additional appeals came in 1743, 1748, and 1749 with the first requesting data for goods shipped to Edo in bottoms from regions other than Ōsaka.[22]

The relevance of these notices to the Ōsaka cotton market is not readily apparent. It is important to note, however, that merchant institutions in Ōsaka were sufficiently well developed to supply the necessary statistical information. It should also be noted that cotton goods were included in the surveys. The sophistication of the Ōsaka market relative to that of Edo removed the necessity for the establishment of new *kabu nakama* in Ōsaka. Ōsaka was to serve as a source of price and export data to assist the *bakufu* in its efforts to correct the imbalance between the price of rice – the basis of government finances – and general price levels in Edo. The existing institutional structure was sufficient to satisfy the *bakufu* objectives. At the same time, the position of the Ōsaka merchants was secure and there was no demand for additional governmental support for their commercial operations. Consequently, the Kyōhō reforms in Ōsaka differed significantly from those in Edo and the Ōsaka cotton trade was not meaningfully affected.

LATE EIGHTEENTH CENTURY 'KABU NAKAMA' AUTHORIZATION

Seed Cotton and Ginned Cotton

During the late eighteenth century a second wave of *kabu nakama* authorization occurred in the Ōsaka commercial sector. Several considerations underlay this reassertion of government involvement in mercantile activity and it is necessary to examine the conditions which led to this action in order to place it in a proper perspective. During the first half of the eighteenth century little change occurred in the Ōsaka cotton trade. The *nakama* which had been authorized in the seventeenth century continued their traditional patterns of operation and there is little evidence of threats to their continued economic stability. With the exception of the government calls for statistical reports, interaction between merchant institutions and government officials was kept to a minimum.

As is evident in the case of the *wataya nakama*, membership in the merchant associations associated with the Ōsaka cotton trade was not necessarily stable over the course of the mid-eighteenth century. Membership in this organization fluctuated considerably between 1730 and 1760. As successive corrections were entered into the official *nakama* registers they became increasingly cumbersome and difficult to read. By 1760 the number of corrections became excessive and the Ōsaka city magistrate granted permission to the association to rewrite the membership register and submit a revised copy to the city officials. This was subsequently completed, but the rules of the association were left unchanged from those authorized in the late seventeenth century. While the internal composition of the association varied over the century, the external form remained the same.[23]

During the years immediately following the submission of the revised register, the *wataya nakama* proved progressively less able to compete with outsiders who were making inroads into the cotton processing industry. From around the 1730s on, cotton cultivating villages increased the volume of processed goods which they produced. This was particularly true for ginned cotton production and the dominant position of the Ōsaka cotton ginners began to be seriously challenged. Local cloth production increased as well and this began to threaten the predominant position occupied by the Ōsaka cotton processing industry.[24] As the *wataya nakama* declined in influence efforts were made to rehabilitate the association. In 1772 the Ōsaka city government issued an order directing all persons engaged in competitive activities to join the *wataya nakama*. This order enjoined all outsiders as well as former members to enter the *nakama* and abide by its rules of conduct and operation. Direct purchases by outsiders were to cease immediately as they were creating difficulties for the *nakama*

67

membership.[25] In effect, the inability of the *nakama* to maintain its position by economic means was being given new support in the form of government directives.

The price of official intervention in favor of the *wataya nakama* was a redefining of its relationship with the Ōsaka city government. The association agreed to pay annually a fee of 10 *mai* silver, equivalent to 430 *momme* silver, to the city government for this support.[26] Licensing payments of this sort, known as *myōga* fees, functioned as a tax upon the *nakama* for government protection of their commercial prerogatives. In keeping with the spirit of the edict of support, the *nakama* established an initiation fee of 215 *momme* silver for all new members, although this was apparently reduced for many of the new initiates.[27] Associated with the redefinition of the status of the *wataya nakama* was an effort to clarify its commercial prerogatives. Late in 1772 the name of the association was altered and the suffix *kuri* (ginned), which had often been added to its title in documents, was eliminated in an effort to substantiate the association's claim to business rights for both seed and ginned cotton sales. As of 1772, the association had reaffirmed government support for its commercial activities, agreed to pay licensing fees, and taken action to make more credible its claim to official trade rights for both seed and ginned cotton sales.[28]

The business procedures of the *wataya nakama* during the late eighteenth century can be reconstructed from an association agreement dating from 1785.[29] This agreement was sealed by ten *wataya nakama* officials and stipulated the regulations to which all members were expected to adhere. It insisted that, first, commissions were to be paid on all transactions, regardless of their size, and that no direct purchases were to be made from nearby rural cotton merchants. Second, when cotton was brought to market, 1 percent of the purchase price was to be deposited on account at the time of sale. Third, members were not to give special discounts to their associates when engaged in intra-association transactions. Fourth, no goods were to be sold until they had been processed into reeled yarn, striped cloth, or loose weave cloth, except for transactions within the association. Fifth, all cotton carding was to be conducted by artisans employed by the *nakama*. Finally, all new employees were to be introduced by their former employers with proof that they had not defaulted on outstanding debts or former contractual obligations. At the end of the regulations were the seals of the 381 members of the *wataya nakama*.

Even a cursory analysis of these rules reveals more than the customary business practices of the *wataya nakama*. Clearly indicated in the regulations are the varieties of 'customary' violations which characterized the business dealings of the membership. The first regulation indicates that buying procedures were by no means uniform and that exceptions to commission payments were made in instances when the volume of business did not seem to justify them. The third rule suggests that special terms were offered to *nakama* associates. Prohibition of this activity was probably directed at satisfying complaints from non-*nakama* members and assuring the city government that uniform standards were being maintained. The fourth and fifth rules indicate that rather hazy lines of demarcation existed between the business rights of the *wataya nakama* and other groups active in the Ōsaka cotton trade. These rules were an attempt to designate the association's special sphere of influence and monopoly power.

During the 1770s other merchant groups associated with the cotton trade were also authorized to form *kabu nakama* and were accorded official protection for their special position within the Ōsaka market. The cotton *tonya nakama*, including Yamashiroya Chōbei and four other *tonya* houses, was authorized to form a *kabu nakama* in 1772 and agreed to pay an annual licensing fee of 7 *mai* silver (301 *momme* silver). The preamble to the association register dated 1772/7, submitted by the *nakama* to the city government at the time of authorization, illustrates the conditions of its status as a *kabu nakama*. It stated:

We, engaged in the occupation of cotton *tonya*, calling ourselves the cotton *tonya nakama* and recipients of membership certificates granted to us by the authorities, agree to pay annually the sum of seven *mai* silver to the government for this privilege. Acceding to our petition, the government issued membership shares to five of us and granted permission to engage in business on the condition that we would not engage in new enterprises or other breaches of conduct which would result in difficulties. Should such difficulties arise it is understood that our membership certificates will be revoked, our goods confiscated, and we will be censured.

From the eleventh month of 1772 we will pay our annual licensing obligations promptly without fail in the eleventh month. In addition, when memberships are transferred, or names, addresses, or seals changed we will notify the authorities and make the appropriate changes in the membership register. Further, we will respectfully obey all orders from the government and jointly place our seals hereon to signify our compliance.[30]

The five *tonya* houses associated with the cotton *tonya nakama* were in 1772 accorded revised status as authorized and protected merchants in the Ōsaka cotton trade. In return for the privilege they agreed to abide by the regulations contained in the *nakama* charter and to pay the licensing fee assessed by the Ōsaka city government. The traditional operations of the *nakama* were given additional prestige and were now backed with new vigor by the legal powers of the Ōsaka city magistrates.

The distinction accorded the cotton *tonya nakama* as the result of its new relationship with the government led to an increase in its membership. By 1774 Wataya Zenemon, Amagasaki Kihei, and six other cotton *tonya* houses had joined the association and its license fee was increased to eighteen *mai* per year.[31] The new members already belonged to the *wataya nakama*. They had been forced to join the cotton *tonya nakama* after complaints had been lodged against them with the Ōsaka city magistrates for infringement of trade rights. Thus, as of 1774, it can be assumed that the new members of the cotton *tonya nakama* were concurrently members of the *wataya nakama* and that their activities included practices which had been granted as monopoly rights to both associations. Despite the admission of *wataya nakama* members to the cotton *tonya nakama*, friction between the associations continued. During the 1780s the cotton *tonya nakama* repeatedly complained about the activities of *wataya nakama* members and charged them with violating the monopoly rights assigned to the cotton *tonya nakama*. Distinctions between the trade rights of these two groups were obviously not clearly defined, and the joint membership of several of the member houses did not ameliorate the situation.

After a series of confrontations between these two merchant groups the Ōsaka magistrates took steps to bring the conflict to a conclusion. A survey of the membership of both associations was taken in an effort to determine more explicitly what the traditional business rights of each association were understood to include at the time of authorization. The survey showed that the cotton *tonya nakama* was engaged in receiving shipments of seed and ginned cotton sent to Ōsaka from various production regions. These goods were then sold to the *wataya nakama* and other customers at a fixed commission. Regarding the *wataya nakama* primarily as a processing operation, the cotton *tonya nakama* sold its seed and ginned cotton in the form in which they were received from the producers. In addition, the association expected that the *wataya nakama* would purchase all of its seed and ginned cotton within the Ōsaka market. As a consequence, each time *wataya nakama* members were discovered engaged in direct transactions with cotton production regions the cotton *tonya nakama* filed a complaint with the Ōsaka city officials.

The *wataya nakama*, however, disputed this interpretation of their activities by the cotton *tonya nakama*. It claimed that the cotton *tonya nakama* members had initially been urban market *tonya* and were not authorized to make direct purchases from cotton production regions. Rather, they had received goods from regional shippers and had primarily engaged in commission sales and profit-taking from the interest received from bills of exchange. The *wataya nakama* claimed for itself traditional rights to make direct purchases of both seed and ginned cotton from production areas as well as the right to market its goods in other parts of the country.

In 1785 a suit was brought by the cotton *tonya nakama* against the *wataya nakama* and one of its members. In the decision of 1786, both sides were criticized by the Ōsaka city magistrates for their inability to maintain amicable relations. The official report went on to describe the customary activities of the two *nakama*. Although at one time the cotton *tonya nakama* had temporarily declined in membership, leaving only Yamashiroya Chōbei to purchase seed cotton from the production areas, this had not given the *wataya nakama* the right to engage in competitive transactions. From the business records of the *wataya nakama* it was established that the association had not traditionally purchased seed cotton as no records of such purchases could be discovered. Further, while direct purchases of ginned cotton had been made, it was on the condition that it would be further processed before being sold.

As the result of the inquiry, the *wataya nakama* was enjoined from making direct purchases of seed cotton. Seed cotton purchased by the association from the cotton *tonya nakama* was to be sold only after it was further processed. Merely ginning this cotton and selling it on the Ōsaka market was forbidden by the city government. Although the *wataya nakama* received the majority of the official criticism, the cotton *tonya nakama* did not escape all censure. It was advised that, while many of its complaints were accurate, it had overstepped the jurisdictional limits granted to the association by complaints lodged against the ginned cotton purchases of the *wataya nakama*. This activity was a right accorded to the *wataya nakama* and was not an activity for which the cotton *tonya nakama* could claim monopoly rights. The legal settlement thus laid out the specific rights of the two merchant groups and directed both to avoid violating the prerogatives assigned to the other.

Contrasting with this official description of the spheres of influence assigned to the *wataya nakama* and the cotton *tonya nakama* is the analysis advanced by Yagi Akihiro and Yamaguchi Yukio, who have both studied the cotton trade in Hirano-*gō*.[32] Located about five miles east of Ōsaka, Hirano-*gō* was closely associated with the Ōsaka cotton trade. The studies of both men suggest that the *wataya nakama* was authorized to make direct purchases of seed and ginned cotton in Settsu and Kawachi and that it in turn sold a portion of the goods collected to the cotton *tonya nakama*. The cotton *tonya nakama*, as the more powerful of the two associations, was able to dominate this function of the *wataya nakama*.[33]

The inconsistency between these two descriptions suggests that the *wataya nakama* played a number of separate roles and was by no means a tightly structured, centralized association. On the one hand the *wataya nakama* purchased seed and ginned cotton from the cotton *tonya nakama*. On the other, it seems to have sold seed and ginned cotton to the same group of merchants. This anomaly can be explained by examining what we know about the internal structure of the *wataya nakama*. Internally the *wataya nakama* was divided into subgroups (*kumi*) defined by functional characteristics. The number of *kumi* is unclear, but three types of subgroups are known to have existed. The first engaged in the cotton trade in Ōsaka and other regions, the second was involved with retail sales, and the third was composed of various types of cotton processers.[34] The first type of subgroup could have sold the cotton it collected to the cotton *tonya nakama* as well as to the other two subgroups within the *wataya nakama*. The third type of processing group could have purchased seed and ginned cotton from both the cotton *tonya nakama* and the first type subgroup. The inconsistency can thus be explained by the existence within the structure of the *wataya nakama* of separate functional units which were not restricted to transactions within the association. Because of its composite nature, the *wataya nakama* should be visualized not as a coherent group of merchants engaged in similar commercial undertakings, but rather as a series of functionally dissimilar groups which interacted and were all contained within the same trade association.

In addition to the cotton *tonya nakama* and the *wataya nakama* were other groups active in the Ōsaka cotton trade. These other groups engaged in cotton exports from the city or internal distribution for local consumption. One of these was the cotton buying and shipping *tonya nakama* (*wata kaitsugi tsumi tonya nakama*).[35] The cotton shipping *nakama* purchased seed and ginned cotton for export from Ōsaka to other regions of Japan. In the 1720s and 1730s it included around forty *tonya* houses. By 1771 it had declined to eleven *tonya* active in the Ōsaka cotton trade. In an attempt to stabilize its commercial operations and gain official protection for its trade rights, in 1771 the *nakama* applied to the Ōsaka city government for permission to become an authorized *kabu nakama* with additional government protection. It agreed to pay an initial licensing fee of thirty-five *mai* silver, with the charge to be reduced in subsequent years to thirty *mai*. In 1772 the request was granted and the cotton shipping *nakama* was established as a *kabu nakama*.

In the beginning the *nakama* issued eleven membership shares. This was increased to twelve in 1787 and the license fee was increased accordingly. In 1787 the association agreed to a series of regulations on discounts, sales commissions, and shipping commissions. Purchases made through the *wataya nakama* included a commission of 1.3 percent and those from the cotton *tonya nakama* a 1.8 percent commission. All goods shipped by the cotton shipping *nakama* were subject to an 8 percent commission rate for services rendered.

Within the Ōsaka seed and ginned cotton trade we have thus identified three merchant associations which played primary roles in its operation. The cotton *tonya nakama* purchased seed and ginned cotton from production regions and then resold them in Ōsaka. Among its customers were the *wataya nakama* and the cotton shipping *nakama*. The *wataya nakama* purchased seed and ginned cotton from the cotton *tonya nakama* merchants as well as directly from the production areas and was required to process these goods before resale. The cotton shipping *nakama* purchased seed and ginned cotton from the cotton *tonya nakama* and ginned cotton from the *wataya nakama* for export from Ōsaka. It also was able to purchase at least small quantities of these two commodities from regional intermediary merchants. While there were areas of overlapping business rights to direct purchases, each one of the associations was limited in the manner in which the goods purchased could be used. When conflicts arose, it was because one *nakama* violated the special trade rights assigned to some other organization in the Ōsaka cotton trade. Given the areas of mutual interest and mutual access, it is not surprising that such conflicts were a regular feature of the cotton trade in the Kinai region.

LATE EIGHTEENTH CENTURY 'KABU NAKAMA' AUTHORIZATION

Cotton Cloth

Complementing the associations concerned with the seed and ginned cotton trade were a series of organizations which dealt primarily with cotton cloth. These groups purchased and sold cotton cloth produced in Ōsaka as well as that produced in rural areas as a by-industry. During the 1770s and 1780s these groups as well were authorized to form *kabu nakama* and received official support for their special functions within the Ōsaka cotton trade.

Among the groups which received official status during this period were the cotton cloth *tonya nakama* (*momen tonya nakama*) and the seven *kumi* cotton cloth dealers *nakama* (*nanakumi momenya nakama*).[36] The cloth *tonya nakama* was composed of twenty-five members. In the preamble to its membership register of 1781, the background and conditions under which it was accorded *kabu nakama* status were described as follows:

We, who receive cotton cloth shipped to Ōsaka from the various production regions and who have for years been engaged in selling this cotton to the Ōsaka warehousing and shipping merchants, have continued to the present to engage in this trade. Previously we were organized in a private *nakama* and recently we have received permission to form a twenty-five-member *kabu nakama* by the authorities for the payment of an annual licensing fee of five *mai* silver in return for this privilege.

As the result of our payment of licensing fees, outsiders who engage in similar pursuits will be ordered to cease their operations. Those who have engaged in this trade until now as well as those who in the future attempt to enter into activities of this type without becoming members of our association will be prevented from receiving and selling cotton cloth. If there are individuals who wish to begin new enterprises in this trade and express the desire to enter our association they will be added to our membership if they are able to pay their portion of the license fee.[37]

The cloth *tonya nakama* was engaged in receiving cotton cloth which it subsequently sold to the seven *kumi nakama* for storage and distribution.

Its new status as a *kabu nakama* gave it monopoly rights to this business in the Ōsaka cotton trade and the police powers of the city government were on call to protect these rights. While an exclusive group, the *nakama* expressed willingness to incorporate outsiders who requested admission and were financially able to bear the burden of membership fees.

The seven *kumi nakama* was a larger and more comprehensive collection of merchants active in the Ōsaka cotton cloth trade. It consisted of the Edo *kumi* of cotton cloth warehousing and shipping *tonya* (*Edo kumi momen shi-ire tsumi tonya*), made up of ten members who shipped cloth to Edo; the Kita *kumi* of regional cotton cloth traders (*Kita kumi shokoku momen shōbainin*), which had twenty-three members and traded cotton cloth to various areas of Japan; the twenty-member Higashibori *kumi* of cotton cloth warehousing and shipping *tonya* (*Higashibori kumi momen shi-ire tsumi tonya*); the Uemachi *kumi* of cotton cloth *nakagai* (*Uemachi momen nakagai kumi*) with fifty members; the Abura-*machi kumi* of regional cotton cloth warehousing merchants (*Abura-machi kumi shokoku momen shi-ire shōbainin*) which had forty-three members; the twenty-member Sakai-*suji kumi* of regional cotton cloth warehousing merchants (*Sakai-suji kumi shokoku momen shi-ire shōbainin*); and last, the Temma *kumiai* of cotton cloth traders (*Temma kumiai momen shōbainin*). The seven *kumi nakama* was granted new *kabu nakama* status during the 1780s. Each of its component parts had functioned as a private association prior to its reception of official status. The Edo *kumi* of the seven *kumi nakama* was the oldest group within the association with a history of operation dating back to 1616.[38]

In the case of all the associations enumerated above, the quest for official status was initiated by the cotton merchants.[39] In 1773 the Edo *kumi*, Higashibori *kumi*, Abura-*machi kumi*, and Sakai-*suji kumi* petitioned the Ōsaka magistrates for official support to protect their position in the Ōsaka cotton trade. The initial petition was rejected but the activities of the private associations were not affected. In 1780 the Edo *kumi* petitioned the city office again and once more tried to obtain from the city officials an improvement in its commercial status. The request emphasized the traditional involvement of the Edo *kumi* in cotton cloth shipments to Edo and other areas of the country. The association indicated its willingness to pay licensing fees to the government and in order to counter objections to its projected official status suggested that all those who might object were in fact interlopers in the trade. It was further stated that if chartered as a *kabu nakama* the association would be willing to absorb outsiders and increase its payments to the government accordingly.

Before acting on the petition, the city magistrate sent for members of several other groups active in the Ōsaka cotton cloth trade and consulted with them on the merits of the request.[40] They verified that outsiders were making inroads into the operations of the established cotton cloth traders. Consequently, the Edo *kumi* petition was granted and licensing payments were set at ten *mai* annually.

Subsequently, in 1781 the Edo *kumi* presented to the Ōsaka city officials a twenty-two-article agreement sealed by its ten members. According to this agreement, the primary business of the Edo *kumi* was to accept orders for cotton cloth from Edo merchants and then conduct the related purchasing and shipping transactions. Large quantities of goods shipped from Owari, Mikawa, and Ise to Edo were to be carefully checked for quality to insure that they were not inferior to goods produced in Ōsaka and areas of western Japan. Goods produced in western Japan were purchased from the associated *tonya* in Ōsaka and the Edo *kumi* merchants were to keep the burden of freight costs and commissions as low as possible. If this was not done successfully, cloth purchased in Ōsaka would be unable to compete with goods purchased elsewhere and shipped directly to the Edo market. Auction sales were mentioned as a disruptive influence on the traditional business activities of the cotton cloth *tonya*. The association agreed not to withhold goods or to take advantage of the price fluctuations which would result from such actions.[41]

The Edo *kumi* members agreed to make all purchases through legitimate channels, as direct purchases from the production areas often resulted in the reception of goods of substandard quality. The savings accrued by such direct purchases were judged not worth the trouble entailed. Known sources were seen as a guarantee of quality merchandise. All transactions conducted with customers in Edo were to be done in good faith. The Ōsaka merchants were responsible for maintaining fair prices, shipping in reliable bottoms, and clearly stipulating payment procedures. Any difference between the current market price and that charged to Edo customers was to be reported to the association. Within the *nakama* rigorous standards of propriety were established. The membership was at all times expected to adhere to the professional and ethical standards which had been codified in the association regulations.[42]

Requirements for entrance to the association were also covered in the Edo *kumi* regulations. All potential members were to be first cleared with the Ōsaka membership as well as with *nakama* associates in Edo as a means of ascertaining their character and reliability. Transference of membership shares required the permission of all association members. In cases when members objected to the individual or house which inherited a membership share, it was to be withdrawn and kept by association officials until acceptable arrangements for its transfer could be made. New entrants were to pay an initiation fee of 300 *ryō* gold and also give an elaborate banquet for all those active in the association. The initiation fee was to be saved by the *nakama* as part of an emergency fund and in some cases was returned to the member at the time of his retirement from the association. Because of the burden of initiation fees and associated entertainments, only well-established merchants could aspire to membership in the Edo *kumi*. In addition to the barriers to association entrance, efforts were also made to exclude undesirable individuals from employment by association members. Clerks or apprentices who had been discharged by one association member were not to be employed by other members on even a day to day basis. Those who failed to meet the expectations of one association member would thus jeopardize their future with all those associated with the Edo *kumi* and might find themselves barred from employment in the entire seven *kumi nakama*.

The Edo *kumi* regulations suggest a conservatism and rigid attachment to traditional business practices. It has been suggested by several historians that this attitude was characteristic of the urban merchant associations, that they stolidly adhered to the wisdom and operational patterns of their predecessors.[43] This was no doubt true to a great extent, but other factors were also involved. The need for official status as a *kabu nakama* in the late eighteenth century illustrates the declining ability of the private merchant associations to hold their own against new sources of competition. Unable to maintain their status, they turned to the government for additional support, indicating their willingness to pay for official protection. Licensing fees were only one part of the price the associations were forced to pay. From the government perspective two separate objectives existed. The first was to develop new revenue sources. The second was to insure the stability of the cotton trade and the supply of cotton goods to the cities. This second objective was achieved by enforcing adherence to the very trading procedures which were proving ineffective within the Ōsaka cotton trade. Stability to the government meant rigid adherence to a progressively outmoded model of the status quo.

The nature of the restraints placed upon the various cotton cloth associations by the reception of official status is clear from the preambles to the membership registers which they submitted to the Ōsaka city government.[44] The preamble submitted by the Edo *kumi* of cotton cloth warehousing and shipping *tonya* is representative of the adherence to tradition by these authorized groups of cotton traders. Discussing the nature of *kabu nakama* status the preamble stated:

As the result of our license fee payments, outsiders will be barred from engaging in competitive business activities by government authorities. Should outside merchants wish to join our association, they will be considered for membership if they are found of suitable character, are able to pay their portion of the fees, and no objections are raised by the Sakai-*suji*, Abura-*machi*, Higashibori, and Uemachi *kumi* which are engaged in the same trade. Conditions for membership will include as well the pledge that they will obey all association regulations and have no intentions of introducing new business procedures. All cases will be subject to the decision of the entire *nakama*.

Within the *kumi*, the penalty for non-compliance with *nakama* procedures was harsh. The preamble went on to state: 'If members attempt to introduce new business procedures they will be expelled from the *nakama*, their goods will be confiscated, and they will be censured as directed by the official agreements of authorization.'[45] Adherence to tradition was required by the acceptance of official status. Violation of association patterns of activity could result in expulsion from the trade. With the government standing behind the *nakama* and defending its business rights, expulsion could deny one one's livelihood and cause great hardship to the individual or merchant house which was affected.

The Edo *kumi* is but one example of the cotton cloth merchant groups which received official status in the early 1780s. Similar arrangements were reached between the government and the Sakai-*suji kumi*, the Abura-*machi kumi*, the Uemachi *kumi*, the Higashibori *kumi*, the Kita *kumi*, and the Temma *kumi*. In each case the *kumi* agreed to pay the government a fixed licensing fee annnually and pledged adherence to a series of regulations which covered the trading procedures of its membership. In most respects, the operations of these groups were similar to those of the Edo *kumi*. Their status within the seven *kumi nakama* placed the restraints of tradition on their operation as well.[46]

A pattern of operation can thus be seen for the Ōsaka cotton cloth trade. Each of the authorized associations played a particular role in the overall pattern. Prior to the 1770s, private and authorized merchant *nakama* in Ōsaka had defined their spheres of activity and had managed to control the operations of the Ōsaka cotton cloth trade. Distinctions were maintained between groups specializing in purchases of cotton cloth in Ōsaka or from rural producers and those involved in exports of the cloth from Ōsaka to other regions of the country. Processors and exporters were distinguished from retailers by a series of informal agreements between merchant organizations and by official distinctions set by the Ōsaka city government. By the 1770s these formal and informal boundaries were no longer effective and the Ōsaka city government was called in to establish clearly defined, protected trade rights for the cotton cloth merchants. This served to refine the spheres of interest granted to Ōsaka merchant groups and also gave them a new source of support against the increasing competition which they faced from outsiders, to be discussed in Chapter 7.

By the 1770s the growth of competitive activity in the cotton trade was beginning to have a significant impact on the position occupied by the established Ōsaka merchants. This included the expansion of direct sales by rural cotton producers to itinerant buyers as well as increasingly independent marketing activity by middlemen in the transport routes to Ōsaka. The neatly defined and regulated marketing networks from the cotton cultivators to the Ōsaka merchants and shippers were disintegrating. Authorization of *kabu nakama* was directed at retarding this process of decomposition and reinforcing the traditional mechanism established in the cotton trade.

It should be kept in mind, however, that this process of decomposition was characteristic of the Kinai region and was not common throughout Japan. Ōsaka and Kyōto were the centers for *kabu nakama* formation during the 1770s and 1780s. Similar actions were not taken in Edo. Conflicts between the Edo merchants and their suppliers had not yet developed to the extent that new *bakufu* support was required to maintain their position of predominance. It was not until the early nineteenth century that comparable policies were applied to the Edo commercial scene.[47]

Efforts by the Ōsaka merchants to control developments outside the city took several forms. In 1773 a request was presented to the Ōsaka city magistrates for permission to form a *kabu nakama* for all merchants dealing in seed cotton, ginned cotton, or cotton cloth in Settsu and Kawachi. An association of 1500 members was projected with an annual assessment of 150 *ryō* gold in licensing fees. All cotton ginners and weavers were to be incorporated. Total membership would have included over ten times the 1773 membership of the 137-member *wataya nakama*. The purpose of the proposed association was to control the increasingly independent processing and marketing activities of villagers and rural merchants. By incorporating them into a *kabu nakama* the Ōsaka cotton merchants were attempting to impose a monopoly structure upon cotton production in these two primary cotton cultivating provinces.

Village opposition to the establishment of more rigorous monopoly controls over cotton sales in Settsu and Kawachi was immediate. Suits opposing this proposal were submitted to the *bakufu* in 1773 and 1774 from groups of cotton producing villages. Both suits were directed against the establishment of *kabu nakama* in general and against the *wataya nakama* in particular.[48] Had it not been for the vigorous opposition of the village producers to the establishment of rural *nakama* the plan probably would have been approved. Because of the intensity of the opposition, the *bakufu* rejected the proposal and the projected monopoly for Settsu and Kawachi was never realized.[49]

Despite the failure of the attempt to establish a broad-based monopoly in Settsu and Kawachi, the *wataya nakama* continued its efforts to extend its direct control. With official support it recruited members in villages which lay near the city of Ōsaka and met with considerable success. The result of these recruitment efforts was an increase in the membership of the *wataya nakama* from 137 to 381 members by 1785. Much of the growth was from outside the city of Ōsaka. This greatly enhanced the influence of the *wataya nakama* and enabled the association to pressure outsiders into either joining the expanded association or directing their efforts into different trades. The *nakama* was thus able to consolidate its control over the supply network which fed into Ōsaka and impose new restrictions on the commercial activities of the cultivators and rural merchants. By enlisting rural merchants into the *nakama* the position of the *wataya nakama* was reinforced in the Ōsaka cotton trade and the negative impact of increased rural trade upon the economic position of the association was delayed.[50]

A basic question must be raised at this point: What was the significance of *kabu nakama* formation in the Ōsaka cotton trade during the 1770s and 1780s? Some of the *nakama* which were authorized to issue membership shares in the 1770s had received official recognition as early as the 1660s. Why, if they already possessed government sanction, was it necessary for them to apply for *kabu nakama* status in the late eighteenth century? Was the reception of *kabu nakama* status in the 1770s equivalent to official recognition in the 1660s? If not, what differences are apparent and how meaningful were they to the operation of the Ōsaka cotton trade?

The most obvious difference between *kabu nakama* authorization in the 1660s and that of the 1770s was the process of authorization. During the seventeenth century, the *nakama* were established by government decree as a means of regulating commercial activity and directing supplies of necessary commodities to the cities. In the case of the cotton trade this included the authorization of the cotton *tonya nakama*, the cotton shipping *nakama*, and the *wataya nakama*. Each of these groups was active in collecting cotton, processing it for sale, or shipping it to urban consumption areas. All thus conformed to the objectives advanced by the government for *kabu nakama* authorization.

Conditions during the late eighteenth century were considerably different. Merchant institutions within the cotton trade in Ōsaka were finding it difficult to maintain established business procedures in the face of growing competition. Supply lines to the Ōsaka market were being endangered by new marketing patterns which the cotton merchant associations were unable to regulate. By turning to the government and requesting status as *kabu nakama* the associations had their commercial prerogatives clearly stipulated and areas of overlapping interest clarified, and the legal authority of the city government was brought to the defense of the Ōsaka merchant organizations. Imposition of *bakufu* controls justified the seventeenth century *kabu nakama* authorization in the cotton trade. In the late eighteenth century, this was changed to a policy of reinforcing the traditional marketing system centered on Ōsaka.

A second major difference between the seventeenth and eighteenth century establishment of merchant associations was the relationship between the merchants and the government. In both cases the government required that records of association membership and procedures be submitted to the city magistrates' office. Contact between the associations and the city government was transformed by the introduction of licensing payments in the late eighteenth century. By increasing the dependency relationship between the cotton merchants and the city government, the late eighteenth century associations limited the capacity of their members to accommodate to changes within the cotton trade as they were under increased pressure to conform to *nakama* regulations. As a consequence, the short-term gains which were realized as the result of government assistance after 1770 were to leave the cotton merchant associations less able to compete as government support weakened in vigor and influence in the nineteenth century.

THE GINNED COTTON FUTURES MARKETS

One of the most interesting developments in the Ōsaka cotton trade during the second half of the eighteenth century was the establishment of the ginned cotton futures market (*kuriwata nobebaibai sho*). Superficially, the futures market appeared to offer an alternative mechanism for ginned cotton sales. The assumption was that the cotton *tonya nakama* and the *wataya nakama* would be by-passed and the rural producers would get an additional outlet for their ginned cotton. This was not the case, however. The futures markets were instead a means of restricting the activities of the rural cotton merchants by encouraging speculation in ginned cotton futures. The underlying theory was that merchants engaged in direct buying from rural producers would make ginned cotton purchases through the Ōsaka futures market and consequently be forced to deal through the institutionalized mechanism of the Ōsaka market. Operation of a speculative market also placed the cultivators in a less desirable position. They were encouraged to make advance sales of ginned cotton when tax payments were due and the competition for crops had not yet begun, and many found this difficult to resist. Sale guaranteed that their crop would be sold at a competitive price and the payment advanced removed much of the pressure of meeting tax obligations. In this fashion, the Ōsaka merchants could buy up ginned cotton futures and undercut local competition.[51]

The first recorded effort to establish an officially authorized futures market in Ōsaka was made in 1759 by Nomuraya Gorōbei. The market was to serve as a meeting place for shipment underwriters, *tonya*, ginned cotton dealers (*kuriwataya*), and various intermediary brokers. Transactions were to be conducted for ginned cotton futures to give the producers an advance on their product and guarantee them a market as well as to give the buyers the opportunity to purchase goods at less than the market price at the time of delivery. Prices were to be established at the futures market and accounts settled within 300 days – stated in terms of five successive 60-day periods. Commissions were to be charged for the use of the futures market and applied to licensing payments.[52]

Gorōbei's request resulted in an official inquiry under the Ōsaka magistrate Okabe Tsushima no kami Motoyoshi. After study he recommended that the request be approved and in an official edict (*furegaki*) of 1760/3/3 Gorōbei received permission to establish a ginned cotton futures market in Ōsaka. Gorōbei was given a free hand to establish a market monopoly and was given government protection from outside competition. The only conditions for authorization were that he avoid disputes and conduct all business in an amicable manner.[53]

In 1770/11/19 a second *furegaki* was issued which stated that control over the futures market had been transferred to Matsuya Riemon. The market was to be moved and was authorized to conduct futures sales under Riemon's direction. Outside competition was prohibited and the need for judicious business transactions emphasized. This, like the previous notice, was to be distributed to the three districts of Ōsaka to notify all those in the cotton trade of the change in management and location.[54]

Management as well as the location of the futures market changed frequently. In 1772 a petition was submitted to the Ōsaka city office by Kashiya Rihei and Wataya Chōemon requesting permission to open a branch of the futures market in Hirano-*gō*, a growing market center in Sumiyoshi *gun* of the province of Settsu. Both the location and management of the Ōsaka market had changed since 1770. The new location and the request for a branch office were to improve the business prospects of the futures market. The government responded favorably and the petition was granted together with an increase in license payments.[55]

Also in 1772 a request was submitted for a second ginned cotton futures market in Ōsaka. The petitioner was Tōemon of Seibeidana, an Edo merchant. He proposed moving to Ōsaka and setting up a second Ōsaka futures market. The management of the existing facility objected and claimed that a second market would interfere with business. After an official inquiry, the second Ōsaka futures market was approved with the reservation that it would be abolished if business at the original market declined. Authorization was accompanied by the establishment of a suitable licensing fee.[56]

As of 1772 three *bakufu*-authorized ginned cotton futures markets were located in the Ōsaka region. Two were within the city, and one was in nearby Hirano-*gō*. All three were officially protected and paying licensing fees. Fifteen years later in 1787/12, all three offices were eliminated under the Kansei reforms.

Behind the abolition of the ginned cotton futures markets was a combination of business instability, a revision of *bakufu* commercial policy, and growing dissatisfaction by cotton cultivators. The 1787 edict which abolished the futures markets included a somewhat different history of their activities than that related above. The original participants were listed as Nakajimaya Yahei and Matsuya Riemon, and Nomuraya Gorōbei was not even mentioned. The manager of the Ōsaka office was given as Nagasawaya Tōemon and no mention was made of his former domicile in Edo. The justification of the abolition was 'difficulties at this time' combined with an order from Edo to abolish all such futures markets.[57]

'Difficulties at this time' included a large component of irritation on the part of cotton cultivators in Settsu and Kawachi. Between 1777 and 1779 five suits were brought before the Ōsaka magistrates by cotton producing villages against the ginned cotton futures markets. All of the suits called for the elimination of the futures markets and the prohibition of subsequent operations of this type.[58] These suits testify to the success of the futures markets in restraining the development of rural commerce in the cotton trade. Because of their effectiveness in undercutting local buyers and itinerant merchants, they were able to maintain low purchase prices and control the marketing of ginned cotton. This success being consistent with the objectives of their formation, what was it that brought about their elimination?

Basic to the policies implemented under the Kansei reforms was the conception 'back to Yoshimune,' the effort to turn the clock back to the first quarter of the eighteenth century. Part of this policy was the elimination of innovations which had been introduced by subsequent administrations. The ginned cotton futures markets were institutional innovations of the 1760s and 1770s. They were one of a series of deviations which the Kansei reformers felt had tampered with the traditional orientation of Tokugawa economic policy. From a contemporary perspective they seemed to offer no benefit to the government and, moreover, they were a source of rural unrest. What better solution than to abolish them as part of the rectification program carried out during the Kansei reforms? The loss of income from licensing payments was of minor importance when compared to the benefits which would result from their abolition.

The problems of managerial instability and relocation of the Ōsaka ginned cotton futures market deserve comment. Between 1760 and 1787 at least four individuals or partnerships are mentioned as managing the original market. Its location changed with equal frequency. The assumption is that each transfer represented an infusion of new capital and new confidence in its eventual success. The establishment of a branch office in Hirano-*gō* illustrates an attempt to go to the producers and expand the scale of the undertaking. The addition of a second Ōsaka market suggests that by 1772 the futures markets were proving profitable and that access to this activity had become more attractive. This interpretation is confirmed by the complaints brought to the *bakufu* by cotton cultivators at the end of the decade. More specific material on market operation and profits would further substantiate this analysis. It is safe to conclude that the ginned cotton futures markets successfully retarded rural commercial activities and turned a profit for their merchant managers until their abolition in 1787.

THE WAKAYAMA 'HAN' OFFICE

In 1785, there appeared in Ōsaka a new source of competition in the cotton trade. Wakayama *han* established an office in the city to purchase cotton for use in the domain-sponsored reeled yarn industry. Reeled yarn production in Wakayama *han* operated as a domain monopoly. Because ginned cotton production within the domain did not supply enough raw material to keep yarn production at the desired level of output, the domain government turned to the Ōsaka market as a source of supplementary supplies.

The objective in creating a ginned cotton buying office in Ōsaka was to purchase large volumes of ginned cotton without having to deal with the institutionalized Ōsaka cotton merchants. Ginned cotton was to be purchased directly from the shippers in Ōsaka. Goods judged of suitable quality for reeled yarn production were to be exported from the city to Wakayama *han* for further processing. Goods of lesser quality were to be resold in Ōsaka by the domain business office.[59]

Here we have an example of a daimyo domain attempting to interfere in the normal operation of the Ōsaka cotton trade. Although merchant groups within the city had formed *kabu nakama* and monopolized specific aspects of the cotton trade, the *han* was attempting to short-circuit the officially sanctioned and supported market mechanism. Objections were naturally raised by the cotton *tonya nakama*. It claimed that the Wakayama *han* scheme violated *nakama* prerogatives and it was joined in the complaint by the *wataya nakama* and the two Ōsaka ginned cotton futures markets.

Faced with complaints from officially authorized merchant institutions, the Ōsaka city government instructed the *han* office to change its pattern of operation. Kawamoto Jihei, manager of the Wakayama *han* office, was forced to rely on established sources of supply within the city of Ōsaka. Purchases were made from the Ōsaka cotton *tonya*, the goods were graded by quality, and that portion suitable for reeled thread production was exported to Wakayama *han*. The remainder was sold to Ōsaka merchants with the consent of the cotton *tonya* and other merchants involved.[60] The authority of the city government was thus utilized to protect the Ōsaka cotton trade from being disrupted by new sources of competition.

In this instance the official position of the *kabu nakama* within the Ōsaka cotton trade was used to impede the development of new institutions and patterns of operation which challenged their traditional business activities. Complaints from the *kabu nakama* were backed by the legal authority of the Ōsaka city government. This insured that cotton purchases in the city of Ōsaka were conducted according to established business procedures and adhered to the market mechanism which had been supported and stabilized by the authorization of *kabu nakama*. Granting of official status insured that goods would be routed through 'normal channels' within the city. The stable trade mechanism which was thereby sanctioned protected the established cotton merchants and worked for the interest of the city government as well. Stability was to the advantage of both.

SUMMARY

Our discussion of the establishment and consolidation of the Ōsaka cotton trade has proceeded from its origins in the early seventeenth century to its successful efforts to attain *kabu nakama* status and retard competitive activities at the end of the eighteenth century. Concentrating on the institutional aspects of this process, we have illustrated the nature of commercial activity in Ōsaka, the cooperative interaction of different groups within the cotton trade, the character of the disputes which erupted between these merchant groups, the appearance of competition and efforts to restrain incursions into the trade, and the changing relationship between the cotton merchants and the Ōsaka city government.

Initially, the cotton merchants were independent agents who united for common advantage in the seventeenth century. The early merchant associations arose to regulate business practices and protect the interests of the individual merchant houses by group support. By the second half of the century the city government officially sanctioned several groups of cotton merchants as a means of regulating the trade and channeling cotton goods to major centers of samurai class consumption. In the early eighteenth century these merchant associations were utilized as a source of statistical data which the shogunate tried to use as the basis of its price control policies during the Kyōhō reforms. By the latter half of the eighteenth century the established Ōsaka cotton merchants were beginning to feel threatened by competitive developments both in the city and from rural cotton production areas. *Kabu nakama* were authorized as a means of reinforcing their commercial positions. In return the merchants paid licensing fees to the *bakufu* and agreed to conform to traditional patterns of operation. This buttressed the Ōsaka merchants' position in the 1770s and 1780s, but, as we shall see in the next chapter, proved of considerably less value in the early nineteenth century.

Following the modification of *bakufu* economic policies in the Kansei reforms, the monopoly position of the Ōsaka cotton traders was increasingly subjected to competition from outside the *kabu nakama* system. Processing industries proliferated in cotton production regions. *Han* monopoly organizations increasingly challenged the authority of the shogunate in the commercial sphere. Rural merchants increased in number and scale of activity. The Kansei reforms can thus be seen as a watershed in the history of the Ōsaka cotton trade. Vigorous support was given to a tradition in which the Ōsaka cotton *nakama* played an accepted economic role. While some institutions were subjected to censure and dissolution, the *kabu nakama* were supported and closely identified with the Tokugawa system of government. This identification with the status quo was welcomed at the time, but diminished in value and failed to protect the Ōsaka cotton trade from changes which were occurring in Tokugawa society in the nineteenth century.

5 The Ōsaka Cotton Trade: Institutional Decline

THE KANSEI REFORMS

The Kansei reforms of 1787 to 1793 are, among the three reform efforts undertaken by the Tokugawa *bakufu*, the least studied and least understood. Matsudaira Sadanobu and his associates, who dominated the policy councils of the shogunate during this period, were faced with what they interpreted as a fiscal and moral crisis. Expenditures of the *bakufu* consistently exceeded income. Vigorous measures were needed to counter the high prices of basic commodities and reverse the innovative policies initiated under Sadanobu's predecessor in the seat of influence, Tanuma Okitsugu. With the Kyōhō reforms as his primary guide, he undertook a program he felt would rectify the problems of his time.[1]

As has been noted in Chapter 4, within the Ōsaka cotton trade the Kansei reforms had a number of effects. To begin with, the ginned cotton futures markets were abolished. Government opposition to market construction was consistent with the effort to strengthen the operation of the *kabu nakama* system. Efforts were directed at tightening internal controls in an attempt to support the market mechanism which had been in operation throughout the eighteenth century. One aspect of this policy was the concern with regulating the conduct of the merchants engaged in ginned cotton transactions. The *Ōsaka shishi* contains seventeen edicts addressed to the problem of wetting ginned cotton before sale to increase its weight, and six are clustered in the years 1787 and 1793. Prohibitions against this form of fraudulent activity were issued in 1787, 1788, 1791, and 1792. Two such edicts appeared in 1789. The second carried the admonition that the traditional marketing system in the countryside was not to be interrupted by outsiders accompanying the cotton buyers on their collection trips in the Kinai region. Evasion of established trade routes had become excessive. Firm measures were taken to try and correct the situation.[2]

Secondly, the *kabu nakama* active in the cotton trade were confirmed in their monopoly rights and an effort was made to reaffirm *bakufu* support of merchant institutions which were consistent with *bakufu* policy objectives. At the same time, merchant institutions which were felt to be inimical to *bakufu* interests were disbanded. Among them were the ginned cotton futures markets. A change in the orientation of Kansei reform policy was that the *kabu nakama* were seen primarily as a means of enforcing price

86

controls, while under the leadership of Tanuma Okitsugu they had been viewed as a prime revenue source. This change in viewpoint does not appear to have significantly altered basic policy toward the cotton *nakama*. The Kansei reforms asserted, with new moral fervor, government support of the Ōsaka cotton traders.[3]

CONFIRMATION OF RIGHTS – THE COTTON SHIPPING 'NAKAMA'

Throughout the late eighteenth and early nineteenth centuries, a constant source of conflict among the merchants engaged in the Ōsaka cotton trade was the question of monopoly jurisdiction. From the beginning, the limits of the *nakama* spheres of influence were not clearly stipulated and this led to a series of disputes which were periodically referred to the Ōsaka magistrates' office for adjudication. By the 1780s, the three *kabu nakama* active in the Ōsaka seed and ginned cotton trade had, as we have seen in Chapter 4, established guidelines which defined their monopoly prerogatives. The cotton *tonya nakama* purchased seed and ginned cotton from production regions and then resold it in Ōsaka. The *wataya nakama* purchased seed and ginned cotton from the cotton *tonya nakama* as well as from the production areas and was required to process it before resale. The cotton shipping *nakama* purchased seed and ginned cotton from the cotton *tonya nakama*, and ginned cotton from the *wataya nakama* for export from the city of Ōsaka. While rights to direct purchases of goods overlapped to an extent, each one of the *nakama* was limited in the manner in which the goods purchased could be utilized. Disputes arose when the latter rights were violated.

Despite the effort to establish special monopoly rights for these three *nakama*, in the 1780s disputes arose between the *wataya nakama* and both the cotton *tonya nakama* and the cotton shipping *nakama*. Conflicts continued into the 1790s and in 1797 three members of the *wataya nakama* were sued by the cotton shipping *nakama* for violation of its monopoly rights. The three merchants charged in the suit had initially desired entrance to the cotton shipping association. The *nakama* had considered their names and they had engaged in business transactions through intermediaries. They purchased goods in production regions or through the *wataya nakama* and cotton *tonya nakama* and engaged primarily in transshipment of cotton goods to Edo. Since the *wataya nakama* included merchants active in many aspects of the cotton trade, including a few who actively shipped goods to other regions, the three *wataya nakama* members never completed their initiation into the cotton shipping *nakama*. Consequently they were accused of violating the monopoly rights of the cotton shipping association.[4]

The *wataya nakama* did not regard the charge as an isolated case. General principles were involved and the accusation was contested in the name of the association. It claimed traditional rights to ginned cotton exports dating back to 1666. It charged the shipping *nakama* with interference in *wataya nakama* activities and accused it of violating the conditions of its *kabu nakama* status. The *wataya nakama* claimed the shipping *nakama* was illegally attempting to monopolize ginned cotton exports for itself.[5]

Ruling on the dispute was the Ōsaka city magistrate Yamaguchi Naokiyo. He called representatives of both *nakama,* advised them to respect the established customs of their trade, and launched an investigation of cotton shipments to Edo. It was discovered that, while the *wataya nakama* had engaged in ginned cotton shipments to Edo, it had largely neglected this type of activity since the 1720s. One member, Kaseya Rimbei, made a small shipment to Edo in 1772, but no other activity of this type was noted in the *nakama* records. In his decision of 1797/7, the magistrate ruled that the 1772 shipment did not constitute a precedent for *wataya nakama* ginned cotton exports to Edo. Further activities of this type would constitute engaging in 'new enterprises,' forbidden under the terms of the *kabu nakama* charter agreement. Consequently, if in the future *wataya nakama* merchants wished to engage in ginned cotton exports from Ōsaka, they would first have to join the cotton shipping *nakama.*[6]

Confirmation of the monopoly rights of the cotton shipping *nakama* gave new strength to the association and by 1807 it had increased its *kabu* from twelve to thirty-two. A set of revised regulations was submitted at this time which clarify the operating procedures of the *nakama.*[7] Buying procedures stipulated that all purchases were to be made through intermediary merchants, and auction buying and direct purchases from producers were prohibited. Orders for cotton from the Ōsaka region were to be supplied via the *wataya nakama* and dealings with non-*nakama* merchants were forbidden. Goods from western Honshū and Shikoku were to be purchased from the cotton *tonya nakama.* All goods were to be inspected and certified before shipment.

Shipping activity was to be confined to a time period designated annually by agreement within the *nakama.* No shipments were to be made before the beginning of the established shipping season and shipments were to terminate promptly at the season's end. All orders were to be handled by the house which received them and direct shipment from other merchants for the convenience of the customer was discouraged. All bottoms used in shipments were to be certified fit, and goods were to be shipped by the contracted date with all prices listed in the shipping documents. When goods were contracted for future delivery, the liability of the cotton shippers was to cease when the goods were delivered to the docks. No compensation for damage during shipment was to be paid by the *nakama.* Commission rates were fixed and were not subject to negotiation.

As a consequence of its monopoly for seed and ginned cotton exports from Ōsaka the cotton shipping *nakama* was able to direct the activities of merchants engaged in similar activities in Kyōto, Hachiman, Hirano-*gō*, Sakai, and Nishinomiya. Twenty-five merchant houses from these locations were grouped under the Ōsaka *nakama* and known as the Go-Kinai merchants. Goods shipped by the Go-Kinai merchants necessarily passed through the hands of the cotton shipping *nakama*. Cotton goods originating from one of the twenty-five forwarding merchants in the Kinai region would thus pass through one of the Ōsaka shippers and then be directed by them to one of the Edo merchant houses with which they had direct associations. Four Edo *kumi*, including sixty-two *tonya* houses, were associated with the cotton shipping *nakama*. They were the Ōdemma-*chō* ginned cotton *tonya kumi* (*Ōdemma-chō kuriwata tonya kumi*), the Ōdemma-*chō* piece goods stores (*Ōdemma-chō futomono mise kumi*), the Moto-*machi* ginned cotton *tonya kumi* (*Moto-machi kumi kuriwata tonya kumi*), and the Kawagishi ginned cotton *tonya kumi* (*Kawagishi kuriwata tonya kumi*), all of which were merchant associations engaged in the cotton trade in Edo. All orders which the Ōsaka shipping *nakama* received from eastern Japan were sent via one of these *kumi tonya* and forwarded to the customer from Edo. Thus all shipments from the Kinai region to the Kantō region passed along an established supply network incorporating all the customary *tonya* in transit. Initially goods could be shipped from Ōsaka on either the Higaki shipping line or in other bottoms. After 1810 the Edo *tonya* demanded that all goods be sent via the Higaki shipping line, with which they were linked in the *Tōkumi tonya nakama*, to assure that they would control all cotton goods landed in Edo.[8]

The example of the cotton shipping *nakama* illustrates the effort by the *bakufu* to maintain the institutionalized structure of the cotton trade and adjudicate disputes which developed between the authorized *kabu nakama*. This was a continuation of the policies which had been reaffirmed under the Kansei reforms. The *kabu nakama* system was protected and supported as a basic element of the Tokugawa economic order. It was considered essential that the system be maintained and that it be protected from both external competition and internal division.

NEW ENTHUSIASM FOR COTTON MARKETS – EDOYA YAHEI

One element of the Kansei reforms in Ōsaka was the abolition of the ginned cotton futures markets in 1787. At the time of their dissolution, three markets had been in operation. Two were located within the city of Ōsaka and the third in nearby Hirano-*gō*. The futures markets had been designed to encourage speculation on ginned cotton futures and lure buyers away from the villages and thereby reduce the volume of direct sales in the production regions.[9] The success of these markets is revealed by their establishment in three separate locations, the number of requests to construct new markets made in cotton centers such as Hirano-*gō*,[10] and the number of complaints against their activities raised by the cotton producing villages.[11] It is consequently no surprise to discover that interest in further cotton market construction remained active after the *bakufu* dissolution policies were enforced.

Wataya Yohei, an Edo merchant, showed interest in reestablishing a ginned cotton market in Ōsaka in 1793. He petitioned the Ōsaka city magistrates for authorization and suggested that such a market would establish a monthly price level for ginned cotton transactions. It also would serve to curtail illegal cotton sales which were threatening the position of the Ōsaka cotton *nakama*. Yohei promised to pay the sum of 100 *ryō* gold annually in license fees if authorized to carry out his proposal.[12] Yohei attempted to introduce a means by which ginned cotton not purchased by the *nakama* could be funneled into Ōsaka and thereby reduce the volume of direct sales which had proliferated outside the city. Operational procedures are not given, but it is apparent that what was intended was a reintroduction of a cotton marketing control mechanism similar to that established by the ginned cotton futures markets.

Several months later, Hiranoya Shichiemon of Ōsaka petitioned the city magistrates for permission to rent an area in Ōsaka destroyed by fire for use as a ginned cotton drying area. Construction of these facilities had been requested by a group of ginned cotton dealers in the city and Shichiemon proposed to apply a portion of the fees collected as land rent to the city government. Objections were raised by the cotton *tonya nakama* to both the ginned cotton market and the ginned cotton drying area proposal. As a consequence both requests were rejected by the city government.[13]

Bakufu opposition to the construction of a new market mechanism for the collection and sale of ginned cotton after 1787 did not discourage merchant interest in government-authorized cotton markets. In late 1799, Harimaya Seibei petitioned to be allowed to establish collection areas for seed and ginned cotton at two sites in Ōsaka. This, he claimed, would encourage transactions between cotton merchants in the city and limit the volume of direct sales between cotton processors or forwarding agents and the regional shippers. Should permission be granted he agreed to pay an annual licensing fee of twenty *mai* silver with exemptions for years of bad harvests.[14]

Here again, the object of market construction was limitation of the commercial activities of the village producers and the growing class of rural merchants. Seibei's collection operation was designed to focus sales of cotton, which were conducted outside the regular trade network of the Ōsaka *nakama*, into the city where they could be controlled. On the one hand this offered a potential means of directing cotton into Ōsaka and on the other implied doing this outside the normal channels of the *nakama* system. A second proposal which was entered at around the same time suggested a further alternative to the established system of authorized *nakama*.

Ōsakaya Yahei, who in 1799 was resident in Edo, requested permission to establish a ginned cotton market in Settsu, Kawachi, or Izumi. Yahei proposed to receive shipments of cotton from the various production regions at his market. In the presence of witnessing *nakama* he would establish a fair price for the goods received. On the basis of his knowledge of cotton price levels he would accept and handle orders from various consumption areas which were sent to his market. For each pack-horse load of cotton sent to his market a fixed commission of 2 *momme* would be charged, of which 1.3 *momme* would go to the income of the market and the remaining 0.7 *momme* would be paid to the participating *nakama* as a rebate. Each pack-horse load was to consist of three bales of ginned cotton with each bale weighing 9 *kan* 300 *me*. As part of his proposal Yahei planned to issue licenses to 500 members of the participating *nakama* (*tachiai nakama*) with a 10-*ryō* charge made for each license. Funds collected in this manner were to be loaned to shippers or participating *nakama* members at an interest rate of 1 percent per month. From the interest received a monthly dividend of 3.6 *momme* per license was to be paid to each license holder as income. The combined income from interest on loans and sales commissions was expected to be of sufficient magnitude that a fee of 200 *ryō* could be paid annually to the government as compensation for its authorization and support.[15]

Yahei's proposal was an attempt to institutionalize with government support the ginned cotton trade in the region around Ōsaka. In effect, he appears to have anticipated the creation of a formalized mechanism to monopolize ginned cotton transactions outside the control of the Ōsaka cotton *nakama*. A new association was to be established. Membership fees were to be used to finance the operation and all participants were guaranteed a return on their investment. Participation was to be limited to cotton merchants who paid the 10-*ryō* fee for licensing and their numbers – he anticipated 500 participants – would ensure that sales would be at competitive prices. Commissions were to be distributed between the market and the association of participating merchants and an additional source of income was anticipated from interest on loans to shippers and traders active in the market. Yahei apparently thought the chances for success to be good, as his offer to pay an annual licensing fee of 200 *ryō* to the government suggested considerable confidence in his proposed operation.[16]

Reactions by authorized merchants to the proposals offered by Harimaya Seibei and Ōsakaya Yahei were hostile. Objections were raised by the cotton *tonya nakama*, *wataya nakama*, and cotton shipping *nakama*. Each of these groups claimed infringements on the trade rights guaranteed them as *kabu nakama*. All were working to maintain their control over the seed and ginned cotton trade in the Ōsaka region and none were willing to accede to the establishment of competitive institutions with official support and protection. As a consequence Harimaya Seibei's petition was rejected and Ōsakaya Yahei was induced to withdraw his request.[17] Committed to the maintenance of the Ōsaka *kabu nakama* system in the cotton trade, the government maintained its post-1787 policy of opposition to innovation.

After withdrawing his initial request to establish a ginned cotton market, Yahei changed his house name from Ōsakaya to Edoya. As Edoya Yahei he requested permission in 1801 to open a seed cotton market in Ōsaka. He proposed to operate an auction market within the city for seed cotton purchased and shipped from regional production areas. His commission was set at 1 *fun* silver for each 12-*kan* bale of cotton sold. Advance payments were to be made to the shippers as security on each shipment and were to equal 20 percent of the market value of the cotton received. These payments were to be in the form of loans to the producers and were to be at the rate of 0.8 percent interest per month or 8 *momme* per *kan* silver advanced. The combined profits on loans and commissions were projected to enable Yahei to pay an annual license fee of 100 *ryō* gold for government support.[18]

As could be expected, objections were once again raised by the cotton *tonya nakama*. It claimed that the loans were a form of futures buying. It also opposed the levy of a 1-*fun* commission per bale of cotton and suggested that a commission of 13 *momme* per *kan* silver of the purchase price of the cotton would be more consistent with current practices in the trade. This commission could then be added to the sale price and passed on to the buyer as was customary in the dealings of the cotton *tonya nakama*. The *nakama* advised that the loans be dispensed with and that the rate of licensing payments be lowered to 100 *mai* silver per year. Advice on the operation of the proposed market did not constitute acceptance by the association. It feared that the market would compete with its own activities and complained of this prospect a second time in 1802. The basis of the complaint was that the proposal would give official status to competitive activities conducted by an outsider. Further, it would deprive the *nakama* of a portion of its business and this was business they could ill afford to lose.[19]

Undaunted by the opposition, Edoya Yahei persisted in his efforts to win approval for his cotton market. In 1806 he once again requested authorization for a somewhat modified proposal which conformed to some of the suggestions made by the cotton *tonya nakama* to his proposal of 1801. Yahei agreed not to engage in activities which would directly challenge the trade rights of the cotton *tonya nakama*. Shipments were to be conducted by the *nakama* and commissions were to conform to their established rates.[20]

Faced with continued opposition from the Ōsaka *kabu nakama*, Yahei looked to the production areas of Settsu and Kawachi for sources of support. In 1806 and 1807 he visited cotton producing villages and discussed with the cultivators the benefits that his market would open up to them. Winning their support he again tried to gain the approval of the government. Yahei's market promised to widen the opportunities for the cultivators to sell their seed cotton. This had been the cotton producers' objective throughout the late eighteenth century and they had several times presented formal petitions to the government. In 1807, a group of cotton producing villages in Settsu and Kawachi sent a formal complaint to the Ōsaka city authorities. They objected to the opposition against the market proposed by Edoya Yahei and offered their support for the auction markets that he had proposed. In 1807 Yahei had altered his proposal and requested permission to have auction sales of seed cotton in Ōsaka and the cotton cultivators were supporting him in his request.[21]

Persistence and ingenuity finally were rewarded in 1810 when Yahei was authorized to establish a seed cotton market in Ōsaka. Producers wishing to sell their harvested cotton in the market were to ship or bring it to the Ōsaka market for sale. Book sales of cotton futures were not permitted and an edict to this effect was circulated in the three districts of Ōsaka.[22] Over a ten-year period Yahei had worked to obtain authorization for the establishment of a cotton market. All his efforts had been directed toward obtaining official sanction for a market operation which would rival, at least to an extent, the operations of the Ōsaka *kabu nakama* in the cotton trade. Outside the city the growth of merchants in the production regions and the growing awareness of the producers had begun to challenge the dominant position of the Ōsaka merchants. As an outsider wishing to operate within the Ōsaka cotton trade, Yahei attempted to win official sanction for competitive activities within the city of Ōsaka itself. In 1810, with the cultivators' support, he obtained his goal. As we shall see, however, official sanction did not constitute a guarantee of financial success.

In 1810 Edoya Yahei opened his seed cotton market in Ōsaka. Business did not, however, develop as he anticipated. With similar markets forbidden in the nearby provinces of Settsu, Kawachi, and Izumi, Yahei expected to have a prosperous operation. Cotton cultivators who traditionally sold their cotton to merchants who travelled from village to village found that to utilize the new market they had to transport their goods to Ōsaka, as well as pay sales commissions. As a consequence, they made little use of the market. Although direct sales were infrequent at the market, futures sales appear to have been rather common, despite the official prohibition. Faced with a failing operation, Yahei in 1811 requested permission to open a market in one of the nearby production areas, but the cotton producing villages objected to his proposal. They claimed this would prevent buyers not associated with the seed cotton market from making direct purchases and restrict their sales outlets. They also feared that futures sales would increase and that they would be subjected to the same sort of exploitation they had experienced under the cotton futures markets prior to 1787. Because of this opposition the proposal to construct a rural market was dropped.[23]

Yahei's initial failure caused him to close the market and default on the licensing payments which he owed the government. He petitioned to have the defaulted payments lowered to twenty *mai* silver annually on the condition that he make up the defaulted payments at the reduced rate. This was agreed to in 1820.[24] Subsequently, in 1822 he requested and received permission to move his market to another site in Ōsaka. The market was reopened under the original agreement and as before the terms stressed that no futures sales were to be transacted.[25] In 1825, Yahei was mentioned in an edict circulated in the city as having moved his market operations once more and as still operating under the initial agreement. The edict expressed concern that direct buying and selling of harvested cotton had increased in the Ōsaka region and that this was resulting in a rejection of the traditionally authorized marketing system. Because these activities were violating the prerogatives of the seed cotton market operated by Yahei they were ordered to cease. It was further directed that book sales of cotton futures were not to be conducted.[26] Yahei's efforts were apparently proving unsuccessful and it is obvious that he was dabbling in futures transactions to make ends meet.

By 1829, conditions in the seed cotton market operated by Edoya Yahei had deteriorated even further. The original founder had retired and his son had assumed his name as well as control over the operation of the market. The younger Yahei found it unprofitable, and wishing to rid himself of the burden requested to be relieved of his contractual obligations. In addition, he requested that he be allowed one hundred years to pay off the balance of defaulted licensing payments. These had accumulated to the value of 32 *kan* 130 *momme* silver – over 747 *mai* silver.[27]

As a consequence, in 1829 the Ōsaka city government issued an edict declaring the intention of Edoya Yahei to discontinue the market operation. Parties interested in taking over the market operation were asked to come forward. The justification for closing the market was given as 'financial difficulties.' If no one stepped forward to assume responsibility for its operation the market was to be terminated.[28] The search for a replacement was a failure and the market was closed. All market rights which had been issued by the government were ordered returned until interest was shown in renewing its operation. Steps were also taken to reduce the financial burden on the younger Yahei. Of the accumulated licensing fees 70 percent were excused and the remaining 30 percent, totalling 9 *kan* 639 *momme* (around 224 *mai*), were to be paid in annual instalments over a forty-year period.[29]

Although operation was suspended and the market rights were retired, the seed cotton market had not been permanently removed from the scene. In 1833 a merchant by the name of Daiku Rihei from Hirano-*gō* took over the retired market rights and opened a seed cotton market. His request had been entered in Yahei's name and he agreed to pay license fees of three *mai* silver per year in addition to the back payments for which Yahei was responsible. Located in a center of cotton production the market appears to have prospered, as in 1839 permission was requested to establish a second market in Ōsaka. Payments for this market were set at six *mai* per year.[30]

Opposition to the Ōsaka market came from a familiar source. The cotton *tonya nakama* claimed that reestablishment of the seed cotton market would violate its special trade rights. The *nakama* expected its position to be protected by the city magistrates from outside interference. It did, however, suggest that, if the market operators would pay the regular cotton *tonya nakama* commission on goods sold, the *nakama* would withdraw the objections to its reestablishment.[31] Traditional trade rights were used to claim income from seed cotton sales in Ōsaka conducted by a non-affiliated market. Whoever the seller, the *nakama* demanded a percentage. Outside interference within the city of Ōsaka would be tolerated only at a price. Faced with increasing competition with its activities in the region around the city, the cotton *tonya nakama* was fighting to maintain its grip on the Ōsaka cotton trade.

Despite his persistence in fighting the Ōsaka *kabu nakama* and his eventual acquisition of government authorization, Edoya Yahei failed in his efforts to establish a successful cotton market. His focus shifted from ginned cotton to seed cotton, he altered his projected operation to conform to criticism advanced by the established *kabu nakama*, and he managed briefly to win the support of cotton cultivating villages in Settsu and Kawachi. Yet, all his efforts notwithstanding, once in operation the seed cotton market proved to be unprofitable. Given his failure, what is there about Edoya Yahei that makes him worthy of consideration in a discussion of the Ōsaka cotton trade? Why bother with his vain attempt to offer a direct challenge to the established commercial order?

To begin with, the failure of Edoya Yahei is illustrative of changes which were occurring in the Ōsaka cotton trade. It was noted earlier that the Kansei reform, with its abolition of the cotton futures markets and its effort to strengthen the *kabu nakama* system, marked a turning point in the development of commercial institutions dealing with cotton in Ōsaka. Yahei, in effect, was stepping into the void left by the abolition of the futures markets. His seed cotton market provided a means for directing cotton which was outside the *kabu nakama* marketing system into the city. At the same time, it provided the cotton cultivators with an expanded market for their goods and the potential of an increased return from their labor. His failure suggests that on the one hand he was unable to tailor his market operation to current economic needs and that on the other the city of Ōsaka was no longer a viable site for market operation.

The availability of village support for his undertakings in 1806 and 1807 suggests that at one stage his projected operation appeared to offer a positive alternative to the *kabu nakama* system. Utilization of the new market presented a means of breaking the dominant power of the Ōsaka *kabu nakama* in the cotton trade. A catch was introduced when the market was established in Ōsaka. The cultivators were faced with the necessity of transporting their cotton to the city. This was both costly and inconvenient and other alternatives were developing locally. Lacking an established mechanism for transporting cotton to his market, Yahei found himself unable to compete either with the established *kabu nakama* system or with the rural merchants operating out of the villages and local market towns. While offering an alternative outlet for seed cotton he lacked an efficient supply mechanism to transport the cotton from the producers to the city.

Associated with this problem was the fact that the focus of institutional innovation was in the countryside, not in the city. Had Yahei established his market in Hirano-gō in 1810, it is conceivable that it would have been a success. Given the supply problems and the fact that much of the activity of the rural merchants was directed away from the city of Ōsaka, establishment of a market in Ōsaka had little chance of success. Much of the rural trade went directly to consumption centers including the shogunal capital at Edo and the castle towns of the daimyo. By locating in Ōsaka, Yahei was denied the flexibility which was increasingly available to his unauthorized rural competitors.

Authorization of Yahei's market operation raises some additional questions. Given the hostility of both the *bakufu* and the *kabu nakama* to new market mechanisms, why was Yahei authorized to begin operation in the first place? Was it his willingness to conform to the established practices of the *kabu nakama*? Was it the pressure from the cotton producing villages? Or did this indicate a shift in the commercial policies of the *bakufu*? At this stage it is difficult to know whether one or all of these factors resulted in his receiving official authorization in 1810. It is clear that the *kabu nakama* system was under assault from several different directions. It seems likely that in Edoya Yahei the *bakufu* saw a means of extending its control over the expanding activities of the rural merchants.

The increasing marketing activities of cotton cultivators and rural merchants in the Kinai region are discussed in Chapters 6 and 7. Their impact on the Ōsaka cotton trade is suggested by the complaints raised by authorized Ōsaka cotton traders. The validity of these complaints is substantiated by the data on the growth of the Kinai cotton trade. In areas of Settsu, Kawachi, and Izumi provinces, there is considerable evidence of increases in both rural cotton processing and rural cotton marketing. Village processing activities were increasingly undercutting the dominant position occupied by the Ōsaka *wataya nakama*. The growth of new marketing systems and the increase in rural trading of cotton goods served to direct commodities which previously were controlled by the Ōsaka cotton *nakama* into new trade routes which avoided the Ōsaka market entirely. Despite efforts to reinforce the position of the Ōsaka cotton merchants, the competition for cotton goods in the Kinai region was increasing in intensity.

By the first quarter of the nineteenth century, it was proving increasingly difficult to contain commercial activity in the city of Ōsaka. Hirano-*gō* and other local centers were expanding their role in the Kinai cotton trade. The failure of Edoya Yahei was symptomatic of this change. The following discussion of the 1007-village dispute of 1823 illustrates the growing independence of the cotton cultivators as well as their increasing disdain for the limitations imposed on them by the Ōsaka *kabu nakama*.

THE 1007-VILLAGE DISPUTE OF 1823

During the first quarter of the nineteenth century, a gradual change in the relations between the cotton producing villages in Settsu and Kawachi and the Ōsaka cotton merchants became evident. Following the Kansei reforms and the effort to strengthen the *kabu nakama* system in the late 1780s and early 1790s, the Ōsaka cotton *nakama* had extended their sphere of influence from the city of Ōsaka to cotton production and marketing areas surrounding the city. Coinciding with this extension of *kabu nakama* jurisdiction was a growing discontent on the part of the cotton producing villagers. Expansion of the number of rural merchants and the volume of direct sales during the first quarter of the nineteenth century resulted in increased expectations on the part of the cultivators, as well as a heightened awareness of the advantages of multiple outlets for their cotton goods.

A primary barrier to direct cotton sales to non-*nakama* buyers was the regional shipping monopoly enjoyed by the Ōsaka cotton *tonya nakama*. This meant that all purchases of seed and ginned cotton in Settsu and Kawachi had to be directed through the shipping facilities of the cotton *tonya nakama* and that its regular commission was levied on all such transactions. This enabled the *nakama* to control much of the business of both the *wataya nakama* and the rural cotton merchants. By the 1820s efforts to guarantee these monopoly rights were hardening the antagonism to cotton *tonya nakama* control.[32]

Efforts by the *nakama* to extend its control are illustrated by its suit against Hiranoya Shinhei in 1822. Shinhei was a *wataya nakama* member from Settsu. When he purchased sixty-seven bales of seed cotton in Settsu and shipped them directly to a Hyōgo merchant the cotton *tonya nakama* claimed infringement of its monopoly rights. While this dispute is not representative of developments in the Settsu-Kawachi region, it does show how the *wataya nakama* was being dominated by its more powerful associate.[33]

More dramatic evidence of the growing independence of the rural merchants and the cotton cultivators in Settsu and Kawachi is the series of suits brought against the cotton *tonya nakama* by groups of villages in 1823.[34] In 1823 a series of complaints were made to the Ōsaka magistrates' office against the cotton *tonya nakama* for restraint of the cotton trade in Settsu and Kawachi. The *nakama* was accused of interrupting shipments in Ōsaka, Sumiyoshi, Sakai, and Nada and confiscating goods until the shipper paid the *nakama* its regular commission. The suits complained that this limited the market for village cotton and that the monopoly privileges of the *nakama* enabled it to unilaterally determine the price of cotton. This caused considerable hardship for the cotton producing villages in Settsu and Kawachi. Villages to the number of 1007 were involved in the final suit and they complained that the eight or nine member houses of the cotton *tonya nakama* threatened the economic well-being of over 10 000 households of cotton cultivators.

Replying to the charges made by the cotton producing villages in Settsu and Kawachi the cotton *tonya nakama* defended itself as follows. To begin with, *nakama* members were not the only merchants engaged in buying seed cotton in the villages of Settsu and Kawachi. *Wataya nakama* members also made direct purchases on a smaller scale, and this group included close to 400 member households. The charge that the smaller cotton *tonya nakama* could dominate the numerically larger *wataya nakama* and determine the price level for seed cotton was contested. It was further suggested that, since the cotton *tonya nakama* charged only a 1.3 percent commission on the purchase price of cotton, its activities did not influence the profits or losses on sales made by the cultivators.

Secondly, the *nakama* reminded the producers and the city government that prohibitions against direct shipments of seed cotton from rivers within the city of Ōsaka, which by-passed the cotton *tonya nakama*, had been in effect for many years. Violation of this prohibition authorized the *nakama* to impound goods until the required 1.3 percent commission was paid. The right to this commission was reinforced by the notes of apology which were sent by outside merchants in cases when seed cotton shipments had been seized.

The third point which was stressed related to goods which were loaded at sea off the ports of Sakai, Sumiyoshi, and Nada. While this was prohibited, the *nakama* was unable to prevent such transshipment and force payment of its regular commission. The final point dealt with the claim by the cotton producing villages that *nakama* trade restrictions inhibited their ability to meet their land tax obligations. The *nakama* claimed that it was unable to prevent direct sales by the villagers to local merchants. It suggested that in fact direct sales by intermediary merchants who formerly had operated within the institutionalized supply system had increased. This interfered with the operations of the Ōsaka cotton *nakama*, as regional buyers were able to illegally purchase their goods directly and thereby avoid the charges levied by the Ōsaka merchants. This reduced the quantity of goods handled by the cotton *tonya nakama* and it objected to this open violation of its monopoly rights.[35]

The Ōsaka city magistrate was required to adjudicate this complaint from 1007 cotton producing villages in Settsu and Kawachi against the cotton *tonya nakama*. The substance of the complaint was that the monopoly rights of the cotton *tonya nakama* threatened the livelihood of cotton producing villagers and that continued abuse might force them to discontinue cotton cultivation. The basis of the defense was that the actions of the *nakama* were consistent with the monopoly rights granted to it by the city government, and that implementation of these rights was not sufficient to cause the hardships claimed by the plaintiffs. In effect, the Ōsaka magistrate was forced to decide whether or not to continue *bakufu* support of the *kabu nakama* system in the cotton trade. A strong decision in favor of either side was certain to cause repercussions from the other. The basis of government commercial policies was being directly questioned.

The government decision did not deny the monopoly rights of the cotton *tonya nakama*, but it effectively sanctioned increased free trade outside Ōsaka. The village producers were authorized to continue direct sales transactions with non-*nakama* merchants. This meant that the government was effectively withdrawing the vigorous support of the *kabu nakama* system which had been affirmed in the Kansei reforms. This decision set a precedent for official response to the reduced influence of the Ōsaka cotton *nakama* in the Kinai cotton trade. The decision abrogated the responsibility of the city government to protect the Ōsaka cotton *nakama* from the growing competition they were encountering from outsiders. The result was to reduce the legal barriers to institutional change in the Kinai cotton trade.

The possibility that antagonism between the cotton *tonya nakama* and the *wataya nakama* may have played a role in the 1823 dispute is suggested by Asao Naohiro. In analyzing the leaders of the village dispute he noted that several of the organizers were *wataya nakama* members. These men were important figures in the cotton trade in the villages around Ōsaka and

99

functioned as intermediary merchants. Since they lacked a buying mono-poly, Asao suggests that their activities were less antagonistic to the cotton cultivators than the cotton *tonya nakama*. At the same time, they had the most to lose from the restrictions placed on direct sales and shipments by the *nakama*. This limited the scope of their operations and forced them to adhere to the claims of their officially supported rivals. Abolition of cotton *tonya nakama* monopoly rights would greatly enhance their business posi-tion. It is thus plausible that members of the *wataya nakama* allied them-selves with the cotton cultivators against the cotton *tonya nakama*, as both would benefit from the liberalization of trade in Settsu and Kawachi.[36] The rapid growth of the rural merchant population dealing in seed and ginned cotton after 1823 suggests that this may well have been the case. *Wataya nakama* members were also exposed to new sources of competition. The victory by the cultivators served other interests as well.

GOVERNMENT AWARENESS – THE ABE REPORT

The weakening of the *kabu nakama* system in the Ōsaka cotton trade accelerated after the 1823 decision in favor of unrestricted rural trade. By failing to support the monopoly rights of the cotton *tonya nakama* in Settsu and Kawachi, the *bakufu* sanctioned further expansion of rural trade. Following the decision, direct sales and shipments by rural cotton traders increased. Cotton cultivators took a more active interest in the price they received for their crops and began to withhold goods until favorable price levels were attained. Buyers came from distant regions to compete for Kinai cotton and auction buying became an integral part of the rural cotton trade. This resulted in a decline in the quantity of cotton which was shipped to Ōsaka as well as a rise in its price, as the supply to this central marketing and processing center failed to satisfy the demand. By 1841, although Kinai cotton production appeared to be increasing, the volume of cotton imported into the city had levelled off and a relatively high price was being maintained.[37]

A major question relating to the period up to the Tempō reforms of 1841 revolves around the problem of *bakufu* awareness of the changes which were occurring in the commercial sector. In the face of what was an obvious failure of government policy is the problem of the degree to which the *bakufu* understood the inroads which rural commerce was making into the marketing network established under the Ōsaka *kabu nakama*. Of particular interest to this problem is a report submitted by Abe Tōtōmi no kami Masazō, then Edo city magistrate, on the subject of commodities and their prices. This report, dated 1842/3, is a detailed analysis of eco-nomic conditions under the Tokugawa *bakufu* in the nineteenth century, as seen by one of the principal officials in the *bakufu* administrative struc-ture. It shows that the government had at its command considerable information on developments which were occurring in the commercial sector. This information was the basis for *bakufu* policy during the 1840s. Since our current concern is with the Ōsaka cotton trade, our inquiry will be limited to this one aspect of merchant activity as revealed in the report.[38]

In his discussion of the trade in seed and ginned cotton, Abe reported:[39]

The seed and ginned cotton which is shipped to Ōsaka from various regions is received by the Ōsaka cotton *tonya nakama*. The local cotton *nakama* ship it to Edo and other regions. The above-mentioned cotton *nakama* members not only purchase cotton from the cotton *tonya* but also make direct purchases from various production regions. The seed cotton they purchase they process into ginned cotton, various types of cloth, reeled yarn, waste cotton, and also rough cotton cloth which they either sell locally or ship to Edo and other areas.[40]

Recently we have heard that the price of cotton has been very high. Upon investigation we found that cotton from the principal production areas of Settsu and Kawachi as well as that from other areas received by the Ōsaka cotton *tonya* and cotton *nakama* is around 1 500 000 *kan* by weight of seed cotton and 2 000 000 *kan* of ginned cotton per year. The price of 1 *kin* [220 *momme* in weight] of seed cotton was around 1 *momme* silver and 1 *kan* of ginned cotton sold for 20 *momme* silver.[41]

The report goes on to discuss the 1823 dispute between the cotton *tonya nakama* and the cotton producers in Settsu and Kawachi:

In 1823, the peasants in the 1007 primary cotton producing villages in Settsu and Kawachi requested that they be allowed to sell the seed cotton they produced as well as the seed and ginned cotton handled by rural cotton merchants directly. They claimed that required sales to the Ōsaka cotton *tonya* caused them great hardship because of the narrow constraints placed upon their sales opportunities. They asked that the above *tonya* be restrained from interfering with their sales to a more diversified group of buyers. This complaint was made to the Ōsaka magistrates' office, then under the direction of Takai Yamashiro no kami.

After inquiry into the matter, it was decided that cotton sales by the farmers, together with that directly sold and shipped to regional buyers by rural cotton merchants, would be allowed to continue outside the city of Ōsaka despite the claims of the Ōsaka cotton *tonya*. The *tonya* were directed not to interfere in the unrestricted activities of the villagers engaged in the cotton trade.[42]

Subsequently, the number of merchants engaged in the cotton trade in the Ōsaka region increased. All engaged in independent transactions and joined with the producers in limiting trade for their own benefit and conducting auction sales as a means of maximizing their profits. They also processed seed cotton into ginned cotton in order to maximize the return on their goods and resorted to hoarding their seed cotton supplies until prices rose to desired levels. Auction sales in rural areas and decreased supply to the Ōsaka market worked together to raise the price on both commodities.

Although he was concerned with the nature of the changes which had occurred in rural commerce, Abe seemed resigned to their permanence. He went on to state:

The above conditions, the proliferation of rural cotton dealers, auction selling, the hoarding of cotton by farmers, and the selling of cotton to buyers from other regions as well as the increase in the number of merchants active in the cotton trade, continue and will become the base desire of those engaged in agriculture even if we were to attempt to prevent participation by the farmers.

While suggesting the difficulty of controlling these tendencies, Abe was very apprehensive about their implications. Cotton was regarded as an essential commodity in Tokugawa Japan. It had a wide variety of uses and as a daily necessity its price fluctuations influenced the well-being of a large portion of the population. Consequently, it was imperative that some means be found to control the cotton price to ensure that cotton would not become so expensive that the price would be a source of general distress. The question remained what measures the government could take to deal with the problems presented.

Abe felt that the changes which had occurred in the status of the cotton cultivators were not appropriate to their station. At the same time he was objective in his awareness that government efforts to stem the decline of the Ōsaka cotton *tonya* and the growth of rural trade had been ineffective. Even when local complaints were settled in favor of the Ōsaka merchants the general trend was not reversed. Government efforts notwithstanding, the proliferation of rural traders continued. The villagers were exposed to commercial forces which had turned them from their primary concern with agricultural production. The stability of the entire commercial order was being threatened.

Continuing his discussion of the cotton trade in the region around Ōsaka, Abe reported:

Currently, the cultivators and their companions engaged in the cotton trade, and in particular the buyers from other regions who purchase cotton in the Ōsaka area, are operating on such a wide scale that the Ōsaka merchants are unable to compete with them in the trade. The seed and ginned cotton purchased directly from the farmers by the rural merchants are not sent to Ōsaka and are instead sold freely at the current market price and this does not interfere with the payment of land taxes.

Naturally, the above sequence of events has forced the Ōsaka cotton *tonya* and the cotton *nakama* to engage in irregular transactions in order to compete with their rivals, as well as constantly complain to the government when they have difficulties with their suppliers. In each case, after an investigation, the necessary instructions have been issued.

In the three districts of Ōsaka as well as throughout Settsu and Kawachi we have issued strict orders to the farmers to correct their habits, increase the volume of cotton they ship to Ōsaka, and lower their prices. Nevertheless, the volume of cotton shipped directly to Edo and other regions by rural merchants has continued to increase and the high prices from these sales have become dominant.

The decline in the traditional pattern of commodity distribution through the Ōsaka *kabu nakama* was a cause of grave concern to the *bakufu*. Efforts to ameliorate the situation by strengthening the *kabu nakama* had proved inadequate by the 1830s. Of more importance, perhaps, was the change in the outlook and expectations of the rural producers. Fear was expressed that they would neglect their primary concern with agricultural production in favor of their growing fascination with the possibilities of commerce. The growth of rural merchants and the increased exposure of the cultivators to commercial activities threatened the very basis of the Tokugawa political order. It was emphasized that this process must be changed. The problem was where constructive measures could be introduced, given the failure of previous *bakufu* policy in this area.

Commercialization of the cotton cultivators resulted in efforts on their part to ensure a high price for their product. The Abe report mentions several times that hoarding of goods to force up the price and auction sales for the same purpose had become widespread. Working together with local merchants in the villages, the cultivators were taking a more active role in the marketing of their goods. This threatened the productive process at its very roots and had to be controlled if a stable commercial order was to be maintained. Identification of local interest in the cotton trade was not limited to the villages. As we shall see in the next section, the *han* as independent political units were also beginning to take advantage of the opportunity offered by commercial controls. Here was a threat from a new and powerful quarter which had ramifications of both a political and an economic nature.

THE ABE REPORT – THE HIMEJI 'HAN' COTTON MONOPOLY

Rural merchants and cultivators were not the only source of difficulties for the Ōsaka cotton trade. Conflicts of interest began to arise between the *bakufu* and the *han* as the latter asserted themselves in programs designed to improve their own financial position. In the cotton trade the monopoly established by Himeji *han* over local cotton cloth exports is of particular interest to our discussion.

Bleached cotton cloth was a distinctive product of Himeji *han*. Cloth production developed into an important by-industry in the villages and by the nineteenth century all cloth purchases within the *han* were controlled by the cotton cloth *tonya* in the castle town of Himeji. Exports from the *han* were directed to the Ōsaka market, so that while much of the cloth eventually was consumed in other areas of Japan, it passed through the Ōsaka cotton traders en route. With the establishment of a *han* monopoly buying office for cotton cloth in 1821, the established marketing system was abruptly altered.[43]

Behind the decision to establish a *han* monopoly for cotton cloth was the increasingly dangerous financial plight of the domain treasury. Expenditures were far surpassing income and the *han* debt was increasing with little evidence it could be repaid from regular revenues. Searching for new sources of income, the *han* established a monopoly buying office to purchase commodities which were exported from the *han* in large quantities. Among these was Himeji bleached cotton cloth.

Operation of the system was relatively simple. Cloth was collected by the established cotton *tonya*, passed through the hands of the cotton bleachers for processing, and was then sent to a freight office at the port of Shikama. Upon presentation of a warehousing receipt at the monopoly buying office, the cloth was purchased by the *han*. Of the purchase price, 70–80 percent was paid in currency issued by the *han* for local use and the balance was paid after the goods were sold in Edo. The cloth was then shipped directly to the Edo market, by-passing the Ōsaka cotton merchants, and consequently gaining direct access to the higher prices in Edo and areas of north Japan. In Edo the cloth was consigned to cotton *tonya* appointed by the *han* government. After the cloth was sold the proceeds were paid directly to the *han* residence in Edo with the Edo *tonya* taking a fixed commission on the sale price. At the completion of the sales transaction the *han* monopoly office then completed payment to the local cotton *tonya* in Himeji *han*.

From the viewpoint of the cotton *tonya* within Himeji, the monopoly system was similar to the consignment sales they had formerly conducted with the Ōsaka cotton traders. From their perspective it was as convenient to sell to the *han* as to other merchants. Direct shipment to Edo was conducted by the *han* monopoly office and it was consequently liable for any losses which resulted during shipment or sale in the Edo market. An additional advantage to the local merchants was the system by which the *han* advanced them 70–80 percent of the final purchase price as a means of guaranteeing the *han* monopoly. This provided them with more rapid turnover of their capital and enabled them to increase the scale of their operation within the *han*. With sale to the monopoly office assured, local productive capacity was the only limitation on the quantity of goods they could handle.

Benefits to the *han* were also extensive. Profits from the sale of cotton cloth in Edo were significant, but of even more importance was the income derived by means of currency exchange. The *han* residence in Edo received payment in hard cash. Payments to the *tonya* within the *han* were made in paper currency issued by the *han* government for local consumption. Income derived from currency manipulation was considerable and, combined with the profits from merchandising activities, greatly improved the financial condition of Himeji *han*. During the first twenty-seven years of its operation, the monopoly system enabled the *han* to repay debts totalling 730 000 *ryō* gold.[44]

Within the Ōsaka cotton trade the impact of the Himeji monopoly system and of other efforts to by-pass the Ōsaka market was extensive.

Bakufu awareness of the dislocation of the cotton cloth trade is revealed in the Abe report. Discussing the breakdown of the monopoly which had been enjoyed by the Ōsaka cotton cloth *tonya*, Abe commented:

The white cotton cloth which is shipped to Ōsaka from the various production regions is received by the seven *kumi* cloth *tonya* in Ōsaka. Cloth received is sold to local cotton merchants. Members of this *nakama* also engage in direct purchases in the Kinai region and other areas. They also arrange for further processing of the cloth including various types of dyeing and printing. They further engage in regional sales of cotton cloth as well as shipping it to Edo and other areas of the country.

Recently we have heard that cotton, in particular, was not circulating as previously had been the case. Upon inquiry, we discovered that white cotton cloth comes largely from western Japan, Shikoku, central Japan, and from the San-in region on the Japan Sea coast. Until around 1810, the quantity of cloth received by the Ōsaka *tonya* averaged around eight million *tan* per year of ordinary white cotton cloth.

From this time [actually from 1821], the daimyo of Himeji *han* in Harima began to purchase all the cotton cloth produced in his domain and ship it directly to the market which offered the highest price. Cotton from this *han* as well as cotton from other areas was sold at auction and this type of activity became extensive. As a result, the volume of cotton which was received by the Ōsaka *tonya* gradually declined. Ōsaka merchant trips to the production regions and along the primary shipping routes and attempts to exert pressure on their suppliers brought no relief to their declining proportion of the market. From 1832 to 1841, the annual quantity of white cotton cloth received by the Ōsaka *tonya* was no more than three million *tan* and this has resulted in the decline of the *tonya* merchants.

This condition notwithstanding, production of cotton cloth has in recent years continued undiminished and the number of weavers has not decreased. By withholding their stocks or by other forms of intereference, the price of cotton cloth has been raised and at present white cotton cloth has a price of about nine *momme* per *tan*.

Corresponding to the decline in the volume of goods shipped to Ōsaka has been a decline in the quantity of goods which the Ōsaka *tonya* have been able to purchase directly. This has consequently reduced the quantity of cloth they are able to process and this condition has been further complicated by an increase in the price of dyestuffs. As a result, the price of dyed cloth has risen by 20–30 percent. The problems involved in the circulation of cotton cloth are very complex and cannot be easily understood or corrected.[45]

While admitting the difficulty presented by changes in the cotton trade, Abe recommended at least one step which would focus on one of the more visible areas of interference. He suggested that

those houses dealing with the various products of the provinces should, as previously stated in government edicts, cease making purchases at auction sales operated by Himeji *han*. If this was done the volume of cotton received in Ōsaka would increase to its previous levels and the price would be reduced. Further, the quantity of cotton cloth shipped by Ōsaka merchants to Edo and other regions would increase in the same manner. The tendencies revealed in the Ōsaka market would be reflected elsewhere and the average price of cotton cloth would be lowered by this program.[46]

From the Abe report we can see dramatic evidence of the decline of the Ōsaka cotton trade. Imports of white cotton cloth declined from eight million *tan* in 1810 to an official average of three million *tan* from 1832 to 1841. At the same time the price of cloth increased by 50 percent from six to nine *momme* silver per *tan* of cloth. In contrast to the apparent decline of imports to Ōsaka was the continued rise in total production of cotton cloth, including an increase in cloth production in Himeji *han*. Efforts by the Ōsaka *nakama* to reconstruct their supply lines were unsuccessful and it appeared to Abe that only by inhibiting the operation of the Himeji monopoly could the *bakufu* hope to gain control over the cotton trade in the Kinai region. Himeji was only one of the *han* operating a successful monopoly system. Other domains had similar programs to maximize their profits from local products. *Han* monopolies were not the only problem with which the *bakufu* was forced to contend. It is in this context that we shift our concern to the Tempō reforms.

THE TEMPŌ REFORMS

As is evident in the Abe report, by 1841 the Ōsaka cotton trade was being assaulted from several directions by outside sources of competition. Rising prices combined with sharp declines in the volume of cotton goods which were marketed through Ōsaka brought the role of the Ōsaka *kabu nakama* in the cotton trade seriously into question. The results of the 1823 dispute clearly indicated the unwillingness of the *bakufu* to continue its comprehensive support of the Ōsaka cotton merchants. The justification for the existence of the *kabu nakama* was increasingly subject to official doubts, since they were ineffective as a mechanism for implementing *bakufu* economic policies. Rising commodity prices in the 1830s, combined with other problems, forced the government to reconsider its economic policies. The Tempō reforms of 1841 to 1843 were a dramatic effort to find new solutions to the economic problems faced by the Tokugawa *bakufu*.

The first shock of the Tempō reforms in Ōsaka came with an edict of 1841/12/23 (24 January 1842). The Edo Higaki shipping *tonya nakama* and all other *nakama* and *kumiai* were officially abolished. All commodities, irrespective of their origin, were to be marketed without restrictions.[47] This was followed in 1842/3/13 by an edict which abolished all *kabu* membership certificates and eliminated the official trade rights which were assigned to *kabu nakama* members. Advance payments to rural producers, sales stoppages, and local hoarding by merchants were prohibited.[48] A third edict of 1842/5/12 suspended the payment of licensing fees. Gifts traditionally presented to city officials on New Year's Day and the first day of the eighth lunar month were forbidden. Special payments for river control, sewer repairs, peddler and coolie contracts, river shipping licenses, and the licensed cotton markets were to continue as before.[49] The *bakufu*, searching for new means for controlling commodity prices and supply lines to the major cities, withdrew its support of the *kabu nakama*. By governmental fiat it eliminated the authorized institutional structure of the Ōsaka cotton merchants.

Following the abolition of the *kabu nakama* came edicts directed against the activities of rural merchants and *han* monopolies. Termination of the *kabu nakama* system was to be accompanied by new controls over sources of outside competition as well. The reassertion of *bakufu* authority was designed to develop a fresh approach to commercial control and assure that consumer goods would be supplied to the cities in an unrestricted flow.

The pre-1841 decline of the Ōsaka cotton *nakama* is confirmed by an 1839 document on business procedures submitted by the cotton *tonya nakama*. Within the association, the need to conform to established trading practices was strongly emphasized. Members were prohibited from submitting to trade terms demanded by their clients. Those who violated *nakama* regulations in order to protect their position in the cotton trade were threatened with censure and ejection from the association. All requests for shipping assistance by non-members were to be referred to *nakama* officials for consideration. No shipments were to be made until payment of the fees stipulated in the *nakama* regulations was agreed to by the customer.[50]

Despite the changes which had occurred in the cotton trade in the Ōsaka area the cotton *tonya nakama* was trying to operate as it had been licensed to conduct business in the late eighteenth century. Members were threatened with fines or expulsion if they departed from the procedures which were outlined in the *nakama* regulations. Those who managed to modify their approach to the cotton trade and defend themselves against new sources of competition were seen not as innovative businessmen but as a disgrace to the association. As an institution the *nakama* was structurally unable to change and many of its members were unwilling to entertain the notion that new techniques were necessary for maintaining their position in the cotton trade. Tradition had resulted in a form of institutional calcification which made altering procedures an anathema.

Thus, despite changes in the cotton trade in the Ōsaka area, many of which are discussed in Chapter 7, the cotton *tonya nakama* continued to adhere to established patterns of operation. What was the impact of the Tempō reforms on this and other *kabu nakama* in the cotton trade? Documentation for the period from 1842 to the 1851 reestablishment of the *nakama* is scanty, but from external evidence some sense of the effect of the reforms on the cotton trade can be gained. To begin with, it should be kept in mind that the focus of the Tempō reform economic policies was the Kantō region rather than Kinai. Commercial agricultural expansion was far more pronounced in the Ōsaka region than around Edo, as were the inroads made by rural traders into the marketing systems of the urban merchant associations. As a result, the abolition of the Ōsaka cotton *nakama* merely accelerated the processes which had increased in intensity with the 1823 decision against the cotton *tonya nakama*. The growth of local marketing systems continued as before, with the major change being a further disruption of the links between the Ōsaka cotton merchants and their associates in Edo. Abolition of the Higaki shipping monopoly linking the two cities opened up additional possibilities for direct shipments of cotton goods from the Kinai area to Edo and the Kantō region. While this enabled outsiders to compete more openly within the city of Ōsaka, the change was less of substance than of degree. Outside competition was nothing new to the Ōsaka cotton merchants.

Second, it should be kept in mind that while the abolition of the *kabu nakama* removed the formal support of the *bakufu* for the Ōsaka cotton *nakama*, they continued to function as unofficial merchant associations. External restraints were removed, but the internal structure and ties of tradition remained the same. Merchants who had failed to modify their business procedures prior to 1841 were under minimal new pressures to do so with the abolition of the cotton *nakama*. The loss of institutionalized ties with other merchant groups, for example those in Edo, caused some realignment, but there is little to suggest that the new groupings differed significantly from the old. This is evident in the ease with which the *nakama* were reconstructed after 1851. The Ōsaka cotton *nakama* received less and less support from the *bakufu* after 1823, so their official abolition in 1842 did not have a severe impact on their position in the cotton trade. Although a careful analysis of individual house records would be necessary to substantiate the impact of the Tempō reforms on the Ōsaka cotton merchants, it is safe to assume that their position continued to deteriorate and that the major impact was probably on the rate, rather than the form, of their decline.

This is confirmed by the lack of impact which the Tempō reforms had on the *han* monopolies and rural trade. With few exceptions, there is little evidence that the prohibition of *han* monopolies had any significant result as the abolition order was never effectively enforced.[51] Similarly, as noted in Chapter 7, government efforts to halt auction sales and hoarding of cotton goods were ineffective. The major period of change in the Kinai cotton trade was after 1823, not after 1841, suggesting that the Tempō reforms were of far less importance to the Kinai cotton trade than might be expected from the significance normally attached to them.

This merely emphasizes a point about pre-modern Japanese history which is often overlooked, namely that regional variations were far more important than is sometimes realized. The fact that the Tempō reforms had a major impact in Edo and the Kantō region is not sufficient justification for the assumption that similar results obtained in Ōsaka and the Kinai region. In the case of the Ōsaka cotton trade, the Tempō reforms served largely to accelerate tendencies which were well under way prior to their implementation. Neither the data for Ōsaka nor those used in Chapters 6 and 7 from Settsu, Kawachi, and Izumi support any claims to a major influence of Tempō reform economic policies on the Kinai cotton trade.

THE TEMPŌ REFORMS – COTTON PRICES

In the absence of business records of the Ōsaka cotton merchants for the period after 1841, any evaluation of the impact of the Tempō reforms on the cotton trade has to be constructed from other sources. One readily available measure of the degree of economic dislocation resulting from *kabu nakama* abolition is a series of price statistics for ginned cotton and cotton cloth for the period from 1830 to 1860.[52] Presumably, any significant disruption in deliveries to the Ōsaka market would be reflected in the prices for that period. Thus a sudden price rise would indicate that demand

TABLE 9. Ginned cotton prices in Ōsaka, 1830–60
(Weight in *kan* per 100 *momme* silver annual average value)

Year	Place of origin		Year	Place of origin	
	Settsu	Kawachi		Settsu	Kawachi
1830	3.78	3.98	1846	3.51	3.86
1831	3.99	4.22	1847	3.84	4.21
1832	4.57	4.77	1848	3.65	4.03
1833	4.20	4.40	1849	3.51	3.99
1834	4.32	4.53	1850	3.54	3.95
1835	3.67	3.88	1851	3.60	4.00
1836	2.60	2.82	1852	3.50	3.78
1837	2.86	3.08	1853	3.49	3.77
1838	4.17	4.36	1854	3.83	4.07
1839	3.57	4.09	1855	4.43	4.66
1840	3.83	4.23	1856	4.57	4.94
1841	3.83	4.45	1857	4.04	4.52
1842	3.61	4.19	1858	3.35	3.88
1843	3.73	4.30	1859	3.16	3.58
1844	3.67	4.22	1860	2.75	3.23
1845	3.27	3.77			

SOURCE: Miyamoto (ed.), *Kinsei Ōsaka no bukka to rishi*, pp. 205–14.

exceeded supply, while a sudden drop in the price would reveal the reverse condition of supply exceeding demand. Price statistics should then be of value in our analysis of the Tempō reforms and the Ōsaka cotton trade.[53]

Let us begin with the price statistics for ginned cotton in the Ōsaka market included in table 9. The crucial period for our consideration is that between 1840 and perhaps 1850. Any radical disruption in the ginned cotton trade should be evident in the statistics. Upon examination of the data, however, no significant fluctuations are visible. The price of ginned cotton produced in Settsu and Kawachi rose slightly from 1841 to 1842 and fell the following year. Neither fluctuation is abnormal, if it is compared with the previous ten-year period. What is most striking about the data is that the period from 1840 to 1850 is significantly more stable than the previous or following ten-year period. This is true for both Settsu and Kawachi ginned cotton.

What does this suggest about the impact of the Tempō reforms? Can we assume that the statistics confirm the government's success in stabilizing the price of ginned cotton? Perhaps, but other factors seem to be involved. Stability here would seem to point to a relative equalization of supply and demand. With no data on the volume of goods traded it is impossible to evaluate the real significance of this equalization to the Ōsaka cotton trade.

In the case of white cotton cloth a rather different picture emerges, as is evident in table 10. The price of Harima cloth rose almost continuously

TABLE 10. White cotton cloth prices in Ōsaka, 1830–60
(Price for 1 *tan* of cloth in *momme* silver)

	Place of origin			Place of origin	
Year	Harima	Bingo	Year	Harima	Bingo
1830	5.00	7.20	1846	7.20	8.50
1831	4.35	6.80	1847	7.60	8.50
1832	4.90	5.60	1848	6.50	8.20
1833	4.90	7.00	1849	6.10	8.00
1834	5.25	7.00	1850	6.00	7.80
1835	5.22	7.50	1851	6.20	8.00
1836	5.60	8.00	1852	6.10	8.30
1837	5.80	8.20	1853	5.90	8.50
1838	6.50	8.50	1854	5.40	7.50
1839	6.50	7.80	1855	5.40	7.20
1840	7.00	8.00	1856	5.50	7.50
1841	7.60	8.30	1857	6.50	8.70
1842	6.00	8.00	1858	6.40	9.60
1843	6.00	8.00	1859	6.00	9.50
1844	6.60	8.10	1860	6.00	9.13
1845	7.00	8.30			

SOURCE: Miyamoto (ed.), *Kinsei Ōsaka no bukka to rishi*, pp. 219–20.

from 1831 to 1841. The price of Bingo cloth rose from 1832 to 1838, declined slightly, and then continued to increase from 1839 through 1841. Both experienced price declines from 1841 to 1842, remained low from 1842 to 1843, and then rose again to attain their former high levels in 1847 and 1846 respectively. Thereafter, the prices of Harima and Bingo cloth experienced declines until the mid-1850s, with those for Harima cloth being the most significant. Here we find some evidence that seems to correlate with the Tempō reforms.

The price drop from 1841 to 1842 could be taken as evidence of considerable disruption in the Ōsaka white cloth trade. Although the data could be said to indicate an increase in the supply of white cloth shipped to Ōsaka or a significant drop in demand, the latter explanation seems most likely. The disruption of shipping and credit systems would have curtailed orders to the Ōsaka cotton merchants from regional customers and resulted in a drop in the demand for white cloth. It is also reasonable to assume that the abolition of the *kabu nakama* slowed trade down to a mere trickle as retail merchants disposed of their accumulated inventories and waited for conditions to settle. It is also likely that Ōsaka retail merchants by-passed the traditional supply system and went to the producers for their goods until the Ōsaka cotton merchants had reorganized. The decline can then in part be explained by the slowing of commercial activity caused by the Tempō reforms.

The sharp rise in prices after 1843 can also, at least in part, be reasonably attributed to the dislocation brought about by the abolition of the *kabu nakama*. If it can be assumed that inventories were exhausted during the period from 1841 to 1843, then the demand for cloth would have risen thereafter. This could account for some of the price rise from 1843 to 1846 or 1847. The Ōsaka merchants managed to reconstruct their marketing system in an unofficial manner as suggested in Chapter 3. This resulted in an increased demand for cotton cloth in the Ōsaka market as the Ōsaka traders tried to recover business. Their supply network was disrupted outside the city, however, and this could not be easily reconstructed. As a result, the demand for cotton cloth exceeded the supply, Ōsaka merchants were forced to compete for their goods with other buyers, and they no longer had any competitive advantage in the form of government support.

For comparative purposes it is useful to examine the price of rice over the period from 1830 to 1860. In table 11, the first thing evident is that the price of rice fluctuated much more violently than that of cotton goods. The difference between the high and low prices is of a different order of magnitude, with a rise of over 100 percent in the price of rice from 1835 to 1837 as the result of disastrous climatic conditions and low yields. With the exception of 1843, the price of rice rose continuously from 1840 to 1846,

TABLE 11. Price of Higō rice on the Ōsaka market, 1831–60, in *momme* silver[a]

Year	Price	Year	Price
1831	81.3	1846	92.5
1832	73.7	1847	87.5
1833	94.0	1848	87.4
1834	107.7	1849	90.2
1835	79.1	1850	126.8
1836	113.4	1851	116.2
1837	168.5	1852	85.4
1838	122.1	1853	97.5
1839	90.6	1854	96.6
1840	68.2	1855	81.4
1841	71.3	1856	81.5
1842	77.4[b]	1857	93.6
1843	74.0	1858	122.5
1844	78.2	1859	121.4
1845	86.9	1860	153.0

SOURCE: Miyamoto (ed.), *Kinsei Ōsaka no bukka to rishi*, pp. 122–4.
[a] Units of 1 *koku* split into three bags.
[b] 11-month average discarding the figure for the first month because of its inconsistency with the other data.

though rather slowly when compared to the 1830s experience. The period from 1845 to 1849 was relatively stable, and the amplitude of the fluctuations for the 1840s as a whole is much less than for either the 1830s or the 1850s. It appears, then, that the decade of the 1840s saw relative stability for the price of rice, ginned cotton, and to a lesser extent Bingo cotton cloth. This confirms the claim that the Tempō reforms failed to have a major impact on the Ōsaka commercial scene. While the data on Harima cloth differ from the other data, Himeji *han* monopoly policies and conditions in Edo may well have influenced Harima cloth price levels and made them inconsistent with the Ōsaka price data.

THE TEMPŌ REFORMS – THE AFTERMATH

Bakufu policy from 1842 through early 1851 attempted to impose controls on commercial operations without the assistance of the *kabu nakama* system. Although the price statistics for cotton during this period suggest a levelling off of prices, other sources suggest that the supply mechanism which directed goods into the major cities deteriorated further. Within the *bakufu*, support for the policies imposed by the Tempō reforms was of limited duration. Mizuno Tadakuni was forced out of office in 1843, though, as noted in Chapter 3, not because of the failure of his commercial policies. Enforcement of the restrictions imposed under the reform rapidly deteriorated, but the basic policy remained in force until 1851 when the *kabu nakama* were restored. Restrictive membership, licensing payments, and several other characteristics of the pre-1841 merchant associations were eliminated in the reconstructed *nakama*. The policy directive of 1851/3/21 in Ōsaka stated:

> In 1842 *kabu* certificates along with *tonya nakama* and *kumiai* were suspended. All payments of licensing fees were excused, together with coolie labor, runner services, and other payments to the *bakufu*. Existing commercial laws were abolished. However, since prices did not fall and reports of breakdowns in commodity distribution have been received, we at this time order the reestablishment of the *tonya kumiai* [associations]. However, membership certificates will not be issued and no payments of fees are to be made. For this reason, monopoly buying, selling of inferior goods, short weighing and other illegal practices are to cease. Prices are to be lowered and all transactions will be conducted honestly.
>
> If there are those who wish to enter a *nakama*, this shall be permitted without fail. Unless there is a clear need for membership limitation it will not be permitted. When new members are initiated large fees and expensive entertainment must not be required of the new initiates.
>
> In addition to the above, the present conditions of all the *tonya kumiai* are to be investigated and reports will be made to the various city officials regarding commodities and their prices.[54]

The restoration order was an attempt to reconstruct the *kabu nakama* system. Restrictive elements which had contributed to the decline of the *kabu nakama* were eliminated. Price control was one of the objectives, but regulation of business conduct was also a primary consideration. While failing in many other capacities, the *kabu nakama* had been effective in regulating business conduct and regularizing business procedures. This was a very important factor in their reestablishment. Increased commercial corruption, combined with the failure of the Tempō reforms to lower prices, resulted in a decision to restore the commercial associations minus those characteristics which were regarded as no longer necessary or desirable.

As part of the restoration process all the *tonya kumiai* were ordered to submit their membership registers and regulations to the government for inspection. Efforts were made to adhere to the spirit of the Tempō reforms by forbidding limited membership and license fee payments. Initially, some of the *nakama* attempted to reintroduce exclusive membership policies and charge exorbitant fees for initiation. In subsequent orders, the *bakufu* cracked down on these violations. One of the offending *nakama* was the cotton shipping *nakama* and an order of 1852/7 prohibited its illegal activities.[55]

Within each of the reestablished *nakama* were two groups of merchants, the first composed of pre-Tempō-reform members, and the second of post-1851 initiates. Eventually government pressure on the associations forced the two groups to merge so that their business procedures would be consistent. *Bakufu* policy on *nakama* activities shifted as the fiscal condition of the government deteriorated. In 1858 licensing fees were reintroduced and by 1861 fees were being collected from fifty-six of the Ōsaka *nakama* as a source of additional revenue.[56]

By 1860 the *kabu nakama* system in Ōsaka was reestablished. The merchant associations were made more comprehensive by the government's trying to include in them all merchants active in the cotton trade, regardless of their status prior to the Tempō reforms. The dominant position of the Ōsaka merchants had been broken and *bakufu* policy now acknowledged this change. The merchant associations established after 1851 were merely a modification of the old *kabu nakama* system. However, economic institutions which had proven unequal to government and merchant needs prior to 1841 could not be expected to inject new vigor into the Tokugawa commercial scene in the 1850s and 1860s. Past inadequacies could not be overcome so easily.

Just how well or badly the reconstructed *nakama* worked is difficult to judge. The difficulties imposed by the opening of the country to foreign trade and the declining authority of the *bakufu* complicate any effort at analysis. Although they continued to play a role in the Ōsaka cotton trade, they failed to effectively absorb their rural competitors, as is evident from the discussion in Chapter 7. Yet they continued to function on a limited basis until abolished again in the 1870s.

SUMMARY

The Ōsaka cotton trade has been discussed from the Kansei reforms to the 1860s. The process by which the Ōsaka cotton merchants gradually lost their position of dominance has been illustrated. Specific episodes which occurred during this transitional period from 1790 to 1860 have been discussed in some detail. Yet a more intensive analysis of a particular house or one of the cotton *nakama* over the course of the period would be very helpful. Documentation available in published form is not yet sufficient to allow this type of inquiry.

Given the limitations of the documentation it is still possible to analyze the process by which the position of the Ōsaka cotton *nakama* was gradually undermined. The Kansei reforms have been presented as a reaffirmation of *bakufu* support for the *kabu nakama* system. By the late eighteenth century, the merchant associations were an accepted instrument of government policy in the commercial sector. When the cotton futures markets were abolished and discredited, the *nakama* were regarded as traditional elements of the Tokugawa economic order. They were given comprehensive support against competitive pressures which, as noted in Chapter 7, were increasing in cotton production regions.

The 1797 decision by the Ōsaka city magistrate in favor of the monopoly rights of the cotton shipping *nakama* was indicative of the primary concern of the *bakufu* with maintaining the urban-centered status quo. Although the countryside was rapidly developing as the dynamic source of institutional innovation, *bakufu* determination to maintain stability focused its attention on developments within the Ōsaka market.

Edoya Yahei and the enthusiasm shown for reestablishing cotton markets at the turn of the nineteenth century illustrate the vacancy created by the abolition of the cotton futures markets. Enterprising merchants saw in market operation a potential source of considerable profit. Yahei, as the most persistent of the group in Ōsaka, managed to gain official authorization for his enterprise in 1810. By this time, however, innovations within the Ōsaka market were less effective than unauthorized innovations in the cotton cultivating areas of Settsu, Kawachi, and Izumi. While Yahei was failing in Ōsaka, the activity of rural merchants was rising to a new peak. Yahei's bankruptcy and market closure symbolized the movement of commercial innovation from the city to the countryside.

It is also evident that *bakufu* concern with tradition did not blind it to the growing unrest in the cotton producing villages. The suit from 1007 cotton producing villages brought to the Ōsaka city magistrates in 1823 met with a very different response than could have been expected at the turn of the nineteenth century. The *nakama* sphere of influence was limited to the city of Ōsaka, and the rapidly growing class of rural merchants and cotton cultivators were given a free hand to conduct their affairs as they saw fit. *Kabu nakama* monopoly rights had lost most of their significance in the Ōsaka cotton trade.

Bakufu comprehension of the changes which were occurring in the cotton trade is evident in the report on commodities and their prices submitted by Abe Masazō in 1842. The nature of the threat to the Ōsaka cotton trade and its consequent decline is set forth in some detail in this report. Awareness of the process of change did not prepare the *bakufu* to deal with it, however, as is evident in the so-called Tempō reforms. The effort to deal with the proliferation of commercial activity by removing the last legal barriers to its expansion was greeted by further dislocation of the national distribution system and a resulting upsurge in what the *bakufu* saw as commercial corruption. In an attempt to reaffirm their control, the *bakufu* reestablished the *nakama* system in the 1850s. The revised system took into account newcomers to the commercial scene. Yet this effort to construct a comprehensive system of merchant associations showed both an awareness of the magnitude of the problem and an inability to deal with it in an effective manner.

Commercial control was no longer a problem which was confined to the major urban centers under Tokugawa control. Commercial activity had developed on a national scale. In the next two chapters the process of commercial agricultural expansion and the growth of rural trade will be examined in the provinces of Settsu, Kawachi, and Izumi, as a means of broadening this discussion of the transformation of the Kinai cotton trade.

6 Cotton Cultivating and Processing in the Kinai Region

Fundamental to the development of Ōsaka as a major center for the marketing and processing of cotton was the increase of cotton cultivation in the area surrounding the city during the Tokugawa period. The diffusion of cotton as a major agricultural crop began in the late sixteenth century. Ōkura Nagatsune's *Menpo yōmu* [The important points of cotton farming] of 1833 suggests that cotton cultivation began in the province of Yamato and spread from there to the provinces of Kawachi, Yamashiro, Settsu, Izumi, and elsewhere during the sixteenth century.[1] By the second quarter of the seventeenth century there was an active cotton market in Ōsaka, illustrating that all cotton cultivated in the Kinai region was not consumed in the cultivating villages and that some marketing of cotton was already taking place.

THE EXPANSION OF KINAI COTTON CULTIVATION

Developments in the Kinai region prior to the Tokugawa period gave to this area high potential for rapid growth in agricultural productivity. To begin with, the Kinai region had a high rate of productivity during the medieval period and had already experienced some degree of commercial agricultural development and a relatively highly monetized economy. Because of its proximity to the imperial capital at Kyōto, a rather high level of barter occurred in this region relative to other parts of the country, partially related to the tribute requirements of the nobility and also the temple and shrine proprietors. In addition, demands for consumer goods by the residents of Kyōto resulted in greater contact with a consumption economy and the growth of handicraft industry in the Kinai area.

Of further importance was the relatively high level of urbanization in the Kinai region. This encouraged landowners and other villagers to engage in various processing activities in their free time from farming, as the towns and cities of the region offered a ready market for their products. With the rapid increase in the demand for cotton cloth for clothing needs in the Tokugawa period, the Kinai region had both the physical requirements and the economic foundations to become a center for cotton cultivating and processing.[2]

Associated with the increases in cotton cultivation were technological advances in farming. Cotton cultivation required high inputs of labor and fertilizer, both of which were available in the Kinai region. The high productivity of the area from medieval times resulted in rather high population density relative to other parts of Japan, and the development of water transport to Ōsaka and along the river systems in the Kinai region made possible the large-scale shipments of commercial fertilizers required for cotton cultivation.[3]

Cotton required massive inputs of cheap fertilizers and the Ōsaka region saw the development of extensive trading in dried sardines, pressed oil wastes, *sake* brewing wastes, and human excrement from early in the seventeenth century. Dried sardines and oil wastes were shipped by *kensakibune*, shallow-draft pointed vessels which worked the rivers in the Ōsaka area, while human excrement was collected by the cultivators in urban centers and then transported to the villages in village-owned boats. Surface transport by packhorse or ox was also a means of transporting fertilizers.[4]

In the fertile plain east of Ōsaka irrigation facilities were good, the weather was relatively warm, and good transport facilities were available by both river networks and roads. Cotton was being cultivated in this area by 1600, particularly in Wakae and Shibukawa *gun* (districts) of the province of Kawachi. Although official policy forbade the growing of cotton in paddy fields, there is considerable evidence that this practice received the tacit approval of local officials. For example, when in 1633 the villagers of Jingūji, part of modern Minami Takayasu, were unable to pay their land taxes because of a bad cotton harvest, their taxes were waived for the year, thus authorizing their concentration on cotton cultivation.[5] Further south, in the area of modern Izumi-sano city, cotton cultivation was important by 1629 and continued as a major crop into the late nineteenth century. Taxes from Nakasho village were paid in ginned cotton and cotton cloth as early as 1601.[6]

In the Fuse region, land surveys from the late sixteenth century indicate the existence of *handa*, fields which mixed elevated dry sections and lower wet sections so that cotton and rice could be grown simultaneously in the same field. This shows that cotton was being cultivated in this area in the late sixteenth and early seventeenth centuries. In the second quarter of the seventeenth century, cotton was being cultivated in Nishi Tsutsumi village. By mid-century, Miyage and Kuboji cotton cloth from this area had developed a national reputation. Official concern over the increased cultivation of cotton in paddy fields was reflected in a 1642 *bakufu* edict forbidding this practice.[7] By the late seventeenth century cotton cultivation was extensive throughout the Kinai region. For example, in the 1690s villages near Sakai had around half their land planted in cotton during the summer months, indicating a major involvement in commercial agricultural production of cotton.[8]

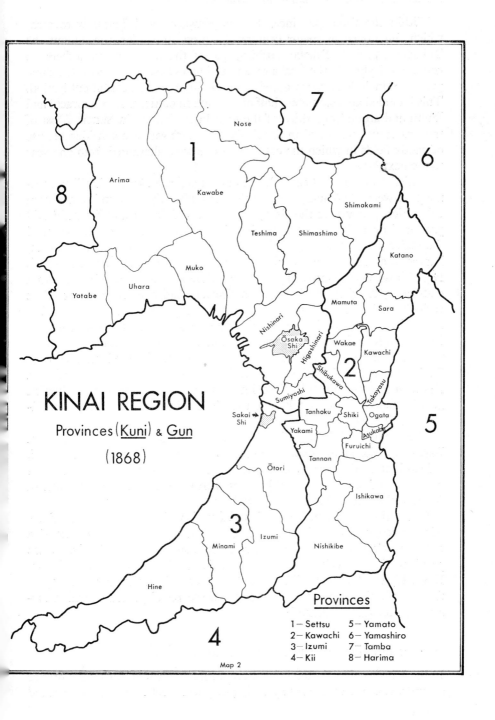

KINAI REGION

Provinces (<u>Kuni</u>) & <u>Gun</u>

(1868)

Nose

1

Arima

Kawabe

8

Teshima

Shimashimo

Shimakami

7

6

Muko

Katano

Yatabe

Uhara

Mamuta

Sara

Nishinari

Ōsaka Shi

Higashinari

Wakae

Kawachi

2

Shibukawa

Takayasu

Sumiyoshi

Sakai → Shi

Tanhoku

Shiki

Ogata

5

Yakami

Asukabe

Furuichi

Tannan

Ōtori

Ishikawa

3

Minami

Izumi

Nishikibe

Hine

4

<u>Provinces</u>

1— Settsu   5— Yamato
2— Kawachi   6— Yamashiro
3— Izumi   7— Tamba
4— Kii   8— Harima

Map 2

Within the three provinces Settsu, Kawachi, and Izumi were areas which functioned as major centers of cotton cultivation throughout the Tokugawa period. Takebe Yoshito, one of the foremost researchers on cotton cultivation in the Ōsaka region, estimates that in the 1830s the three provinces included approximately 21 000 *chō* of land in cotton cultivation. This included approximately half of the land in cultivation in Kawachi and Izumi and around one-third of the land in cultivation in Settsu. Most of the cotton was cultivated in dry fields, but there was also considerable use of paddy fields in which the cotton and rice were alternated from one year to the next.[9]

Statistics on national agricultural output collected by the Meiji government between 1876 and 1878, considerably after the peak in Kinai cotton cultivation, show that the former provinces of Settsu and Kawachi still produced over 20 percent of total national cotton harvested. In Kawachi the major areas of cotton cultivation were Wakae, Shibukawa, Tanhoku, Kawachi, and Shiki *gun*, while in Settsu the major areas were Nishinari, Higashinari, and Sumiyoshi *gun*. Map 2 shows the location of these cotton cultivating districts. Each of these districts had over 20 percent of its agricultural land in cotton cultivation in the 1870s, and can be assumed to have had more extensive cotton cultivation during the Tokugawa period. Muko and Kawabe *gun* in Settsu, and Ogata and Takayasu *gun* in Kawachi were of lesser importance for cotton farming.[10] Despite the introduction of foreign yarns into Japan, cotton cultivation continued to be extensive in Kawachi into the 1880s.[11] Yarn imports and machine textile production notwithstanding, cotton cultivation in Kawachi was not completely eradicated until 1924.[12]

The province of Izumi, with its long coastline with sandy soil on Ōsaka Bay, had major areas of cotton cultivation and processing in Ōtori, Izumi, Minami, and Hine *gun*. This is indicated by the participation of villages from each of the four *gun* in disputes with the cotton futures markets in Sakai during the eighteenth century.[13]

In addition to Settsu, Kawachi, and Izumi, which are the primary focus of the present study of the Kinai cotton trade, there was also extensive cotton cultivation in Yamato and some in Yamashiro as well. These two provinces have received less attention from scholars than have Settsu, Kawachi, and Izumi and I have excluded them from the present study so that I could focus my attention on the three Kinai provinces which surrounded the city of Ōsaka.[14]

COTTON CULTIVATION: PROCESS AND RISKS

In the Kinai region, cotton seeds were normally planted during the first or second week of May. Prior to planting they were soaked in water and rolled in a mixture of ashes and urine for initial fertilization. Normally, the seeds were planted in dry fields or on the ridges of paddy fields or *handa* to prevent rotting from excess moisture. In the dry fields, they were often planted in furrows over the roots of the previously harvested winter wheat crop. During the course of the summer, the plants were fertilized three times, watered occasionally, weeded, and pruned to insure the growth of healthy plants.[15] In good years, one *tan* of land in cotton produced 270 to 300 *kin* of dried seed cotton, with each *kin* weighing 220 to 230 *momme*, depending on the region in which the cotton was cultivated.[16]

Cotton cultivation had a higher potential return than rice farming, but was highly speculative. To begin with, output varied greatly depending on weather conditions. Second, cotton required two to three times the fertilizer inputs required for rice cultivation. Finally, it also required around twice the labor inputs required for rice. It is estimated that rice cultivation required twenty-two or twenty-three man days per *tan*, while cotton required around forty man days per *tan* of cultivation.[17] Consequently, over the course of the Tokugawa period, cotton cultivation fluctuated as the value of cotton and rice and the costs of fertilizer and labor varied.[18]

The fertilizer requirements for cotton cultivation placed a considerable burden on the cultivators. Many of them borrowed fertilizer from local fertilizer dealers at planting time and paid for it with seed cotton or cash after the harvest. In many instances, bad harvests made repayment impossible and this led to payment defaults and the mortgaging of farmland.[19] While evidence for this process is extensive for the eighteenth and nineteenth centuries, there are also seventeenth century examples. A 1694 dispute between the Sakai fertilizer merchant Hoshikaya Shichibei and the villagers of Hikishō over defaulted fertilizer payments is one illustration. Shichibei sued the village through the Sakai city magistrate for the recovery of 3 *kan* 100 *momme* of fertilizer sold to the village twenty years earlier. The villagers, in replying to the suit, explained that they had been buying fertilizer from Sakai since the 1660s. The burden of payments was such that twenty out of the twenty-three farmers who had defaulted on the payments to Hoshikaya Shichibei had either lost some of their land or gone bankrupt. Consequently, they were unable to pay their debts and asked for relief.[20]

This is but one example of the risks of commercial agriculture in the seventeenth century. Not all cotton farmers went bankrupt, however. The story by Ihara Saikaku of Kawabata Kusuke, written around 1685, illustrates the popular notion that with diligence and enterprise great wealth could be gained through cotton cultivation and processing.[21] This potential for profit attracted many farmers in the Kinai region to cotton cultivation. Once they were involved, the lure of further profits or the demands of fertilizer payments sustained their involvement.

The risks entailed in cotton farming were greatest for poor farmers on the lower economic levels of the agricultural population. Farmers with small holdings, those under five *tan*, had little margin for error and a series of bad crop years could be devastating. Those with larger landholdings had other sources of income and could offset the losses of one year with future earnings or returns from other crops and income from by-employment activities. Table 12, from Kowakae village in the Fuse region, is a nineteenth century illustration of the relation between landholding and rate of cotton

TABLE 12. Cotton cultivation in Kowakae village by land farmed, 1842 and 1866

1842			1866		
Land farmed *tan*	Households no. (%)	Percent of land in cotton	Land farmed *tan*	Households no. (%)	Percent of land in cotton
30–40	2 (2.6)	49.9			
20–30	3 (3.8)	47.1	20–30	4 (4.9)	24.1
10–20	17 (21.8)	57.2	10–20	4 (4.9)	37.2
5–10	12 (15.4)	62.0	5–10	10 (12.3)	55.0
3–5	8 (10.3)	75.9	3–5	9 (11.1)	57.8
Under 3	29 (37.2)	75.0	Under 3	33 (40.7)	87.3
0[a]	7 (9.0)	0	0[a]	21 (25.9)	0
Total	78 (100)	58.4		81 (100)	47.1

SOURCE: 1842 data from *Fuse shishi*, II, table 40, pp. 560–1; 1866 data from *Fuse shishi*, II, table 47, pp. 570–1.
[a] 0 indicates no land farmed in Kowakae village.

cultivation. As is evident in table 12, the rate of cotton cultivation varied inversely with the area of land farmed by the cultivators. Those farming less than five *tan* had the greatest dependence on cotton cultivation in both 1842 and 1866, and those farming less than three *tan* had by far the greatest dependence on cotton in 1866. The picture is similar if viewed from the perspective of land ownership, defined in table 13 in terms of productive capacity in rice (*kokudaka*). The relation between land owned and rate of cotton cultivation is not as clear in table 13 as is that between land farmed and cotton cultivation in table 12, but the general trend is the same. This is particularly true for those households owning less than ten *kokudaka* and for tenant farmers. In general, the smaller the scale of the cultivator, the greater the dependence on cotton cultivation. It is from data of this kind that the risks of cotton cultivation can be appreciated.

In 1842, harvested seed cotton in Kowakae village averaged 110 *kin* per *tan* and returned 220 *momme* silver per *tan* of cotton cultivation. Rice output in 1842 was two *koku* per *tan* and returned on the average 120

TABLE 13. Cotton cultivation in Kowakae village by land owned, 1842 and 1866

1842			1866		
Land owned in *kokudaka*	Households no. (%)	Percent of land in cotton	Land owned in *kokudaka*	Households no. (%)	Percent of land in cotton
300–400	1 (1.3)	42.4			
			200–300	1 (1.2)	19.3
100–150	1 (1.3)	44.4			
50–100	2 (2.6)	46.5	50–100	2 (2.5)	18.8
20–30	4 (5.1)	61.7	20–30	1 (1.2)	60.0
10–20	6 (7.7)	55.7	10–20	3 (3.7)	33.9
5–10	4 (5.1)	60.1	5–10	4 (4.9)	56.3
3–5	1 (1.3)	53.1	3–5	2 (2.5)	66.7
Under 3	3 (3.8)	57.9	Under 3	4 (4.9)	55.6
0 (tenants)	49 (62.6)	65.6	0 (tenants)	43 (53.1)	62.9
0[a]	7 (9.0)	0	0[a]	21 (25.9)	0
Total	78 (100)	58.4		81 (100)	47.1

SOURCE: 1842 data from *Fuse shishi*, II, table 41, pp. 560–1; 1866 data from *Fuse shishi*, II, table 46, pp. 570–1.
[a] 0 indicates no land farmed in Kowakae village.

momme silver per *tan* of land in rice cultivation. Of the value of agricultural products in Kowakae village 72 percent came from cotton and the profits from cotton cultivation far exceeded those for rice. No comparable data are available for 1866.[22] Although these output data appear to be impressive, output estimates for Settsu, Nishinari *gun* suggest that this harvest was less than average. In Nishinari *gun*, average cotton output was 180 *kin* per *tan* and in good years 245 to 272 *kin* of seed cotton per *tan* of cultivation was possible.[23]

Variations in cotton output per *tan* of cultivation in the Kinai region are evident in table 14. Using five-year averages, output varied from a high of 172 *kin* per *tan* between 1854 and 1863 to a low of ninety *kin* per *tan* between 1834 and 1838. Use of the five-year averages softens both the peaks and the troughs in this fluctuation. As can be seen in the output index for cotton in table 14, the harvest varied by plus or minus 31 percent from the index of 100 for the years 1769 to 1773. Five of the periods had an output of less than the 131 *kin* per *tan* average for the years between 1769 and 1773, and this figure was considerably less than the 180 *kin* per *tan* average for Nishinari *gun* noted above or the 200 *kin* per *tan* average estimated for Kawachi.[24]

TABLE 14. Fluctuations in cotton output and seed cotton and rice prices in Kinai (five-year averages).

Years	Average price per *koku* rice in *momme* silver	Rice price Index	Average price per *koku* cotton in *momme* silver	Cotton price index	Average output per *tan* cotton in *kin*	Output index
1764–68	64	98	112	138	–	–
1769–73	65	100	81	100	131	100
1774–79[a]	64	98	75	93	148	113
1780–84	79	122	93	114	128	98
1785–89	90	139	96	119	114	87
1797–1803[b]	68	105	78	96	140	107
1804–08	72	111	80	99	128	98
1809–13	60	92	78	96	116	89
1814–18	72	111	77	95	140	107
1819–23	73	112	82	101	144	110
1824–28	68	105	77	95	140	107
1829–33	76	117	81	100	148	113
1834–38	128	197	139	172	90	69
1839–43	77	118	103	127	152	116
1844–48	84	129	115	142	138	105
1849–53	96	148	139	172	132	101
1854–58	96	148	103	127	172	131
1859–63	148	228	171	211	140	107

SOURCE: Shimbō, 'Kinai mensaku ni okeru shōhin seisan,' table 12, p. 522.
[a] Six years.
[b] Seven years. Shimbō omits data for 1790–6.

Annual output per *tan* of land in cotton often varied dramatically, as is evident in table 15. These data for a single household show how output varied, even assuming that inputs were constant, and also show how larger households were able to vary the quantity of land used for cotton cultivation. The seventeen years covered in table 15 show cotton output varying from a high of 211 *kin* per *tan* in 1854 to a low of 54 *kin* per *tan* in 1866. The fluctuation in output was severe and some effort was made to adjust the area of land in cotton cultivation to conform with changing harvests of seed cotton.

Weather was one factor over which the cultivators had no control. Cotton was highly susceptible to damage from excessive or inadequate rainfall, strong winds, and other causes. Table 16 illustrates the frequency with which the elements played havoc with cotton cultivation throughout the Kinai region. It is apparent from the data in table 16 that bad weather was a regular cause of concern for cotton cultivators. Even an incomplete survey of the sort presented here gives ample evidence of the risks of cotton

TABLE 15. Cotton output per *tan* in Minami Kurasaku village – one household

Year	Area in *tan*	Yield per *tan* in *kin*	Year	Area in *tan*	Yield per *tan* in *kin*
1851	8.3	155	1861	11.0	195
1852	8·3	156	1862	11·5	162
1853	8.3	146	1863	15.0	146
1854	8.3	211	1864	10·5	157
1855	8.3	193	1865	9.5	179
Five-year average	8.3	172	Five-year average	11.5	168
1856	15.0	144	1866	8.0	54
1857	11.0	185	1867	9.0	143
1858	15.0	126			
1859	15.0	120			
1860	15·0	85			
Five-year average	14.2	132			

SOURCE: *Kami sonshi* [History of the village of Kami] (Ōsaka, 1957), pp. 155–6.

TABLE 16. Cotton crop damage in the Kinai region by year and location

Year	Location	Cause	Description
1623	Jingūji[a]		Bad crop, taxes waived
1707	Sayama[b]	Wind	50 *kin* of cotton per *tan*
1714	Shimo Kawarabayashi[c]		Bad harvest, relief rice sent
1725	Sayama[b]		25–40 *kin* in paddy, none in dry fields
1728	Sayama[b]	Wind	Crop damage
1740	Sayama[b]	Wind and rain	Crop damage
1741	Sayama[b]	Disease	Entire cotton crop lost
1755	12 villages near Kawarabayashi[c]		Dry-field harvest very bad, relief asked
1758	Hiraoka[d]	Wind and rain	Heavy damage to cotton
1770	Shimokosaka[e]	Drought	Bad water in 75 villages
1778	Kishidadō[f]		Bad harvest
1781	Amagasaki[g]	Wind and rain	Entire crop lost
1782	Amagasaki[g]	Wind and rain	Entire crop lost
1782	Sayama[b]	Weather	Entire crop lost
1782	Tsukado[c]	Weather	All cotton lost, riots, relief asked
1783	Kishidadō[f]		Bad harvest
1786	Sayama[b]	Insects	50% of cotton lost
1787	Shimokosaka, Hishiya Nakashinden[e]	Drought	Damage to fields

Year	Location	Cause	Description
1807	Kurasaku Shinke[h]		56 *kin* of cotton per *tan*
1820	Shimokosaka[e]	Flooding	Water damage, taxes lowered
1821	Nishi Hashinami[i]	Wind	Severe crop damage
1821	Shimokosaka[e]	Drought	Bad harvest, taxes lowered
1829	Sayama[b]		Bad harvest
1831	Shinke[e]	Drought	Bad water in wells as well
1831	Sayama[b]		Bad harvest
1832	Sayama[b]		Very bad harvest, low yield
1833	Sayama[b]	Rain	Very bad harvest
1836	Sayama[b]	Heavy rains	10–40 *kin* of cotton per *tan*
1837	Naruo, Imatsu[c]		20–60 *kin* of cotton per *tan*
1853	Hirano-gō[j]		Bad harvest, tax remission
1858	Yao[a]		Very bad harvest, 0–1 *kin* per *tan*
1866	Minami Kurasaku[h]		54 *kin* of cotton per *tan*

SOURCES: [a] *Yao shishi*, I, pp. 276, 279.
  [b] 'Nakabayashi-ke ruidai nikki' [Nakabayashi house diary from successive generations] in *Sayama chōshi*, II, pp. 20–8.
  [c] *Nishinomiya shishi*, IV, pp. 819, 822, 824; II, p. 230.
  [d] *Hiraoka shishi*, I, p. 424.
  [e] Furushima Toshio and Nagahara Keiji, *Shōhin seisan to kisei jinushisei – Kinsei Kinai nōgyō ni okeru* [Commodity production and the parasitic landlord system – Concerning Kinai agriculture in early modern times] (Tōkyō, 1954), pp. 37–8, 106.
  [f] *Fuse chōshi*, p. 282.
  [g] *Amagasaki shishi* [History of the city of Amagasaki], II (Amagasaki, 1968), p. 630.
  [h] *Kami sonshi*, pp. 154, 156.
  [i] *Moriguchi shishi* [History of the city of Moriguchi], V (Moriguchi, 1966), p. 233.
  [j] *Hirano-gō chōshi* [History of the town of Hirano-gō] (Ōsaka-fu Sumiyoshi-gun Hirano-gō, 1931), p. 143.

farming. When small cultivators concentrated on cotton cultivation, they risked a total loss of their investment in seeds, fertilizer, and labor if the weather was unfavorable. Yet despite this risk, cotton cultivation flourished in the Kinai region during the Tokugawa period, because of high output and high profit ratio in good harvest years.

For a sense of the geographical distribution of crop damage see map 3, which shows cities, towns, and villages in the Kinai region.

COTTON CULTIVATION: FERTILIZER INPUTS

Cotton cultivation required large inputs of fertilizers, and neither the quantity nor the quality of the dried grasses, ashes, or human excrement available in the Kinai area villages was adequate for good cotton farming.

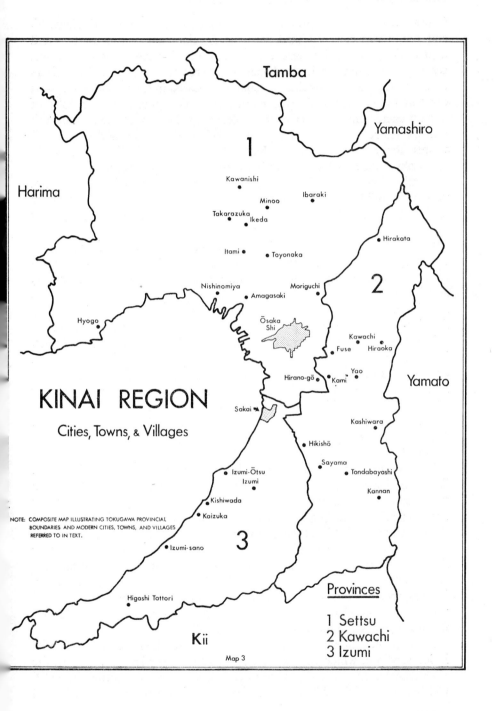

Map 3

Consequently, the rapid diffusion of cotton cultivation in Settsu, Kawachi, and Izumi was closely linked with the development of a marketing and distribution system for commercial fertilizers. By the early seventeenth century cotton farmers in the Kinai area were using commercial fertilizers on their crops. Dried sardine merchants appeared in Ōsaka and Amagasaki early in the century and by mid-century dealers specializing in sales of human excrement were active in Ōsaka.[25] By the end of the seventeenth century instructions on the application of dried sardines and pressed oil wastes for cotton cultivation had received national dissemination in Miyazaki Antei's *Nōgyō zensho* [Complete treatise on agriculture].[26]

Fertilization costs varied significantly over the course of the Tokugawa period. Individual farmers varied the quantity and types of fertilizers applied to their cotton crops, with the wealthier cultivators often investing far more in fertilizers than their poorer neighbors and getting greater output as a result. Fertilizer costs also rose during the Tokugawa period, reflecting the increased demand for commercial fertilizers and the relatively inelastic supply of dried sardines, pressed oil wastes, *sake* wastes, and human excrement. With the diffusion of cotton cultivation in the Kinai region, the cultivators became increasingly dependent on commercial fertilizers to ensure that their efforts would result in profitable harvests.

Fertilizer costs varied significantly within the Kinai region. For example, in the Amagasaki area, farmers in Mantaraji village in 1701 used dried sardines costing 35 to 40 *momme* per *tan* of cotton cultivation. By 1749, fertilizer costs in nearby Shimosakae were 40 to 50 *momme* per *tan*, and by 1782 farmers in Ushioe complained that sardine prices had increased to the extent that whole villages were impoverished by fertilization expenses. By the period 1801 to 1803, costs in Namazu were 75 *momme* per *tan* of cotton.[27]

In other areas, use of different kinds of fertilizer varied cultivation costs. In Nishi village, pressed oil wastes, cotton seed wastes, and dried sardines were used for fertilizer and in 1746 costs were 50 to 90 *momme* per *tan*.[28] Farmers in the Moriguchi area used human excrement, oil wastes, and dried sardines to fertilize their cotton in 1768. Wealthy farmers used human excrement and one *koku* of dried sardines per *tan* of cotton, while poorer farmers used seven or eight *to* of oil wastes and human excrement for each *tan* of cotton farmed.[29] In Shimokosaka village near Fuse, dried sardines, herring roe, herring, pressed oil wastes, and human excrement were all used as fertilizer. One *tan* of cotton cost 70 to 90 *momme* while rice fertilizers cost 50 to 60 *momme* per *tan* in 1787.[30]

By 1746, fertilizer prices in the Yao region had increased dramatically. Dried sardines, which had cost 20 to 25 *momme* per *tan* of cotton in the seventeenth century, now cost 90 to 120 *momme* per *tan* of cotton farmed.[31] Cultivators from Shinke village near Fuse in 1832 used dried sardines and pressed oil wastes at a cost of 30 to 50 *momme* per *tan* for rice and 50 to 90 *momme* per *tan* of cotton farmed. By 1843, farmers in Arakawa village in the same area were spending 120 to 180 *momme* per *tan* for dry-field cotton fertilization, indicating a significant increase in fertilizer costs.[32]

Fertilizer costs were the largest single input for cotton cultivation and fluctuations in fertilizer prices had a great impact on the economics of cotton farming. The price of seed cotton was relatively stable until the late Tokugawa period, as is evident in table 14, so the rise in dried sardine and other fertilizer prices after the mid-eighteenth century put particular pressure on cotton cultivators.[33] Dried sardine prices rose after the 1730s and continued to rise until the late Tokugawa period. In 1740, the *bakufu* attempted to stop fertilizer costs from rising by forbidding monopoly buying of dried sardines and pressed oil wastes. Yet in 1743 eighty-four villages from Shimakami and Shimashimo *gun* of Settsu complained that increased fertilizer costs were driving them out of farming and asked for further government intervention. Efforts to control fertilizer prices continued and edicts against monopoly buying were issued in 1786, 1788, 1835, 1837, and 1849, but despite efforts to the contrary, prices continued to rise as demand increased and supplies failed to keep up with increased demands.[34]

The impact of fertilizer price increases can be seen in the number of disputes between farmers and fertilizer dealers and the repeated requests from cultivators to the government for fertilizer price reductions. For analysis, disputes involving villages incorporated into the modern cities of Amagasaki and Nishinomiya have been divided into four periods.[35] Disputes in the first of these periods, beginning in the 1730s, resulted from a decrease in shipments of dried sardines to Ōsaka. Sardine catches declined, dried sardine dealers competed for the reduced supply, and this drove up the price which they charged to the cultivators. After 1740, Settsu villagers asked for *bakufu* price controls and regulation of the Ōsaka dried sardine merchants. The villagers complained that even with good harvests their incomes were inadequate to support both fertilizer costs and other necessities for their survival. Many complained of defaulted fertilizer payments and associated difficulties in obtaining fertilizers the following year. To ease the burden of fertilizer cost increases, the farmers asked for a government reform of fertilizer distribution and for price reductions.[36]

Village complaints against increasing fertilizer prices continued sporadically until 1763. As dried sardine prices increased, so did the costs of various substitutes such as pressed oil wastes, *sake* wastes, and human excrement. This led to further discontent among the farmers and objections, such as the one of 1743, to the high cost of pressed oil and soy wastes in Ikeda, Itami, Amagasaki, and Nishinomiya. The villagers argued that fertilizer merchants bought up all available fertilizers and then forced up prices to the cultivators. This suit was followed in 1753 by a similar complaint, but neither resulted in relief for the villagers involved.[37]

A second period of agitation over rising fertilizer prices began in the late eighteenth century. Dried sardine prices rose in the 1780s when deliveries to the Kinai region declined and this, combined with government restrictions on *sake* brewing from 1785 to 1795 which reduced the quantity of *sake* wastes available as a substitute, increased complaints from the cultivators.[38] The reduction in supplies of dried sardines and *sake* wastes increased competition for pressed oil wastes and other fertilizers and drove up their prices, leading to a series of complaints between 1788 and 1790. In one complaint of 1788, 836 villages in Settsu and Kawachi united to press home their anger over increased fertilizer costs. Other suits asked for action against speculators and dealers who doubled and tripled their commissions on fertilizer sales. Hoarding and sales to villages in other provinces were pointed to as causes of price increases. A 1790 complaint from fifty-eight villages in Settsu charged that a 40-*kan* horseload of dried sardines had cost 20 to 25 *momme* in the late seventeenth century, had increased to around 70 *momme* in the 1750s, and had risen from 100 to 150 *momme* in 1790. Agricultural commodity prices were not keeping up with fertilizer costs and the strain on the farmers was severe. While fertilizer costs eased later in 1790, the impact of the suits is impossible to measure and other factors may have been more important in the reduction in price levels.[39]

A third period of opposition to increased fertilizer prices began in 1794, when 650 villages from twenty *gun* of Settsu and Kawachi asked for *bakufu* intervention to lower fertilizer prices. The government, aware of declines in dried sardine production, asked for information on hoarding and initiated severe penalties to be levied against dealers who interfered with the distribution of available fertilizer supplies. To implement the new policy, government representatives met with officials of the fertilizer dealers' *nakama* and encouraged them to lower prices and speed up deliveries. Anxious to develop their own system of fertilizer distribution, the 650 villages asked for government intervention against high prices and dishonest marketing practices in the fertilizer trade. This led to the organization of a new distribution system for fertilizer by leaders from the complaining villages.[40]

The fourth period of agitation against fertilizer costs began in 1835 with the largest dispute over fertilizer prices in the Ōsaka area. This dispute included 952 villages from Settsu and Kawachi, among them many villages from around modern Amagasaki. This, like earlier complaints, was directed against high fertilizer prices and trade restrictions and reflected the growing opposition by farmers to monopoly controls on marketing in the Kinai region.[41]

Herring wastes from the island of Hokkaidō replaced dried sardines as the primary fertilizer used in cotton cultivation in the late Tokugawa period. Yet despite this shift fertilizer prices continued to rise and the price of cotton tended to lag behind. With fertilizer purchases normally made in the third, fourth, and fifth months of the lunar year and the cotton crop sold in the ninth, tenth, and eleventh months, the prices of fertilizer and cotton were independent of each other and there was no necessary correlation between their price fluctuations. Table 17 shows these price fluctuations during the late Tokugawa period. As is clear from this table, the costs of cotton cultivation varied considerably in the late Tokugawa period and were often inconsistent with the profits received. Fertilizer costs increased irrespective of the value of ginned cotton per *tan* of cultivation.[42] Per *tan* profits to the cultivators also fluctuated significantly. Table 17 shows that profits declined after 1832, and it was only in the last years of the Tokugawa period, from 1863 to 1867, that inflation pushed profit rates back to their 1830 levels.

TABLE 17. Late Tokugawa income and expenditures for cotton cultivation, in *momme* silver

Period	Average ginned cotton price[a]	Average herring waste price[b]	Ginned cotton value per *tan* (1)[c]	Fertilizer costs per *tan* (2)[d]	Taxes per *tan* (3)[e]	Net profit to cultivator per *tan* (1) less (2)	(1) less (2) and (3)
1756	18.5	–	217.0	52.5	53.7	164.5	110.8
1830–2	25.1	20.4	294.5	54.7	62.3	239.8[f]	177.5[f]
1832–5	24.7	28.3	290.0	72.9	75.1	217.1	142.0
1841–5	20.8	31.9	284.0	85.5	62.7	198.5[f]	135.8[f]
1854–8	25.0	39.8	293.0	107.0	75.1	186.0	110.9
1863–7	101.0	167.7	1158.0	449.0	504.0	709.0	205.0

SOURCE: Furushima and Nagahara, table 51, p. 206.
[a] Average price in Ōsaka for the ninth, tenth and eleventh lunar months.
[b] Average for third, fourth, and fifth months.
[c] Assumes a seed cotton output of 30 *kan* per *tan* and a conversion to ginned cotton at 1 *kan* seed cotton to 390 *momme* ginned cotton, giving a per *tan* output of 11.71 *kan* of ginned cotton.
[d] Based on cost of 26 *kan* 800 *momme* herring wastes.
[e] Computed from 50% of rice productivity estimate and Chikuzen rice price for the period.
[f] Corrected.

A second example of the relation between income and expenditures for cotton cultivation can be seen in table 18, which gives 1842 data for the Kinoshita house of Yaoki village. The major expenditure by the Kinoshita house for cotton cultivation was fertilizer, which exceeded in cost land

TABLE 18. Yaoki village Kinoshita house income and expenditures, in *momme* silver, 1842

	Cotton	Rice	Tenant land
Area	1.15 *chō*	1.23 *chō*	1.33 *chō*
Income	5400.00	2212.00	1834.00
Expenditures:			
taxes, fees	953.53	690.83	934.00
wages	275.00	135.00	–
fertilizer	1719.32	281.92	–
Total	2947.85	1107.75	934.00
Net income	2452.15	1104.25	900·00
Profit per *tan*	213.23	89.77	67.67

SOURCE: Oka Mitsuo, *Kinsei nōgyō keiei no tenkai – Jisaku keiei no shokeitai* [The evolution of agricultural management in early modern times – various forms of self-cultivating management] (Kyōto, 1966), p. 22. *Hiraoka shishi*, I, p. 426.

taxes and wages combined. Fertilizer inputs were 149.5 *momme* per *tan* of cotton cultivation. When the data for profit per *tan* are examined, it is obvious why this kind of expenditure was justified. Profits for cotton were more than twice those for rice and three times those for tenant land in 1842. It was this kind of profit potential which encouraged farmers to make the investments necessary for cotton cultivation. Despite the risks entailed, the income potential was sufficient to justify the gamble, and for this reason cotton cultivation flourished in the Kinai region.[43]

COTTON CULTIVATION RATES

The importance of cotton cultivation to farmers in the Kinai region during the Tokugawa period varied by location. Areas where the soil was sandy had high rates of cotton growing, as did villages where land reclamation had been extensive and water resources were inadequate for rice farming. For example, in the Amagasaki region cotton cultivation was extensive in the northern portion of west Settsu and in villages with reclaimed fields along the coast of Ōsaka Bay. In the southern portions of modern Amagasaki city, rapeseed and rice were the dominant crops.[44]

Seventeenth century data are limited, but Kami Kawarabayashi village, now in the city of Nishinomiya, had 21.3 percent of its wet fields and 55.6 percent of its dry fields in cotton cultivation in 1686.[45] Cotton cultivation rates for villages in Kawabe and Muko *gun* near modern Amagasaki can be seen in table 19. The data are inconsistent, as some are based on land area and some on productive capacity, but it is apparent that cotton was a major crop in this part of Settsu. Cultivation rates varied from a low of under 3 percent in Higashi Ōshima to a high of 70 percent in Imakita,

TABLE 19. Cotton cultivation rates in Kawabe and Muko *gun* villages

Year	Village	Percentage of cotton cultivation
	Kawabe *gun*	
1707	Mantaraji	29 in paddy, 25.5 in dry fields
1757	Tōda	10.3 of *kokudaka*
1779	Shidō	11.3 in paddy, 65.2 in dry fields
1783	Shidō	12 in paddy, 31.8 in dry fields
1786	Kami Kema	73.7 in dry fields
1791	Ushioe	3 in paddy
1825[a]	Noma	32.8 in paddy, no data for dry fields
1827[a]	Shinden Nakanō	18.8 in paddy, no data for dry fields
1864[a]	Nanatsumatsu	12.9
1866[a]	Shinden Nakanō	15.0 in paddy, no data for dry fields
	Muko *gun*	
1734	Nishikoya	42.4 of land
1734	Tsunematsu	22.3 of land
1734	Tsuneyoshi	30.5 of land
1734	Higashi Muko	13.1 of land
1734	Imakita	43.2 of *kokudaka*
1734	Hamada	9.6 of *kokudaka*
1734	Higashi Ōshima	2.4 of *kokudaka*
1734	Higashi Shinden	27.5 of *kokudaka*
1734	Dōi Shinden	37.2 of *kokudaka*
1734	Matabei Shinden	48.9 of *kokudaka*
1777	Tokitomo	28.8 of land
1786	Imakita	56.3 of *kokudaka* in Nagabei and Yasutao Shinden
1788	Imakita	70 of *kokudaka* in Nagabei Shinden
1811	Tomoyuki	27 of *kokudaka*
1815	Tsunematsu	around 40 of land
1819	Nishikoya	42.8 of land (44[b])
1820	Tomoyuki	38 of *kokudaka*
1828	Tomoyuki	21.7 of *kokudaka*
1836	Namazu	29.7 of land
1836[a]	Naka	38.5
1870[a]	Mukonoshō	13 in paddy only, no data for dry fields

SOURCES: [a] *Amagasaki shishi*, II, table 134, p. 629.
[b] Yamazaki Ryūzō, 'Kinsei kōki Settsu nōson ni okeru shōhin ryūtsū' [Commodity marketing in Settsu agricultural villages in the late Tokugawa period], (Ōsaka Shiritsu Daigaku) Keizaigaku Nenpō, no. 8 (1956), p. 61.

with half the villages having 20 to 50 percent of their fields, wet or dry, in cotton.

In the Fuse area, cotton cultivation was particularly extensive in fields reclaimed from the Yamato river after 1704. As the result of a project to reroute the river the productive capacity of this area increased by around 9 percent.[46] Flooding had been a major problem along the Yamato river and its tributaries in the seventeenth century and, after numerous unsuccessful attempts to improve diking systems and deepen the channel to prevent silting, the *bakufu* finally organized a major project to rechannel the river. Sixty years of agitation by villages affected by the flooding resulted in extensive corrective actions by the government.[47]

The new river bed was nine miles long and 600 feet wide, required eight months of labor, and created 788 *chō*, 8 *tan*, 9 *se*, 5 *bu* of new agricultural land in Kawachi. The final reclamation process was completed by Ōsaka merchants, wealthy farmers, and religious institutions under *bakufu* license. Local cultivators were used as the labor force and tax exemptions were granted to encourage the rapid completion of the project.[48]

The reclaimed land was of a sandy consistency and ideal for cotton cultivation. All the reclaimed fields were used as dry fields and used exclusively for cotton farming during the summer season.[49] In addition, many of the villages in the area also utilized paddy fields for cotton cultivation. For example, in Kowakae village, although over 50 percent of arable land was paddy, 62.5 percent of farmland was in cotton and only 37.5 percent in rice in 1739. Nearby Arakawa had 43 percent of its paddy and 94 percent of its dry fields in cotton in 1743, while Aramoto had 64 percent of its paddy and 96 percent of its dry fields in cotton in 1750. Utilization of paddy for cotton cultivation declined after it was forbidden in 1744, but in the Fuse region the practice was extremely widespread.[50]

This area has a very high rate of cotton cultivation, with most villages having 90 to 100 percent of dry fields in cotton during the summer season. In Shimokosaka village, between 1791 and 1809, cotton was cultivated on 55.6 percent and rice on 44.4 percent of village fields, conforming to the approximate distribution of dry and paddy fields.[51] In the nineteenth century cotton cultivation was extensive in Shimokosaka and Kowakae, and continued in a relatively stable manner until the end of the Tokugawa period.[52] In the Fuse area, the role of cotton was relatively constant from the early eighteenth century until 1868 and the area was clearly part of the cotton belt which surrounded the city of Ōsaka.

Around the city of Sakai further south, cotton was also a major crop. Nagasone had around 50 percent of its cultivated land in cotton in 1695 and Ōtori village had a similar percentage in 1694.[53] Cotton was one of the staple crops in Ōtori *gun*: Wada village had 37.8 percent of its land in cotton in the 1740s and Akahata village had around 60 percent of its land in cotton at this time.[54]

In the Sayama area, Handa village had 39.3 percent of its *kokudaka* in cotton in 1765, 43.8 percent in 1817, and 26.3 percent in 1846. Nearby Higashino village had around 40 percent and Shumiki village 54 percent of its *kokudaka* in cotton in 1772.[55] Near Yao, Kamei village had around 30 percent of its farmland in cotton in 1819, while Ōtake village had 34 percent in 1801 and 52 percent in 1815.[56] Around the modern city of

Izumi, cotton cultivation rates varied from 43 percent in Sakamoto Shinden in 1753 to 57 percent in the same village in 1784. Terata village had 46 percent of its land in cotton in 1790. As a whole, villages in the Izumi area averaged around 50 percent of their cultivated land in cotton in the mid and late eighteenth century.[57] Near Kashihara, around half of paddy and all dry fields were in cotton by the 1760s.[58] Here and in the Kami area, cotton was cultivated on both wet and dry fields, despite regulations against cotton cultivation in paddy. For example, Kurasaku village had 32 percent of paddy and 54 percent of dry fields in cotton in 1715 and had increased this to 40 percent of paddy and 60 percent of dry fields by 1736. Minami Kurasaku had 68 percent of paddy and 98 percent of dry fields in cotton in 1743.[59]

Cotton cultivation also flourished in villages east of Ōsaka around modern Itami. This was also true around modern Takarazuka, where cultivation rates varied from 32 to 52 percent between 1736 and 1741.[60]

In 1877, a Meiji government survey of agricultural production showed that the Kinai region was still a major producer of cotton. The five Kinai provinces of Settsu, Kawachi, Izumi, Yamato, and Yamashiro together accounted for 30 percent of total national cotton output. Settsu and Kawachi produced over half the cotton cultivated in the Kinai region, with Wakae, Shibukawa, Nishinari, Sumiyoshi, and Higashinari *gun* accounting for much of this production. Table 20 shows the 1877 rates of cotton cultivation in these districts and also the value of cotton output relative to

TABLE 20. Cotton cultivation in Settsu and Kawachi, 1877

Gun	Percent of farm land	Percent of dry fields	Value of cotton as percent of total agricultural output
Wakae[a]	28.0	58.8	48.2
Shibukawa[a]	26.9	60.0	43.3
Nishinari	18.2	41.3	37.2
Sumiyoshi	21.8	44.3	44.8
Higashinari	12.1	46.4	27.1

SOURCE: Furushima and Nagahara, pp. 161–2.
[a] *Gun* in Kawachi. The other three were in Settsu.

total agricultural output for each of the *gun* included. In each of these districts, it can be assumed that Tokugawa period cotton cultivation was at least as extensive as the figures in table 20, and it is very likely that it was considerably more extensive prior to the opening of Japan to foreign trade and the associated competition with machine produced cotton textiles.

It is obvious from the discussion above that farmers in Settsu, Kawachi, and Izumi had a major involvement in cotton cultivation. In many villages it was the primary cash crop and its success or failure had a tremendous impact on the village economy. In response to rising fertilizer costs many farmers tried to increase the returns on their harvested cotton. Two approaches were available. They could further process the cotton and add the income from processing activities or they could try to raise the price of seed cotton by taking a more active role in marketing their crops. Many cotton farmers used both means to improve their economic position. Either one brought them into conflict with the Ōsaka-centered marketing and processing monopolies. But prior to examining the nature of this conflict, let us first look at the development of cotton related by-employment in Kinai villages in the eighteenth and nineteenth centuries.

COTTON-RELATED BY-EMPLOYMENT

Complementing the diffusion of cotton cultivation in the Kinai region was the gradual development of cotton processing at the village level. In the seventeenth and early eighteenth centuries, most of the cotton sold in Kinai was in its harvested seed cotton form. The limited processing of cotton in the villages was for household consumption and the scale of processing activity was quite small.[61] As a consequence, towns such as Hirano-*gō* specialized in cotton ginning and merchants from the town bought up seed cotton, ginned it in Hirano-*gō*, and then sold it to spinners, weavers, and the Ōsaka ginned cotton merchants.[62]

In the early and mid-eighteenth century many of the cotton cultivating villages began to process a portion of their cotton crop. Cotton ginning became a common form of village by-employment and in some areas carding, spinning, and weaving were extensive. [63] The gradual spread of village level processing can in part be attributed to new technology, as new tools for cotton ginning increased productivity and new looms increased the cloth output of rural weavers.[64] Some of the increase in village processing can be attributed to the putting-out activities of rural merchants who, realizing the profits which could be earned from finished goods, loaned tools and capital to villagers so they would be able to devote their free time from farming to cotton processing.[65] The degree of involvement in cotton processing was by no means constant in the Kinai region. In some areas, much of the cotton crop was processed into cotton yarn or cloth prior to sale by the cultivators. In others, not even cotton ginning, the first step in cotton processing, developed to any significant degree. The diffusion of technology was uneven and patterns of regional specialization led villagers in some areas to devote themselves to other forms of by-employment.[66]

In some villages one step in the production of cotton cloth was completed and the goods sold to farmers from other villages for further processing. This was true for villages which specialized in cotton ginning or yarn spinning. Patterns of regional specialization developed with villages focusing their by-employment activities on one kind of product or specific kinds of cotton cloth. Despite the uneven diffusion of processing technology and the patterns of differential development, it is apparent that during the eighteenth century the dominant position of Ōsaka and Kinai rural towns as processing centers was replaced by village level processing of much of the Kinai cotton crop.[67] In the following pages, we will examine specific examples of cotton processing as village by-employment in order to develop a more complete picture of the changes which were occurring in the cultivating and processing of cotton in the Kinai region.

To begin with, table 21 illustrates the kinds of by-employment found

TABLE 21. Amagasaki area cotton-related agricultural by-employment

Village	Year	Description
Ushioe[a]	1677	Women weave cotton cloth
Mantaraji	1701	Men weave rope and matting, women spin cotton yarn in off-season
Shimosakabe	1749	Women weave cotton cloth in off-season
Ushioe[b]	1782	Men weave rope and matting, women spin cotton yarn
Nishikoya	1803	Women spin and sell yarn
Ushioe	1838	In off-season, men weave rope and matting, women weave cotton cloth for clothing
Tokitomo	1844	Women weave cotton cloth
Ushioe[a]	1867	Men weave rope and matting, women spin cotton yarn
Shidō	1868	Men weave ropes, women weave cotton cloth in off-season
Hōkaiji	1869	Men weave rope and matting, women weave cotton cloth

SOURCES: *Amagasaki shishi*, II, table 143, p. 655.
[a] *Amagasaki shishi*, II, foldout facing p. 664.
[b] *Amagasaki shishi*, II, p. 658.

in the Amagasaki area west of Ōsaka. It should be noted that in the late eighteenth and early nineteenth century, the role of cloth weaving increased in villages from this area.

Further west around Nishinomiya, cotton processing was also a major form of village by-employment. In table 22, it should be noted that in Higuchi Shinden, while no cotton was cultivated, weaving was the major form of female by-employment. Yarn spinning and cloth weaving were both major sources of supplementary income in this area. Closer to Ōsaka in Nishinari *gun*, cotton weaving and spinning were often found as forms of female by-employment.[68]

To the southeast of Ōsaka near modern Fuse, in villages in both Wakae and Shibukawa *gun* the most common types of by-employment were the

TABLE 22. Nishinomiya area cotton-related agricultural by-employment

Village	Year	Description
Namase	1730	Women weave a little cotton cloth
Koshiki Iwashinden	1769	Women are busy spinning and weaving for wages
Komatsu	1790	Shigemon is a cotton cloth merchant
Danjo	1803	Women spin cotton yarn
Kami Ōichi	1803	Men weave straw and women spin yarn and weave cotton cloth
Shimo Ōichi	1803	Men weave straw, women weave cotton cloth from yarn
Shimo Ōichi	1843	Women are employed as cotton weavers
Toiguchi Shinden	1843	Women are employed as cotton weavers
Danjo	1850	Wage labor as cotton carders in nearby villages
Higuchi Shinden	1867	Men weave straw, women weave cotton as by-employment, no cotton grown in village

SOURCE: *Nishinomiya shishi*, II, table 45, p. 241; V, pp. 54, 56, 61.

weaving of sedge hats and cotton cloth. In most villages, part of the cotton crop was sold in seed cotton form, but further processing was common in many households. Both men and women participated in cotton processing in the Fuse area.[69] Table 23 shows the widespread involvement in cotton processing as by-employment in the Fuse region of both men and women. It was not universal, however, as sedge hat weaving was also important and trade played a small role.

Further south around Sakai, cotton processing was a major form of rural by-employment. Carding, yarn spinning, and weaving were found in many villages in this area. In Akahata village in 1843, among forty-three households of non-farmers there were one cotton carder and twenty-two yarn reelers. Ōtori village had one dyer, one carder, six engaged in cloth work, and twenty-six in yarn work in 1854. Most of the non-farming population was engaged in full-time cotton processing.[70]

Both men and women in this area wove from seven to eleven in the evening. Women could weave up to one and one-half *tan* of cloth per day and in one evening one person could spin yarn weighing thirty to fifty *momme*. In Hata village average household cloth production was ten *tan* per year and one house produced thirty *tan*. In 1875, total Hata village cloth output was 231 *tan* of white cloth and 199 *tan* of striped cloth.[71]

In the Sayama area most cotton was sold as harvested until the early eighteenth century, although there was some ginning and weaving. By the nineteenth century production of cotton yarn and cotton cloth was a common form of village by-employment.[72] Similarly, around Yao many cultivators worked in the off-season as cotton ginners and weavers, either for themselves or as wage laborers for local entrepreneurs. Women were

TABLE 23. Fuse area cotton-related agricultural by-employment

Village	Year	Description
Wakae *gun*		
Hishiya Nishi Shinden[a]	1719	Most cotton sold as seed cotton, little weaving
Kowakae	1745	Outside of farming, men and women process cloth
Hishiya Nishi Shinden	1760	In off-season, men and women process cotton cloth
Hishiya Higashi Shinden	1760	In off-season, men and women process cotton cloth
Shimokosaka	1770	In off-season, men and women process cotton cloth
Nagata	1787	Outside of farming, men and women weave cotton cloth
Hishiya Naka Shinden[b]	1787	Men and women weave cloth and sell it
Omido	1788	Outside of farming, men and women process cloth
Tamai Minami Shinden[b]	1791	Men and women weave cotton cloth
Tamai Kita Shinden[b]	1791	Men and women weave cotton cloth
Shinke	1832	Men and women do cloth work as by-employment
Takaita	1861	By-employment is work with white cotton cloth
Tomoi	1869	In free time, men and women weave cotton cloth
Shibukawa *gun*		
Arakawa	1744	In off-seaon, men and women weave cotton cloth and sedge hats
Minose	1754	Men and women weave cotton cloth and sedge hats
Taiheiji	1754	Men and women weave cotton cloth and sedge hats
Arakawa[a]	1758	Men and women weave cotton cloth as by-employment
Ōhasu	1759	In off-season, men and women process cotton cloth
Higashi Ajiro	1767	In off-season men and women weave cloth and sedge hats
Minose[a]	1843	Women spin yarn and weave white cotton cloth
Higashi Ajiro[a]	1845	Three men in seed cotton trade, no cotton weaving in cotton growing season
Nagado	1861	Men and women weave sedge hats in winter and spring

SOURCES: *Fuse shishi*, II, table 10, p. 72.
[a] *Fuse chōshi*, pp. 18–20.
[b] Furushima and Nagahara, p. 74.

particularly active as weavers and weaving skills became a prerequisite for marriage, with brides expected prior to marriage to weave their own clothing and bedding from yarns they had dyed themselves.[73] In many villages near Yao, men and women worked in their free time from farming at cotton-related processing activities and cotton processing was a major form of village by-employment.[74]

Throughout the Kinai region village registers list cotton processing as one form of by-employment. This was true in Higashi Tottori, around the towns of Kashihara, Hiraoka, Izumi, and Izumi-sano and in the Moriguchi area as well.[75] Production of ginned cotton, cotton yarn, and cotton cloth became a regular part of village life and a source of extra income to many village households. The spread of this kind of by-employment activity linked Kinai villages to broadly based marketing networks and was a characteristic feature of rural life in the eighteenth and nineteenth centuries. It reflected many of the dramatic changes which had occurred in the villages and which blurred the distinctions between occupational classes. From map 3 (p. 127) it is possible to see how both cotton cultivation and cotton processing activity were distributed in Settsu, Kawachi, and Izumi. Other areas were also involved, but those shown have preserved documents which have been used in the current study of the Kinai cotton trade. Before going on to a discussion of the growth of rural trade, let us first illustrate the income potential of cotton cultivation in the Kinai region.

INCOME FROM COTTON CULTIVATION

Income from cotton cultivation and cotton processing was a major component of cash income for many Kinai area village households. A good example is that of the Ujita house of Nishikoya village in Muko *gun*, Settsu. The Ujita house was quite wealthy and had rather large landholdings within the village. As can be seen from table 24, it received cash income from various crops other than cotton, it should be noted, however, that income from rice and cotton was by far the largest source of cash and that these crops together provided over 60 percent of total household income from agricultural commodity sales. In table 24, the rather low value of cotton cloth sales relative to cotton sales indicates that the Ujita house sold most of its cotton crop in unprocessed form. Some cotton cloth was produced by the Ujita house, showing at least a partial involvement in cotton processing, but income from this source was limited and only once exceeded 6 percent of total income from agricultural commodity sales. The discontinuous nature of the data makes generalization difficult, but cotton processing does not appear to have been a major by-employment activity of the Ujita house.

During the Tokugawa period rice, cotton, rapeseed, and cotton cloth

TABLE 24. Nishikoya village Ujita house agricultural commodity sales, in *momme* silver

Commodity	1792	1817	1837	1860	1873[a]
Rice	1671.5	2191.8	3795.4	2823.6	64.5%
	(33.3%)	(39.8%)	(33.6%)	(34.7%)	
Wheat	259.1	128.4	499.8	0	0
	(5.2%)	(2.3%)	(4.4%)		
Cotton	1365.6	1893.2	3929.5	3234.8	21.7%
	(27.2%)	(34.4%)	(34.7%)	(39.7%)	
Rapeseed	1081.8	551.3	1952.0	1170.0	8.0%
	(21.6%)	(10.0%)	(17.3%)	(14.4%)	
Beans	106.4	87.9	240.8	563.3	4.3%
	(2.2%)	(1.6%)	(2.1%)	(6.9%)	
Potatoes	233.0	—	299.5	149.2	1.5%
	(4.6%)		(2.7%)	(1.8%)	
Cotton cloth	295.5	657.8	592.0	203.7	0
	(5.9%)	(11.9%)	(5.2%)	(2.5%)	
Total	5012.9[b]	5510.4	11 309.0	8144.6	(100%)
	(100%)	(100%)	(100%)	(100%)	

SOURCE: Yamazaki, 'Kinsei kōki Settsu nōson ni okeru shōhin ryūtsū, table 1, p. 63.
[a] Data are in *yen*, so only the percentage is given.
[b] Corrected.

sales accounted for over 90 percent of the Ujita house income from agricultural commodity sales, while in the Meiji period cotton cloth sales ceased and 95 percent of agricultural income came from rice, cotton, and rapeseed.[76] The data for the Ujita house are consistent with those for the Furubayashi house of Noma village. Here as well, as is evident in table 25, cotton sales were a major source of agricultural income. Cotton and rice

TABLE 25. Noma village Furubayashi house agricultural commodity sales, in *momme* silver

Commodity	1842	1859	1877[a]
Rice	1409.5 (27.2%)	3351.6 (44.9%)	68.0%
Wheat	143.7 (2.7%)	56.8 (0.8%)	1.8%
Cotton	2818.8 (54.4%)	2518.5 (33.8%)	20.3%
Rapeseed	494.2 (9.6%)	1284.8 (17.2%)	7.7%
Beans	319.3 (6.1%)	247.9 (3.3%)	2.2%
Total	5185.5 (100%)	7459.6 (100%)	100%

SOURCE: Yamazaki, 'Kinsei kōki Settsu nōson ni okeru shōhin ryūtsū,' table 2, p. 63.
[a] Data are in *yen*, so only the percentage is given.

sales together accounted for over 75 percent of the income from agricultural commodity sales and were the major revenue sources for the Furubayashi house. In both tables 24 and 25, cotton and rice sales were by far the most important sources of agricultural income. The value of cotton relative to other agricultural commodities varied from one year to the next, and for the Ujita house there is evidence that cotton was withheld from sale in years when the price was low.[77] This illustrates that although cotton was a major source of agricultural income large cultivators could afford to withdraw goods from the market when they felt the price was too low and hold them until the following season. It should be kept in mind, however, that this was not the case for the smaller cultivators, who did not have the capital resources to store their crops and wait for a more favourable price.

Throughout the Kinai region, as can be seen in map 3, cotton cultivation and cotton processing played an important role in the economic life of the villages. In some villages, both cultivation and processing activities were a major source of agricultural income. In others either cultivation or processing predominated. In either case, changes in cotton marketing practices had an immediate impact on the villagers and they became increasingly involved in the marketing of their harvested and processed cotton goods. With the gradual shift from urban-centered marketing systems to town- and village-centered marketing systems in the eighteenth and nineteenth centuries, the role of the cultivators in sales and distribution of their cotton goods changed considerably. As will be discussed in the following chapter, the cotton cultivating villagers became increasingly vocal in asserting their interests in the Kinai cotton trade.

This discussion of cotton growing villages in Settsu, Kawachi, and Izumi illustrates the importance of cotton cultivation and processing to farmers in the Kinai region. With major investments in cotton cultivation and an associated involvement in cotton processing, Kinai villagers had a major stake in the Kinai cotton trade. Changes in marketing procedures which increased the return on their crops and which opened up new channels for the distribution of cotton goods offered them the opportunity to improve their economic status. As production costs increased and the profit margin on cotton cultivation fluctuated, the cultivators took steps to enhance their influence over the marketing of their crops and processed goods. It was this development which lay behind the great legal disputes in the late eighteenth and early nineteenth centuries over cotton marketing in Settsu and Kawachi. The discussion above is intended to give a broader perspective on the background to this process of economic and social change.

7 Changes in Cotton Marketing in the Kinai Region

The development of the Kinai cotton trade in the seventeenth century is known only in fragmentary terms. As in the early history of the Ōsaka cotton trade discussed above in Chapter 4, data are extremely limited, and at best an incomplete picture of an Ōsaka-centered marketing and processing network can be discerned. Most discussions of the cotton trade in the Kinai region in the seventeenth century are based on the limited data for Ōsaka and vary only slightly from the description of cotton marketing in Ōsaka during this period.[1] Yet I will make some effort to describe aspects of the early patterns of cotton marketing in Kinai as a background for subsequent modifications in trading procedures.

THE EXPANSION OF THE KINAI COTTON TRADE

There was little processing of harvested cotton in Kinai villages during the seventeenth century. Most of the crop was sold as seed cotton and then ginned, spun into yarn, and woven in rural towns or Ōsaka. For example, by 1677 the town of Itami had a market for buying and selling cotton, firewood, brushwood, and straw matting opened twelve times monthly. Cotton came from nearby villages and processed goods originated in rural towns rather than agricultural villages. With the exception of cotton processed for household consumption, in the seventeenth century all cotton grown in the Amagasaki area was sold as seed cotton in the markets of Amagasaki, Ikeda, and Itami. Towns in this area served as market centers for villages in a two to five mile radius and the town markets were the source of goods not produced locally.[2]

By the 1660s merchants specializing in cotton goods, such as Momenya Yahei of Daigazuka, in modern Ishikawa village, were active in parts of the Kinai region.[3] By 1695, Sakai officially had 9 seed cotton *tonya*, 17 cotton cloth *tonya*, and 241 cloth retailers, while by 1705 Hirano-gō had 9 ginned cotton *tonya*, 8 ginned cotton *nakagai*, 11 reeled yarn merchants, 186 cotton ginners, 43 cotton carders, and 32 cotton seed buyers, indicating the development of this town as a major center for cotton ginning.[4] In 1710 there were three cotton *tonya* active in Tondabayashi and cotton growing and Kawachi cloth production were found in villages along the Ishi river.[5] By 1701, Ikeda cotton cloth was being marketed in the Kinai region, indicating that weaving was active in the town of Ikeda and Ikeda weavers were most likely using cotton grown in nearby villages.[6]

Between early 1734 and early 1735, seed cotton *tonya* in Hirano-*gō* purchased 10 500 bales of seed cotton. The six buyers of seed cotton were all large-scale, wealthy houses in the 1720s and 1730s, but by the 1760s four of them had retired from the seed cotton trade and a fifth house left the trade in the 1790s. Hirano was widely known for the high quality of its white cotton, but both quality and sales declined in the late eighteenth century, partially accounting for the disappearance of most of the major seed cotton buyers.[7] In the Kaizuka area there were twenty-four cotton dealers by 1710 and they had increased to seventy by 1746, at which time there were also seventeen reeled yarn dealers in the city.[8] Most of the seventy cotton merchants in the city in 1746 were licensed *nakagai* who were paying licensing fees to local officials.[9]

In the Itami area a dealer named Momenya Yojihei bought seed cotton from nearby villages, ginned it, and then sold and shipped the ginned cotton to Edo and other regions in an active business. Yojihei received some kind of special privileges from the Konoe daimyo, but his precise status and its time of acquisition are not clear from the surviving documents. By 1749 the cotton trade in Itami became more competitive. One active merchant was Aburaya Hachirōbei. One of his rivals forged his seal and made a shipment of ginned cotton in Hachirōbei's name to eastern Japan. Hachirōbei complained to the Konoe daimyo that his name and reputation had been abused. In compensation he was granted special rights in the cotton trade as well as a seal which designated him as holding primary trade rights for ginned cotton in the area around Itami controlled by the Konoe house. This new status placed all ginned cotton merchants in Itami under his control. The number of traders involved in 1749 is unclear, but around forty were active by 1772 and thirty were given licenses as ginned cotton *tonya* in 1790.[10]

In 1771 the authority of the licensed ginned cotton merchants in Itami was challenged by Tamaya Shichirōbei and his brother Yoichihei of Kitashoji village. They attempted to compete with the established traders and a complaint made to the Konoe daimyo resulted in an order for them to cease their competitive activities. However, despite the initial censure by the daimyo, the following year both were authorized to engage in ginned cotton sales. The censure of the Tamaya brothers was challenged by their village headman Momenya Kizaemon and also by Furuteya Shinhei of Ebisu village. Both appear to have been active in some aspect of the cotton trade and they encouraged the Tamaya to continue their involvement in ginned cotton marketing.[11]

The conflict described above suggests that by the 1770s a ginned cotton *nakama* was active in the Itami region and was attempting to suppress outside competition. Membership was limited and the Tamaya attempt to enter the ginned cotton trade was initially blocked by *nakama* members. When the Tamaya received support from other established cotton merchants the *nakama* backed down and subsequently absorbed the Tamaya into their organization. At this time the merchant association did not have the strength to block new traders who attempted to compete with them in ginned cotton sales. This interpretation is supported by the creation in 1790 of a new association of ginned cotton traders which received thirty licenses for its members. This group, as well, met with difficulties and was replaced in 1818 by another organization of ginned cotton merchants.[12]

THE COTTON FUTURES MARKETS

After 1749, the ostensible leader of the ginned cotton traders in the Itami area was Aburaya Hachirōbei, who held primary trading rights granted by the Konoe daimyo. These were brought into question when a protracted illness forced Hachirōbei to retire from activity between 1751 and 1763. This eventually led to a series of efforts by rival merchants to establish ginned cotton futures markets as a competitive mechanism for marketing ginned cotton. These markets were similar to those active in Ōsaka in the 1760s and 1770s and in 1783 an effort was made to establish such a market in Itami.[13]

Nagasawaya Tōemon in 1783 requested authorization for a branch of his Ōsaka ginned cotton futures market in Itami. He noted that until the mid-eighteenth century Itami had been a major local marketing center for cotton and that it was an excellent location for a cotton futures market. He presented references for his character, offered to pay a suitable licensing fee, and assured the daimyo that prosperity would result from his projected enterprise. Anticipating some opposition from nearby cotton cultivating villages, Nagasawaya asserted that all such opposition was groundless.[14]

Nagasawaya was not alone in his request for a ginned cotton futures market in Itami. Just prior to his application came a request from Wataya Chōbei for permission to establish such a market in either Itami or Ikeda. Since both towns were surrounded by cotton cultivating villages, he was willing to establish a futures market in either location. He promised that such a market would bring prosperity to the cultivators and offered to pay an appropriate licensing fee for authorization.[15]

How did the cotton cultivators react to futures markets as an alternative mechanism for marketing ginned cotton in the Itami and Ikeda area? To begin with, let us consider a 1779 case in which fourteen villages petitioned to block the establishment of a cotton futures market in Ikeda. The villages, ten in Kawabe and four in Teshima *gun*, were in what are now the cities of Takarazuka, Minoo, Kawanishi, and Ikeda. All cultivated cotton and feared that a futures market would reduce the price they received for their crops and result in economic hardships. They requested that the proposed Ikeda market not be authorized.[16]

Villagers were not the only source of opposition to the futures markets. The Ikeda ginned cotton *nakama* also tried to stop the construction of the futures market by offering to pay a higher licensing fee than that initially offered for market authorization. This was opposed by the cotton growers who feared that a futures market, irrespective of the management, would force them to transport their crops to Ikeda for sale and reduce the return on their cotton harvests. Traditionally, buyers had gone from one household to another purchasing cotton and the villagers had been able to bargain over prices. Establishment of a market would create a unilateral mechanism for price determination and leave the cultivators at the mercy of the market. The village opposition was apparently successful as the futures market failed to receive official authorization.[17]

When in 1783 two additional requests for ginned cotton futures markets were made for the Itami area the villagers were asked again to state their position on the question of market authorization. Villages in both Kawabe and Muko *gun* opposed the futures markets in 1783 and based their opposition on the potential reduction in cotton prices and consequent difficulty they would have in meeting their land tax obligations. They also noted that such markets would unilaterally set cotton prices, restrict sales outlets, and put them at a disadvantage in their dealings with cotton buyers.[18]

In both 1779 and 1783, the cotton growers opposed construction of cotton futures markets in Itami and Ikeda. They saw such markets as a means of forcing them to sell their crops cheaply, limiting their sales outlets, and damaging their interests as cotton cultivators. They added emphasis to their position by noting that decreased revenues from cotton sales would interfere with their capacity to pay taxes, an argument that seems to have carried considerable weight as the futures markets were denied authorization by the local authorities.

South of Ōsaka in the area around Sakai, licensed cotton trading is evident by 1736 when a *nakama* of cotton cloth merchants with forty licenses was established. By 1758 the scale of activity increased and ten additional licenses were authorized raising the total to fifty. Trade began in 1738 and most of the cloth handled was produced in the four *gun* of the province of Izumi. Licensing fees increased in 1745 when the government stepped in to suppress competitive activities by merchants from other provinces and protect the monopsony of the cotton cloth *nakama*. Prohibitions against substandard-size cloth were in force between 1745 and 1764 in an effort to protect the *nakama* merchants and the reputation of Izumi cotton cloth which was being undermined by undersize cloth production. Despite these efforts the demand for Izumi cloth declined, illustrating the ineffectiveness of the *nakama* and the government in their efforts to ensure high quality cloth production and marketing controls.[19]

During this period a seed cotton futures market was operated in Sakai by Kaibeya Tasaburō. The market opened in 1757 and continued in operation until it was closed in 1788 during the Kansei reforms. Most of the seed cotton sold in the market came from Izumi and the increase in licensing fees during its period of activity suggests that it was a profitable venture. [20] Village opposition to the Sakai cotton futures market began in 1762, when 284 villages in the four *gun* of Izumi asked that it be closed. They complained of lowered cotton prices and difficulty in paying their taxes as the reason for their request. Opposition to futures markets increased in 1777–8. On 1777/11/13 twenty-six villages from seven *gun* in Kawachi asked that both the Ōsaka and Hirano-*gō* futures markets be closed. A large-scale protest was organized in central Kawachi against cotton futures markets. This was joined by Izumi villages in 1777/12, and included cotton growers from the Watanabe, Hisae, Koide, Tsuchiya, Okabe, Shimizu, and Tayasu domains, who united in opposition to the Sakai cotton futures market. With limited water resources, they were heavily dependent on cotton cultivation and the futures market limited their ability to sell their cotton crops profitably. This made tax payments difficult and they asked for the market to be closed. More opposition surfaced in 1778 when villagers complained that sales outlets were restricted and cotton prices depressed by the futures markets. Complaints were sent by cotton cultivators to officials in Sakai and Ōsaka. Later that year 720 villages in Settsu, Kawachi, and Izumi complained that cotton futures markets forced down cotton prices and had ruined many cultivators who speculated on their crops. Again, the objective was the closing of the cotton futures markets. Replying to the complaints, the Ōsaka city magistrate noted that cotton prices fluctuated yearly depending on the size of the crop and that the futures markets did not play a major role in price determination. Because of this he rejected the complaints of the cotton growing villages.[21]

The cultivators' opposition to the cotton futures markets resulted from their fear of economic exploitation. The futures markets offered advanced payments to the cotton farmers at price levels current prior to the cotton harvest, at a time when the demand for cotton was low. At harvest time when the demand and the price increased, the cultivators were forced to sell their cotton crops at a prearranged price to the futures markets. This placed them at a disadvantage as they could not benefit from price increases or competitive offers for their goods. Their bargaining position was further weakened by the attraction of the futures markets for cotton buyers. By purchasing cotton through the futures markets buyers were usually able to obtain goods at less than the price set at harvest time on the open market. In addition, by buying through the futures markets they saved themselves the effort of going from village to village and purchasing goods from individual households or individual rural merchants. The futures markets thus saved them both money and effort. Consequently, buyers were less willing to go from village to village and the cultivators who did not utilize the futures markets found fewer buyers for their crops. The net effect was to reduce competition and lower the price of harvested cotton.

The magistrate's decision to continue the futures markets disappointed the protesting villagers. For cultivators with small landholdings, the advances they received from the futures market were critical for buying seeds and paying for fertilizer and they became entrapped in a cycle of indebtedness which forced them to sell their crops to the futures markets at unfavorably low prices. While ineffective in 1777–8, their complaints did not go unheard. In 1787–8 the Hirano-*gō*, Sakai, and Ōsaka cotton futures markets were all closed as part of the Kansei reforms. One of the major justifications for the closure of the markets was the disruptive impact they had on cotton cultivators in Settsu, Kawachi, and Izumi.[22]

THE NATURE OF RURAL TRADE

Northeast of Sakai around modern Yao, the rural cotton cloth trade was organized into three groups under the Yao, Kuboji, and Yamanoneki *kumi*. The Yao *kumi* was made up of merchants from twenty-nine villages including eight now in the modern city of Yao on the right bank of the Nagase river. The Kuboji *kumi* included merchants from twenty-five villages on the left bank of the Nagase river and the Yamanoneki *kumi* was composed of merchants from villages along the hills east of Yao.[23]

The operation and nature of these three associations of cotton cloth traders is apparent from the regulations of the Yamanoneki *kumi* from 1755. In the copy sent to the Yao *kumi*, it was noted that, first, cloth trading along the roadside was forbidden by government order and all three associations were to eliminate dishonest trading activities. All new customers were to be queried about previous sources of cloth and shifting from one association member to another was discouraged. Members who, by allowing customers to go along on buying trips, thereby enabled them to by-pass the association and purchase cloth directly, would be excluded from membership. No new members would be admitted to the association, but relatives or employees could be established as branch houses if the three *kumi* were notified and the appropriate fee was paid to each. Vacated trading licenses (*kabu*) could not be sold and were restricted to the house to which they had been initially assigned. Houses which left the associations were to retire from cloth trading. No substandard-size cloth could be sold and the discovery of such cloth would result in a fine of 300 *mon* for each roll of defective cloth. Half this fine was to be paid to the informer and half to the cloth associations as a means of encouraging mutual surveillance. These regulations applied to each of the three associations and each appointed officers to discipline and expel members who violated the rules of the cloth traders' associations. In addition there was a provision by which the associations would come to the assistance of impoverished members by making donations which would be secured by monthly reports on the business activities of the affected house. The regulations were signed by forty-eight members of the Yamanoneki *kumi* from thirteen villages east of Yao.[24] Supplementing the regulations described above was a memo, also from 1755, which in less formal language emphasized the restrictions imposed on members of the cloth traders' associations and warned of the fines and punitive sanctions which applied to violations of the regulations.[25]

Analysis of the regulations above indicates that all was not well with the three cloth traders' associations. The admonitions against roadside sales and dishonest transactions suggest that both were prevalent. Members, outsiders, or both engaged in trading practices which were inappropriate to authorized cloth merchants. Similarly, the attempt to restrict customers to a single source of goods suggests competition between members in which customers could play off one against another to reduce the price they paid for cotton cloth. Restriction to a single outlet was an attempt to reduce competition and ensure uniformity within the associations. Complementing this were efforts to prevent direct cloth purchases by customers from the association suppliers. This was designed to protect the monopsony position of the associations and assure their continued role in the cloth trade in the Yao area. The presence of this kind of injunction suggests that weaknesses had developed in the control of the three *kumi* over cotton cloth marketing and that efforts were being made to reinforce their position.

The membership restrictions were designed to protect members from internal competition. Numbers were limited to ensure that each house would have access to adequate cloth supplies and only branch houses which would work cooperatively with an established member house could be added to the associations' rolls. Consistent with this was the effort to prevent former members from continuing in the cloth trade and competing with the monopsony of the cotton cloth *kumi*. For this purpose contact with former members was restricted and all such contact was to be reported to the appropriate officials. Expulsion from the cloth traders' *kumi* had little impact if those expelled continued to engage in the cloth trade and these restraints were designed to limit this possibility. The seriousness of the sale of substandard-size cloth to the reputation of the cloth traders is evident from the fine schedule and the encouragement of internal policing. Undersize cloth sales threatened the status of all members of the associations and the reward structure was designed to encourage each member to oversee the cloth sales of its associates.

Each of the regulations was characterized by its punitive nature. All prohibited trading practices forbidden by the government or against the best interests of the three associations. The issuance of the regulations in 1755 and the sending of a follow-up memo illustrate the importance attached to appropriate behavior by the membership. To what degree they were also intended to reassure the government and placate people with complaints against individual members cannot be determined, but each of the regulations added to the status and viability of the cloth traders' associations. Failure to control their membership challenged the effectiveness of the associations, not only in the eyes of the government, but also in the eyes of individual cloth traders. Internal competition brought harm to some members. When self-interest dominated, the merchants included in the associations each lost as a result. The regulations attempted to structure the cotton cloth trade in the Yao area in the interest of all *kumi* members, as well as asserting the capacity of the *kumi* to control the marketing of cotton cloth in their area of jurisdiction.

Among the members of the Yao *kumi* of cotton cloth traders was the house of Wataya Kichibei, which under the shop name of Watakichi was a large-scale trader in cotton cloth during the Tokugawa period and into the twentieth century. Watakichi dealt in ginned cotton, cotton yarn, and other dry goods in addition to cloth, and had extensive direct trade from the Yao area to buyers in Ōmi province and elsewhere, independent of the Ōsaka market. In 1759, for example, Watakichi sold 21 428 *tan* of cotton cloth, including both white and striped cloth, 1720 spools of yarn, and 273 *kan* of ginned cotton. Watakichi had a large volume of business with many employees and was one of the largest cloth dealers in the Yao, Kuboji, and Yamanoneki *kumi*.[26]

Although originally a seed cotton dealer, from the 1750s Watakichi became a major wholesaler of cotton cloth. As a member of the Yao *kumi*, he was incorporated into an organization of cloth traders, but within the villages included in the association were unaffiliated cloth merchants as well. The scale of the Watakichi cloth business fluctuated annually, but it tended to increase in the nineteenth century. For example, in the statistics available for the years from 1826 to 1868 Watakichi sold 52 178 *tan* of cloth in 1826, had fluctuating sales which hit a low of 33 676 *tan* in 1852, then rose to a high of 79 275 *tan* of cotton cloth in 1864, and dropped off to 35 297 *tan* in 1868.[27] The independence of Watakichi from the Osaka cotton cloth *tonya* is apparent in orders and shipping documents which have survived. Both indicate that Watakichi engaged in direct sales and shipments to Ōmi merchants and did not have to go through the Ōsaka cloth traders' associations en route.[28]

Watakichi appears to have been one of the larger cloth merchants in the Yao area, but he was by no means the only trader who was independent of the Ōsaka cotton cloth *nakama* controls. It was just this kind of independent rural cloth trader which caused the Ōsaka cotton merchants in the 1760s and 1770s to request additional monopoly rights and protection from the Ōsaka city magistrates. This effort to increase the control of Ōsaka merchants over rural cotton traders is evident in subsequent attempts to expand the jurisdiction of the Ōsaka *nakama* and incorporate rural cotton traders under their control.

Kinai cotton growers were well aware of the potential impact of the expansion of the Ōsaka cotton *nakama*. During the 1770s, when the Ōsaka cotton merchants received additional monopoly powers from the government, Kinai area villagers expressed concern over the deleterious influence this would have on their marketing activities. An excellent example of this fear was a 1773 petition sent to the Ōsaka city magistrates' office by villagers from Kawachi *gun* of Kawachi province. The petition stated:

Recently there was a request for licenses for seed and ginned cotton and cotton cloth dealers. Should the licenses be granted, villagers who in the off-season work as cotton and cotton cloth traders would be forced out of business, and we are apprehensive that this request will be authorized.

We, who are village traders in cotton and cotton cloth, are not normally merchants and engage in trade only in the off-season. However, should licenses be authorised, all trading in cotton and cotton cloth would be controlled by the licensed merchant associations [*kabu nakama*]. This would reduce the sales outlets in the villages, would interfere with tax payments, and cause us great sadness. We implore you to continue the present system of cotton marketing and we will regard it as a benevolent gesture for which we would be extremely grateful.[29]

It is clear that the cotton growers were well aware that their marketing activities would be severely curtailed by the granting of rural trading licenses under a *kabu nakama*. By-employment as village cotton merchants was an important source of revenue to the villagers in Kawachi. Formation of rural *kabu nakama* was designed to restrict this kind of trading to merchants who could afford to pay license fees and would conform to the institutionalized marketing mechanism which centered on the Ōsaka cotton merchants. The villagers knew that this went against their economic interests and they petitioned the Ōsaka magistrates in an effort to prevent this kind of institutionalized rigidity for cotton marketing in Kawachi.

This effort to preserve flexibility in cotton marketing in Kawachi failed to achieve its objectives, for the *nakama* was authorized. The following year, a group of cotton cultivating villages from Settsu and Kawachi joined in a request to the Ōsaka city magistrates for consideration of their interests in the Kinai cotton trade. The document of 1774/8/27 noted that when in 1773 they were asked about the impact of licensing cotton traders, the cultivators had replied that it would cause them great hardships.

151

Despite this, between 1773/10 and the summer of 1774, merchants from several villages near Ōsaka were summoned to purchase licenses from the Ōsaka cotton and cotton cloth merchants' associations in order to continue trading in cotton goods. As villagers who were heavily involved in cotton cultivation and who were dependent on the income which they received from by-employment as cotton traders in the off-season, they asked that their interests be given consideration.

Because their ability to pay taxes was directly dependent on the returns which they received for their cotton crops and the income which they earned in by-employment as traders, the villagers asked that the restrictions on trading be removed. They noted that in the twelve villages bordering on Ōsaka affected by licensing requirements, many cultivators had experienced difficulties in selling their crops or had been forced to sell at unfavorably low prices. The restriction of trade to licensed merchants enabled them to force down prices and this brought suffering to the cotton growers. From the cultivators' perspective, the authorization of *kabu nakama* for rural cotton and cotton cloth traders could only force down prices and bring hardship. They respectfully asked that the *kabu nakama* be abolished and the old system in which they were able to sell their crops on a wide market be restored.[30]

The cotton cultivating villagers clearly understood the threat which *kabu nakama* formation in the Kinai cotton trade made to their economic position. It provided a means for forcing down cotton prices by limiting the number of cotton buyers and also denied them participation in lucrative off-season by-employment as cotton traders, as few could afford trading licenses. This would reduce their incomes from commercial agriculture by lowering the market price of cotton goods and remove cotton trading as a source of supplementary income. The interests of the government in separating commerce and agriculture and those of the cotton growers in enhancing their economic position were at odds.

From the government perspective, the objective of *kabu nakama* formation was to include rural cloth traders in the marketing system which focused on Ōsaka and thus add a new element of control over rural commerce. The villagers were getting far too involved in commercial pursuits and strict limitation of their mercantile involvements was to result from expansion of the *kabu nakama*. Although this policy was inconsistent with changes in commercial agriculture and trade in the Kinai region, it was consistent with Tokugawa conceptions of propriety and occupational specialization. Farmers were supposed to be just that – farmers – and involvement in trade as a form of by-employment distracted them from their primary concern with agriculture. The interests of social harmony and social control were best served by restricting cotton trading to licensed merchants. It was this kind of argument, combined with the attraction of the income from licensing fees, which lay behind the expansion of the *kabu nakama* in the Kinai cotton trade. The villagers' claims to consideration of their economic position fared badly when faced with the kind of moral and social arguments illustrated above.

A similar case was a petition from villages in Settsu and Kawachi which complained about the extended influence of the Ōsaka cotton *nakama*. This petition of 1774/8 noted that 1500 trading licenses had been authorized and licensing fees established for rural cotton traders active around Ōsaka. A licensing bureau in Ōsaka was to keep records on all licensed traders and ensure that any supplementary licenses issued would not interfere with the trading rights of previously established merchants. Village headmen were to ascertain how many licenses should be issued in each village and were also to report to the government instances of trade obstruction. This system of licensed traders was to apply to villages located within two to five miles of Ōsaka and all cotton traders active in this area were to join the Ōsaka *wataya nakama* and purchase licenses for cotton trading.

The petitioners complained that the licenses would restrict the cotton trade and exclude many village cotton traders. This would cause great hardship to the cultivators, who in bad harvest years concentrated on cotton and cotton cloth sales so that they would be able to pay their taxes and fertilizer bills. As villagers from Settsu and Kawachi, they pleaded that the magistrates consider their interests compassionately, terminate the distribution of licenses from the Ōsaka *wataya nakama*, and allow as, previously, broad-based participation in the Kinai cotton trade.[31]

Here, as in the petition discussed above, the cotton growing villagers objected to the extension of Ōsaka *nakama* controls to villages outside the city. The Ōsaka *wataya nakama* had been authorized to expand its control outside of the city and license rural cotton traders. This enabled it to establish a monopsony of the cotton trade in portions of Settsu and Kawachi and brought economic harm to the cotton cultivators and part-time merchants. The interests of the villagers and the objectives of the government in supporting the Ōsaka merchants were in conflict.

With the government working to strengthen the controls of the urban merchant associations, the pleas of the cultivators were in vain. This suggests that, initially, the expansion of the Ōsaka cotton *nakama* in the late eighteenth century successfully restricted the cotton trade in Settsu and Kawachi. Restrictions on trading by means of a licensed merchant monopsony distinguished between authorized cotton merchants and part-time seasonal by-employment by cotton cultivators and other outsiders. The limiting of market outlets also had an impact on cotton prices, but data are inadequate for statistical analysis. The expansion of *kabu nakama* served to slow down the development of alternative marketing patterns in the countryside around Ōsaka, but it was unable to eliminate the trading activities of the villagers and rural merchants.

This is evident from a 1783 document from the Yao area complaining that cultivators were engaged in cotton trading to the extent that it was interfering with their farming activities. Commerce was forbidden and any farmers found trading cotton were to be reported by their village headmen immediately. This document was widely disseminated to villages in the Yao area, signed by cotton cultivators as proof of their compliance, and was to be adhered to by all.[32] The copy from Ōta village warned that many farmers who engaged in the cotton trade went bankrupt and that to prevent this occurrence future violators of the prohibition on trade would be severely punished. Yet many of the villagers who were forced to pledge their compliance with this regulation, which aimed at terminating the mercantile activities of the cultivators, were very likely already engaged in part-time trade as a form of agricultural by-employment.[33] Because of this, it is unlikely that this kind of punitive sanction had more than a short-term impact on rural cotton trading and over the long term it proved completely ineffective.

LATE EIGHTEENTH AND NINETEENTH CENTURY CHANGES IN RURAL TRADE

By the end of the eighteenth century, the authorized cotton cloth merchants in the Yao, Kuboji, and Takeyasu area appear to have been under the control of the Uemachi *kumi* of the Osaka cotton cloth dealers' association (*nanakumi momenya nakama*). However, new sources of competition appeared in the last decade of the century in the form of rural merchants who maintained independence from the marketing system centered on Ōsaka. Because of the fragmentary data available it is difficult to know whether merchants like Watakichi were included in the licensed trading group or continued to function in an independent capacity. In any case, competition between independent and authorized cloth merchants for limited cloth supplies drove up the price of cotton cloth and the government responded with an order reducing prices and restricting cloth sales to licensed traders associated with the Ōsaki Uemachi *kumi*. The control of the Ōsaka cloth *nakama* was being undermined in the Yao area.[34]

The failure of the monopsony of the Uemachi *kumi* is apparent from a 1790 governmnt edict included in price reduction orders for that year. This attempted to ban direct trade between rural cloth merchants and retail clothing stores in Ōsaka. Also in 1790, a complaint from the Uemachi *kumi* noted that rural buyers for the association were acting on their own and that the competition resulted in higher cloth prices than those authorized by the Ōsaka cloth monopsony. This and a 1791 complaint that outsiders were buying cloth and selling it to retail stores in Ōsaka illustrate the growth of rural competition for cotton cloth and the inability of the Ōsaka cotton cloth dealers' association to suppress rural competitors.[35]

The influence of the Yao and Kuboji *kumi* of cotton cloth dealers extended considerably beyond the immediate area of the two villages located in Wakae and Shibukawa *gun* of Kawachi. As is shown by table 26, associated cloth buyers (*yoriya*) were located in villages in eight of the

TABLE 26. Distribution of Yao and Kuboji *kumi* cloth buyers (*yoriya*), 1791

Gun	Buyers	Gun	Buyers
Shiki	11	Shibukawa	2
Tannan	8	Takayasu	4
Tanhoku	26	Wakae	2
Furuichi	5	Sumiyoshi	4
Ishikawa	3		
		Total	65

SOURCE: Furushima and Nagahara, table 20 (abbreviated), p. 81.

sixteen *gun* of Kawachi and one of Settsu. This made the independence of these merchants a serious threat to the interests of the Ōsaka cotton cloth dealers' *nakama*. With sixty-five buyers spread in thirty-five villages in Kawachi, the Yao and Kuboji *kumi* were able to control a significant portion of Kawachi cloth production. As the control of the Ōsaka cotton cloth merchants deteriorated in the late eighteenth century, the influence of the Yao and Kuboji cloth dealers and other cloth traders increased.

Similar problems appeared in the marketing of seed cotton in the Yao area. Villagers purchased small quantities of seed cotton and sold it directly to itinerant merchants from Ōmi province. While the scale of the activity for most individuals was small, the cumulative impact was considerable and large quantities of seed cotton were sold and shipped to Ōmi without relying on the Ōsaka-centered marketing system.[36]

The weakening of Ōsaka Uemachi *kumi* control over the cotton cloth trade is evident from a 1790 document from Wakae village near Yao, which complained that buyers for the Ōsaka merchants had been unable to force down prices and control local cloth sales. Despite efforts to the contrary, auction sales and competition by unauthorized traders drove the price of cloth upwards. Despite the monopsony guarantees of the *nakama*, short sales by both licensed merchants and outsiders made it impossible to enforce the 10 percent price reductions ordered by the government. *Nakama* monopoly rights notwithstanding, the efforts of the licensed merchants failed to control the rural cloth trade and reduce prices.[37]

The licensed rural cloth dealers were in a quandary. They were under pressure from both the Ōsaka Uemachi *kumi* and the government to lower cloth prices and their monopoly position was supposed to enable them to achieve this objective. But they found it impossible to control the marketing of cotton cloth and this undermined all their efforts at price reduction. The growth of independent traders at the expense of the authorized cloth buyers is apparent by the 1790s and the Ōsaka-based cloth dealer's *nakama* was proving incapable of controlling the rural cotton trade in Kawachi.

In the Sakai area the growth of similar kinds of competition was apparent. In 1791, villages in the four *gun* of Izumi complained that the Sakai cloth *tonya* association was trying to buy up all cotton cloth produced in Izumi and use its monopsony of cloth purchases to force down prices. At the same time, Kishiwada *han*, located in Izumi, was trying to use a similar monopoly mechanism to force down the price of cloth produced in the domain. Both control efforts were evaded by the cloth producers when they wove cloth of substandard size, which was unacceptable to the licensed cloth merchants and which they were able to market without recourse to the government-supported marketing systems.[38]

In 1807, an additional complaint was made by Izumi cloth producing villages against marketing controls imposed on them by the Sakai cloth *tonya*. This was followed by still another complaint in 1810, when the government ordered that all cloth produced in Izumi be sold to the Sakai cloth merchants and banned shipments to markets other than Sakai. Villagers who owned boats were ordered not to accept from rural cloth traders shipments of cloth destined for Ōsaka and other markets. On 1811/4/19, seventeen village elders from Izumi complained that this had forced down cloth prices and caused great hardships for the weavers. They recommended that if 60 percent of the cloth was sold to Sakai merchants, the other 40 percent should be authorized to be marketed freely by the producers and rural merchants. Assuming that total provincial production amounted to around 1.2 million *tan* of cloth annually, this would have sent 720 000 *tan* to Sakai and left 480 000 *tan* for unrestricted sale elsewhere.[39]

The Sakai city magistrate who adjudicated the dispute on 1811/8/15 authorized the cloth producers to sell a portion of their cloth to merchants from other provinces after they sold the bulk of their production to the licensed Sakai *tonya* and their agents. Since this conformed to the objectives of the cloth producers, they welcomed this intervention on their behalf.[40] The decision was conditionally accepted by the Sakai cloth *tonya* and the associated groups of rural cloth buyers, but they insisted that all cloth should first be marketed in Sakai, with that portion not purchased by them later sold in other markets, for example Ōsaka. This intransigence on the part of the licensed cloth merchants extended the dispute, as they feared that liberalization of trade restrictions would reduce their control over the

Izumi cloth trade. Determined to preserve their monopsony, they questioned this weakening of their monopsony rights.[41]

The precedent for this stance came from an order of 1809/11 when, at *nakama* request, the Sakai magistrate had prohibited cloth sales to buyers not linked to the Sakai cloth *tonya* association and a complementary order had been issued in Kishiwada *han*.[42] By 1811 the climate of governmental opinion had changed somewhat and the Sakai magistrate was no longer willing to strictly uphold the monopoly rights granted to the Sakai cloth merchants. By authorizing a degree of free trade by the Izumi cloth producers, the government began to back away from its support of *nakama* monopsony rights in the Kinai cotton trade.

Complementary tendencies can be seen in the Sakai seed cotton trade. Beginning in 1803 the Sakai cotton merchant Yoshikawa Hyōjiro requested permission to establish a seed cotton market in Sakai to provide an alternative mechanism for marketing the Izumi cotton crop. He noted that his market would stabilize the demand for seed cotton and reduce the impact of itinerant buyers when they went to the villages to purchase cotton. He also projected that his market would provide laboring jobs in Sakai and he requested official authorization for his project.[43]

In his proposal Hyōjiro described how his market would operate, the manner of payment and delivery of goods, and its hours of operation. He suggested that such a market would supplement existing sales outlets without interfering with other marketing systems for seed cotton. He anticipated that it would restrain the exploitive actions of rural cotton buyers and offer the cultivators an attractive alternative for marketing their crops. The Sakai magistrate questioned Hyōjiro about his proposal and then asked for the villagers' reactions to the proposed market. Fearing that their marketing outlets would be restricted rather than expanded, the villagers opposed the construction of the Sakai seed cotton market.[44]

The outcome of the 1804 proposal by Yoshikawa Hyōjiro is unclear, but in 1808 a similar request was made by Yamamoto Mohei for a license to control all ginned cotton sales in the Sakai area. He wanted a commission on all sales and his request was strongly opposed by farmers from the nearby Tayasu and Hitotsubashi domains, who feared that a trade monopoly would result from his request. Some kind of compromise was reached, for by 1810 the thirteen licensed ginned cotton *tonya* in Sakai attempted to set up a monopsony on all ginned cotton sales in Izumi. This met with united opposition from the cotton cultivators, as they objected to this effort to restrain trade and what they feared would be an attempt to lower ginned cotton prices.[45]

The opposition from villagers and rural cotton traders to the attempted monopsony of the Sakai seed and ginned cotton *tonya* association resulted in 1810/6 in a government order which again authorized direct sales in the villages of both seed and ginned cotton. The Sakai merchant association continued to play a major role in the trade, however, and by 1812 the seed and ginned cotton *tonya nakama* had increased from 13 to 150 houses of licensed merchants.[46] Despite the reduction in government support of urban merchant control over the seed and ginned cotton trade in Izumi, the *nakama* was able to increase its membership, presumably on the basis of its capacity to enhance 'the economic position and status of its membership. Although the data are fragmentary, the suggestion is that by either the reception of additional governmental support or other means, the Sakai seed and ginned cotton *tonya nakama* was able both to preserve and, in fact, expand its role in the Izumi seed and ginned cotton trade.

In Kishiwada *han*, efforts to control cloth marketing continued despite the increasing activities of rural merchants. In 1816/12, the *han* government ordered that all cotton cloth sales be restricted to buyers licensed by the domain. This was followed in 1817/6 by an edict which demanded that illegal sales of all commodities to merchants not licensed by the *han* should cease immediately.[47] Both these decrees suggest that the attempt by Kishiwada *han* to restrict trade in cotton cloth and other commodities failed to restrain independent cotton trading by the producers and rural merchants.

The effort to restrict trade to authorized merchants in Izumi and within Kishiwada *han* met with effective resistance from the cotton growers and village merchants. Limitation of trade went counter to the tendency in the villages for more open marketing networks and fewer restrictions on the sale of cotton goods. The effort to preserve the distinction between commerce and agriculture and to suppress the participation of villagers in marketing cotton met with broadly based, increasingly effective opposition. The pressure for changes in economic policy increased, but the shift in policy was still to come.

Associated with government efforts to support the position of licensed merchant groups were attempts to utilize these groups for implementing price controls. During the so-called Kyōhō and Kansei reforms of the second, third, and last decades of the eighteenth century price controls to preserve the economic position of the samurai class had been major policy objectives of the Tokugawa shogunate. With samurai incomes paid in rice, increases in general commodity prices which were not matched by corresponding rises in the price of rice caused considerable strains on samurai finances. In the second decade of the nineteenth century this problem again surfaced and the government responded with a series of price control regulations. In 1819, directives were issued ordering reductions in both commodity prices and wages. Associated with them was an effort to retard the development of rural markets so that rural merchants would be unable to fix prices and acquire powers which had been assigned to the urban *kabu nakama*.[48]

The villages in Wakae *gun* of Kawachi received an order for price and wage reductions, as noted in table 27. Most goods were reduced in price by 10 to 20 percent, but merchant commissions on sales were reduced even

TABLE 27. Wakae *gun* detailed price reduction order, 1819

Item	Description	Current price	Reduced price	Reduction
Cotton ginning	Daily wage	2.0 *momme* silver	1.8 *momme* silver	10%
Roof thatching	Daily wage	2.0 *momme* silver	1.8 *momme* silver	10%
Ginned cotton	Price per 1 *kin*	36 *mon*	32 *mon*	11%
Seed cotton	Commission per 100 *momme*	1 *momme* silver	0.5 *momme* silver	50%
Ginned cotton	Commission per 100 *momme*	2 *momme* silver	1 *momme* silver	50%
Rice	Commission per *koku*	5 *fun*	3 *fun*	40%
Soy, bean paste, oil	Retail prices	To be reduced by 10%		10%
Service personnel	Wages	Unchanged		0

SOURCE: *Fuse shishi*, II, table 24 (abbreviated), p. 844.

further. For example, commissions on rice sales were reduced by 40 percent and those on seed and ginned cotton sales by 50 percent in an effort to force down prices to the consumers.

A similar document was sent to villages in the Yao area. In response the Yao *kumi* of cotton cloth dealers sent a document to the government promising that it would try to implement a 20 percent reduction in the price of cloth. The association also pledged that buying of substandard-size cloth, which had been increasing, would cease immediately.[49] In neither case is there evidence that the price reduction orders had a significant impact. Price determination was a complex process which could not be altered by the issuance of a government order. It is highly unlikely that the reductions ordered in Wakae *gun* or Yao were ever implemented or that, if implemented, they had anything other than a short-term effect.

In the ginned cotton trade, the urban-based monopoly associations continued to play an active role into the nineteenth century. The Ōsaka ginned cotton *tonya nakama* included under its control six branch associations known collectively as the Go-Kinai ginned cotton *tonya nakama*. The 1805 regulations of this association illustrate the business practices and monopoly powers of this merchant group. In 1805 there were thirty-two *tonya* houses in Ōsaka and associated ginned cotton *tonya* in Kyōto, Hachiman, Hirano, Sakai, Nishinomiya, and Yamato. Some direct trade by outsiders with Edo was authorized if appropriate consultations were conducted with the authorized *tonya nakama*. Within the Kinai area, all shipments by the association were to be conducted by the thirty-two members in Ōsaka and these shipments were to be sent to the sixty-two members of the associated Edo ginned cotton *tonya nakama*. All orders from eastern Japan were to be shipped via the licensed Edo merchants, irrespective of whether Edo or other parts of the Kantō region or northern Japan was the final destination. All changes in associated regional *tonya nakama* membership were to be reported to the Ōsaka association and all members were admonished to adhere strictly to the regulations of the ginned cotton merchants' group.[50]

To increase control over their regional counterparts, the Ōsaka *tonya nakama* advised the regional associations in Kinai to expel all members who failed to conform to the regulations on ginned cotton trading. A similar document was also sent by the Edo ginned cotton merchants' association to the Ōsaka and the Go-Kinai *tonya* associations, illustrating the cooperation between the ginned cotton traders in Edo and the Kinai area and the uniformity of their norms of commercial behavior.[51] Yet the insistent repetition of the regulations by both the Ōsaka and Edo *nakama* suggests that their control over the Go-Kinai *tonya* was far from complete. The emphasis on proper behavior contained in the regulations implies that variant patterns of activity were not uncommon. Given the growing independence of rural cotton traders in the Kinai region, it is not surprising that the Go-Kinai *tonya* were also acting independently of the Ōsaka *tonya nakama*. New patterns of rural distribution offered them the opportunity to escape the restrictions imposed on their cotton trading by the Ōsaka *tonya nakama*. Here as well are indications of change in the Kinai cotton trade.

THE 1823 DISPUTE

The 1007-village lawsuit of 1823 has been discussed above in Chapter 5, as a major break in the control of the Ōsaka cotton merchants over the Kinai cotton trade. With the resolution of this dispute, the government removed its support of the *kabu nakama* monopolies in the cotton trade and authorized the continued development of alternative rural marketing systems, which were independent of the Ōsaka merchant associations. This step dramatically reduced the controls exercised by the Ōsaka cotton *nakama* over the Kinai cotton trade.

From the village perspective, the 1823 dispute concluded with the cotton growers and rural merchants obtaining their objectives of eliminating *kabu nakama* restrictions on trading and shipping cotton goods. This is evident in the statement sent in 1823/7 by sixty-three representatives from the 1007 villages in Settsu and Kawachi to the Ōsaka magistrates who had ruled in their favor. The statement explains their side of the dispute and is quoted in full.

We, from villages in Settsu and Kawachi, who market cotton which we grow, have in recent years been troubled by the restrictive controls of the Ōsaka cotton *tonya nakama*. In order to widen the market for our crops, on 1823/5/25, we appealed to the Ōsaka city magistrate for assistance. The above *tonya nakama* was summoned for examination by the magistrate and on 1823/7/6 we were summoned and told that, hereafter, both cotton growers and rural merchants who were not licensed by the Ōsaka cotton *tonya nakama* were authorized to sell and ship cotton to customers in other provinces without restriction.

Because of this ruling, the Ōsaka cotton *tonya nakama* is not to interfere with waterborne shipments passing through Ōsaka on river boats or with coolie or packtrain shipments. We have been authorized by the Ōsaka city magistrate to market our goods widely and for this authorization we are most humbly grateful. We thus request no more than the above benevolence from the government. All cotton cultivators in Settsu and Kawachi will be reassured and continue their farming. We will be eternally thankful for the good will of the government and most humbly present this statement.[52]

As is evident in the document above, the cotton growers and rural merchants saw in the settlement of the 1823 dispute a vindication of their marketing activities in Settsu and Kawachi. The government in the decision backed away from its support of the monopsony granted to the Ōsaka cotton *tonya nakama* and liberalized the seed cotton trade in Settsu and Kawachi. Behind the dispute lay the reorganization of the Ōsaka *kabu nakama* in 1772 and the expansion of its influence into Settsu and Kawachi villages in the 1790s. With the conclusion of the dispute in 1823, the restrictive controls of the Ōsaka cotton merchants' association were removed and new conditions initiated in the seed cotton trade in Settsu and Kawachi.

The impact of this decision can be seen in the example of Shimokosaka village in the Fuse area of Kawachi. Flooding and drought in Shimokosaka and nearby villages in 1820 and 1821 had caused unusual difficulty for the cotton growers, and ten households from the village actively participated in the 1823 dispute. The leaders of the Shimokosaka contingent were landowners who were closely tied to the rural cotton trade.[53] Following the settlement of the dispute, ten cotton merchants from the village issued a document which indicated their understanding of the decision and willingness to comply with it. The document stated:

(1) Because of the authorization of direct sales and shipments of seed cotton, we will not assess commissions on merchants and boat captains from other provinces as was the practice of the Ōsaka cotton *tonya nakama*.
(2) When seed and ginned cotton are traded, irrespective of the *gun* or village in which sales are conducted, all villagers may freely participate to broaden the sales outlets with their presence.

(3) No corporate groups will be formed to restrict sales within any villages by cotton merchants.

(4) Sales among cotton merchants will be made at the current market price and we will not engage in dishonest transactions.[54]

This document illustrates that from the perspective of Shimokosaka cotton traders, the restrictions on the seed and ginned cotton trade had been removed. They stated their awareness of this change and also their intent to maintain this new condition of unrestricted trade by promising not to institute local merchant groups which would serve to reassert similar controls over cotton trading in the village of Shimokosaka.

The participation of village elites in the 1823 dispute has been suggested by various writers as the reason for the broad base of involvement. Village headmen, large landowners, and village traders – and some households played more than one of these roles – had the kind of inter-village contacts and organizational experience necessary to organize a movement involving a large number of villages spread over two provinces. The village elites were thus able to utilize their status in the villages to advance their commercial interests as village cotton growers and traders.[55]

Village functionaries were among the major representatives in the dispute and this plus the scale of the final petition to the Ōsaka magistrate suggests that individuals with broad social contacts were integrally involved in the organization of the 1823 suit. The question whether status as village officials and landowners or function as itinerant cotton traders with contacts in many villages should be emphasized as the essential quality for leadership cannot at this point be answered satisfactorily. Both qualities provided access to a broad range of contacts. Further, it is unlikely that without considerable involvement in the outcome of the dispute most village officials would have participated in this challenge to the commercial policies of the government, even in what was basically an indirect manner. In any case, it must be assumed that the leadership of the 1823 dispute was involved in either cotton growing or cotton marketing and was concerned with the economic impact of trade restrictions on the cotton cultivators and cotton traders in Settsu and Kawachi.

The 1823 dispute did not terminate efforts to construct local mechanisms to control the cotton trade in the countryside around Ōsaka. In various areas, groups formed to try to maximize their role in the marketing of cotton, despite countervailing efforts by others to maintain the gains toward open marketing of the 1823 decision. Although relieved of much of their official support after 1823, the various Ōsaka merchant groups in the cotton trade continued their involvement as before. New mechanisms for cotton marketing also received some official endorsement, as is illustrated by the cotton market authorized in Hirano-gō in 1834. Both the ginned cotton *nakama* and the *nakagai nakama* participated in this market

TABLE 28. Price reductions ordered in the Ōsaka area, 1842/5/23

Commodity	Description	Current price	Reduced price	Reduction
Agricultural labor	Daily wage – men	1.5 *momme* silver	1.2 *momme* silver	20%
Agricultural labor	Daily wage – women	0.7 *momme* silver	0.6 *momme* silver	14%
Service personnel	Annual wage		To be reduced by 20%	
Cotton ginning	Daily rate for 2 *kan*	2.5 *momme* silver	2 *momme* silver	20%
	Best cotton per 100 *momme*	20 *mon*	18 *mon*	10%
	Middle cotton per 100 *momme*	22 *mon*	20 *mon*	9%
Dyers' fees	Per 100 *momme* yarn by weight			
	dark blue	3 *momme* silver	2.5 *momme* silver	17%
	red	1.5 *momme* silver	1.3 *momme* silver	13%
	light blue	0.5 *momme* silver	0.4 *momme* silver	20%
Packhorse fees	Carry 1 *kan* for 2½ miles	150 *mon*	100 *mon*	33%
Cotton pongee	Weight per 1 *momme* silver	30 *momme* weight	35 *momme* weight	17%
Cotton yarn	By quality of yarn		To be reduced by 20%	
Seed and ginned cotton		Reduction covered separately according to current market price		
Cotton cloth		Reduction covered separately according to current market price		

SOURCE: *Fuse shishi*, II, table 26 (abbreviated), p. 847.

and their members, as licensed market traders, paid licensing fees to the government from 1834 to 1852 when the official association appears to have ceased.[56]

With the so-called Tempō reforms of 1842, the position of the Ōsaka cotton *nakama* was further undermined by the removal of all remaining monopoly rights. The objectives of these reforms were primarily price controls, the reassertion of Tokugawa authority by extension of the boundaries of both Edo and Ōsaka, the restoration of *bakufu* finances, and moral reforms combined with sumptuary legislation. The price control objectives of the reforms backfired when the abolition of all *kabu nakama* dislocated the marketing systems for major commodities, disrupted currency circulation, and instead resulted in price increases and inflation. Reduced output levels in the 1830s, largely the result of natural disasters and bad weather, were followed by market dislocation and currency debasements in the 1840s. These disrupted the supply mechanism and the flow of currency, and commodity prices soared. In 1842/3, merchants in Edo and Ōsaka received orders to lower price levels and in Ōsaka they were also ordered to improve the circulation of coins. A second order to lower prices came in 1842/5. This was followed in 1843/6 by an order for a 20 percent reduction in prices, rents, and wages in Ōsaka and the surrounding area and for commodity price reductions in Edo.[57]

Table 28 lists some representative price reductions ordered by the government in the Ōsaka area on 1842/5/23. They included wage reductions of 20 percent in many occupations and a 33 percent reduction in packhorse transport fees, as well as other reductions of a similar nature. Supplementing the reductions listed above was an order issued two days later which explained the difficulties in setting price reductions for white and striped cotton cloth, seed and ginned cotton, yarn, and rice because of fluctuations in both the supply and quality of these products. Consequently, no specific price levels were set, but efforts were made to encourage price reductions by the merchants who sold these items. Agricultural wage reductions were directed at lowering the cost of agricultural commodities to the consumers and the severe 20 percent wage cut attempted to compensate for recent increases in the costs of agricultural labor. The order directing these reductions originated in the Fuse area and was to apply to Wakae, Shibukawa, Shiki, and Ogata *gun*.[58]

A further effort at price control came in 1842/8, when the Ōsaka city magistrates Abe Tōtōmi no kami Masazō and Mizuno Wakasa no kami Tadakazu issued the following order to villages surrounding Ōsaka. They noted:

Recently, people from rural areas around Ōsaka have been adopting urban manners, forgetting their occupation as cultivators, and engaging in commerce. Since the 1823 dispute in particular, when cotton cultivators and rural cotton merchants from 1007 villages cooperated in an effort to market seed and ginned cotton and were resisted by the Ōsaka cotton *tonya nakama*, those who have been actively engaged in cotton trading have gradually increased. To maximize their profits they have sold ginned cotton at auction to force up its price. This greed has spread to the cultivators who have reduced their commitment to farming and have been demeaned and hindered in fulfilling their obligations as farmers. Moreover, many of them have been freely acting like *tonya* or authorized merchants in the cotton trade and many farmers have become wealthy. Now, in order to correct this behavior, farmers will be allowed to continue their participation in the cotton trade and will not be obstructed, but hoarding, cornering the market, and auction sales by rural cotton merchants, as well as trading by disreputable merchants who wander from one area to the next, are expressly forbidden. All seed and ginned cotton, including that sold by the cultivators, must be sold freely to local cotton dealers or to other merchants in an open manner. Since the price of cotton will be adversely affected by dishonest trading policies, these are to be reported immediately to the Ōsaka city magistrates and all trade is to be strictly legitimate.

The above should be made known in the villages.[59]

From this it is apparent that the government was going one step further in liberalizing the cotton trade in the Kinai region. Rural trading by cultivators and merchants was authorized, but specific practices, such as auction sales and hoarding, were prohibited because they forced up cotton prices and went against government price control policies. Rural involvement in cotton marketing was increasing. While not trying to restrain its development, the government was attempting to channel it away from activities which conflicted with its efforts at controlling commodity prices.

POST-1823 PATTERNS OF RURAL TRADE

What was the impact of the 1823 dispute on the Kinai cotton trade? Were the Ōsaka magistrates correct in their evaluation of the changes which had occurred? What kinds of evidence do we have of increased participation in cotton marketing by rural traders in the Kinai area? An example of special interest on this point is that of the Ujita house of Nishikoya village in Muko *gun* of Settsu.

The Ujita house was a large and successful farming household. The distribution of their seed and ginned cotton between 1783 and 1890 gives a dramatic insight into the changing nature of the rural cotton trade. During this period, Ujita house seed cotton was sold to buyers from the towns of Amagasaki, Nishinomiya, and Itami, as well as those from the villages of Nishino, Tsunematsu, Tokitomo, and Nishikoya. Between 1783 and 1822, the Ujita sold 221 bales of seed cotton and 21 *kan* of ginned cotton to town merchants, while they sold 244 bales of seed cotton to village buyers. Thus the balance was slightly in favor of village buyers, but town buyers purchased around 48 percent of the seed cotton sold during this period.

After 1824, the balance between town buyers – those from Amagasaki, Nishinomiya, and Itami – and village buyers – those from nearby villages – changed dramatically. Between 1824 and 1867, only 27 bales of seed cotton and 26 *kan* of ginned cotton were sold to town merchants, while during this same period 316 bales of seed cotton and 8 *kan* of ginned cotton were sold by the Ujita house to village cotton buyers. During this second period village cotton buyers increased their share of the Ujita house seed cotton crop from 52 percent to around 95 percent and the importance of town buyers declined sharply.[60] As can be seen in table 29, this trend away from town buyers and towards the increased importance of village buyers continued into the Meiji period.[61]

TABLE 29. Ujita house seed and ginned cotton sales by buyer type

	Town buyers		Village buyers	
Period	Seed cotton	Ginned cotton	Seed cotton	Ginned cotton
1783–1822	221 bales	21 *kan*	244 bales	0
1824–1867	27 bales	26 *kan*	316 bales	8 *kan*
1869–1890	0	0	162 bales	3 *kan*

SOURCE: Yamazaki, 'Kinsei kōki Settsu nōson ni okeru shōhin ryūtsū,' table 12, p. 82.

Merchants from Amagasaki accounted for half the Ujita seed and ginned cotton sold to town buyers. Amagasaki merchants played a far greater role than did merchants from Itami and Nishinomiya in respect to Ujita house cotton sales. In contrast, the Ujita house rice crop went largely to buyers from nearby Itami. This can be explained by the high cost of shipping rice relative to cotton because of its greater weight, but probably was also related to the demand for rice from Itami *sake* brewers.[62] Table 30 illustrates the distribution of Ujita house seed and ginned cotton and rice

TABLE 30. Ujita house cotton and rice sales to urban buyers by location, 1783–1867

Town	Seed cotton	Ginned cotton	Rice[a]
Amagasaki	150 bales	27 *kan*	8.0%
Itami	63 bales	0	87.8%
Nishinomiya	35 bales	2 *kan*	4.2%
Ōsaka	0	8 *kan*	0.0%

SOURCE: Yamazaki, 'Kinsei kōki Settsu nōson ni okeru shōhin ryūtsū,' table 8, p. 82.
[a] For 1782–1885.

among the urban buyers. It is of interest, as shown in table 30, that Ōsaka buyers played such a minor role in Ujita house cotton sales and none whatsoever in rice sales during this period.

166

The shift in the locus of Ujita house cotton sales is clearly visible from year to year in table 11 of the article by Yamazaki Ryūzō cited above. Data for sixty-four of the years between 1783 and 1890 indicate not only the shift from town to village buyers, but also the increased role of cotton merchants from Nishikoya village. Table 31 summarizes these data. During

TABLE 31. Ujita house seed cotton sales by location of buyer, 1783–1890

Period	Urban buyers	Village buyers	Nishikoya buyers
1783–1822	221 bales	189 bales	55 bales
1824–1890	27 bales	353 bales	125 bales

SOURCE: Yamazaki, 'Kinsei kōki Settsu nōson ni okeru shōhin ryūtsū,' pp. 78–81.

the second period, from 1824 to 1890, cotton buyers from Nishikoya increased the volume of cotton purchased from the Ujita house and increased in number from three to four. While some of the cotton purchased by Nishikoya village buyers may have been processed in the village, it is likely that most of it was sold to cotton ginners in other villages for processing.

Cotton cloth sales by the Ujita house indicate the same kind of shift away from town to village buyers after the 1007-village suit of 1823. Between 1790 and 1822, buyers from the towns of Itami and Ikeda purchased 744 *tan* of cotton cloth from the Ujita house, while village buyers purchased 2191 *tan* of cloth. Following the 1823 suit, in the period from 1824 to 1874, town buyers from Itami, Ikeda, and Amagasaki purchased only 44 *tan* of cloth, while village buyers purchased 1468 *tan* of cotton from the Ujita house.[63] Following the dispute, the volume of cloth purchased by town cloth buyers declined from around 25 percent of total cloth sold prior to 1823 to around 3 percent between 1824 and 1874. Town buyers were almost completely displaced by village buyers of cotton cloth.

This shift from town to village cotton buyers was accompanied by changes in the nature of the village cotton buyers themselves. For example, during the years from 1818 to 1829, of ten cotton buyers in Shimokosaka village near Fuse, five had lands assessed at over eight *koku* productivity, including one with almost thirty-four *koku*, and only two were landless. In contrast, twenty years later during the years from 1848 to 1853, the eight cotton buyers from Shimokosaka included only one individual with land assessed at over two *koku*, and he owned less than six *koku*. Four were small landholders, and three were cotton buyers with no land at all. Thus in the later period, the Shimokosaka cotton buyers tended to be smaller landholders or landless merchants who were far more dependent than merchants active before 1829 upon the income which they earned from the cotton trade. This shift was from middle and upper class farmers to lower class farmers and appears to have been characteristic of village traders during the last decades of the Tokugawa period in the Kinai region.[64]

By 1860 there were thirteen seed cotton buyers in Shimokosaka, as well as two cotton ginners and three dealers in carded cotton, who presumably produced the carded cotton which they sold. This increase in commercial activity associated with the cotton trade is thought by Furushima and Nagahara to have accompanied a decrease in the scale of the individual merchant houses.[65]

The abolition of *kabu nakama* in 1842 can be interpreted as a realistic adjustment of government policy to the realities of commodity marketing in the Kinai region. In Ōsaka and most of the Kinai region, termination of the monopoly privileges of the urban merchant associations was consistent with the transition from urban-dominated marketing systems to more flexible and broadly based systems in which new alternatives, founded on widespread involvement of village merchants, had absorbed a significant share of the business formerly dominated by licensed merchant groups. Thus the impact of the so-called Tempō reforms on Kinai commerce and on the Kinai cotton trade in particular was far less dramatic than the impact on the commercial life of the shogunal capital at Edo.

The same can be said with respect to the restoration of *kabu nakama* in the Ōsaka region in 1851. In reconstructing licensed trading associations the government hoped to develop a mechanism for managing commerce which would apply not only to merchants in Ōsaka but also to their competitors in the villages. The restrictive aspects of the old associations were largely eliminated, but regularization of business procedures and marketing controls were the major justifications for the new merchant associations.

Various examples illustrate the influence of the post-1851 merchant associations on the Kinai cotton trade. For example, in the Yao area, the reestablishment of *nakama kumiai* led to the creation of the Yao, Terauchi, Kuboji, Yamadori, and Onchi *kumi*, which were all designed to control cotton cloth trading in villages around Yao.[66] The 1853 regulations of the Yao *kumi*, signed by the eighteen members of the association and representatives of the four associated cloth merchant groups, differed little from their pre-1842 predecessors. Emphasis remained on adherence to trading regulations and the abandonment of ineffective marketing practices. All government trade policies were to be implemented immediately, including the traditional prohibition against roadside sales. Members were to work for the interests of the collective group and not compete with their colleagues for customers. All defaulted or delayed payments by customers were to be reported to the association so that an embargo could be applied to their orders for additional goods. Members were to pay a fair price to weavers for cloth and all cloth was to be examined to ensure that it conformed with the established standards for size and quality. Trade was to be restricted to the geographical area assigned to the Yao *kumi* and trade with other villages was forbidden, thus limiting trade to a seven-village sector. Members or employees who violated the rules of the Yao *kumi* were to be reported to the group leaders and those who ignored the interests of the collective membership were to be excluded from contact with the association.[67]

As had been the case prior to *nakama* abolition in 1842, each of the cloth traders was to cooperate with colleagues in his own and nearby local trading associations. Each of the associations had a clearly defined territory to which it was to confine its cloth purchases and each member was to adhere to the rules of the collective group. While membership limitations and licensing fees had been eliminated, for all practical purposes the associations were similar or identical to the merchant groups which were abolished in 1842.

This was true from the government perspective as well. For example, in 1856 the Ōsaka city magistrate ordered a reduction in cotton cloth prices. To implement this policy he held discussions with the Ōsaka Uemachi, Yao, and Kuboji *kumi* of cloth traders. Following the meeting a 10 percent reduction in cloth prices was ordered as well as a 15 percent reduction on goods sold within the associations. Sales at higher prices were forbidden, but the impact of this price control effort is difficult to measure and it probably had little effect.[68] From the government viewpoint, the new associations had the same purposes as their predecessors, and one of these was price control.

Given the objectives of reestablishing the Ōsaka cotton *nakama*, the question remains how effective they proved to be for imposing new controls on the Kinai cotton trade. The example of the Ōsaka *wataya nakama* illustrates some of the problems which the reconstructed trade associations encountered during the last decades of the Tokugawa period. In 1854, the Ōsaka city magistrates issued a directive which supported the interests of the *wataya nakama* and gave the official view of the role assigned to the reestablished association. The directive stated:

Recently, cotton merchants in the Ōsaka area were organized into a *nakama kumiai*. Trade and direct shipments by outsiders interfered with the trading of association members and complaints were made to the Ōsaka city magistrates. Those who wished to continue in the cotton trade were ordered to join the *wataya nakama*. As has been noted on several occasions since the abolition of *kabu nakama* in 1842, because their former members continued to trade as before it was decided to reestablish these associations in 1851. Since this time, individuals who did not understand the significance of the reconstruction of the *nakama* associations have continued to trade cotton without joining the *wataya nakama*. They are said to have reduced the business of *nakama* members and engaged in dishonest trading. Because of this, we order that those merchants who wish to continue to participate in the seed and ginned cotton trade and to ship to other regions must join the *wataya nakama*. Hereafter, those outside the *nakama* who continue to trade and ship to other areas will be investigated and ordered immediately to cease trading in cotton.[69]

This 1854 directive ordering village merchants to join the *wataya nakama* resulted in a challenge from the rural cotton merchants. They claimed that the *wataya nakama* was trying to utilize the reconstructed *nakama kumiai* to expand its control outside the city of Ōsaka and that this violated the decision of the 1007-village dispute of 1823. This decision had clearly granted new trade rights to rural traders of seed and ginned cotton and the villagers strongly objected to the *wataya nakama* attempt to suppress these rights by imposing new controls over their trading activities. Standing by their victory in the 1823 dispute, the village merchants were unwilling to acquiesce in this incursion into their marketing rights for seed and ginned cotton.[70]

The government attempted to clarify the issue by noting that the regulations of the association, like those issued in 1772 and 1837, were designed to control individuals trading in seed and ginned cotton. Commerce in these two commodities was to be conducted in accordance with these rules, which were not designed to hinder the rights of the cotton growers to freely sell their crops to a wide range of customers. The government agreed that efforts by the *wataya nakama* to restrict village trade violated the spirit of the government attempt to reassert controls over trading in seed and ginned cotton and that complaints against this practice by the villagers were justified. Consequently, the jurisdiction of the *wataya nakama* was limited to Ōsaka and villages bordering on the city and did not include traders from villages elsewhere in the Kinai region.[71]

To further clarify the situation, the government requested in a document of 1854/8 that the villagers explain their understanding of their cotton trading rights. A certified answer was requested and the following example from Shimokosaka village near Fuse was signed by nine villagers active in the cotton trade. Their reply stated:

We, as village cotton merchants understand the following seven points:
(1) The new regulations do not change the settlement of the 1823 dispute. Therefore, we will not challenge the establishment of the *wataya nakama* and licenses will not be required for village cotton traders. Cultivators and rural cotton merchants are free to sell and ship cotton to customers from far and near and shipments via the Ōsaka waterways, or by coolie or packhorse trains, will not be interrupted by the Ōsaka seed and ginned cotton *tonya*. Sales to a wide range of clients are authorized. While cotton is covered in the new trade regulations, it is a special case as the 1823 settlement is still in effect, and, consequently, it may be widely sold.
(2) Cultivators may gin and sell their seed cotton and participate in the cotton trade in their free time as village cotton merchants. They may purchase cotton from nearby areas, gin it, and then sell and ship it to customers from far and near without restriction. Consequently, their expenses should be reasonable and they will be sure to sell at a fair price. If in the village there are conspiracies to violate

this practice they will be reported to the authorities and the guilty parties prohibited from trading cotton.

(3) Rural cotton merchants who buy cotton from nearby cultivators and then gin and sell it will not be required to join the *wataya nakana* as the result of their involvement in cotton processing. Under the trade regulations of 1823 and 1854 they may refuse to join the Ōsaka *wataya nakama*.

(4) In the above regulations, processed cotton refers to cotton which has been carded [*shinomaki*], cotton wadding, reeled yarn, striped cloth, and so forth, and those who trade in these items are required to join the *wataya nakama* according to the regulations of 1772 and 1837, but only if they are active in the following seventeen villages. The seventeen, included in or bordering on Ōsaka, are Tennoji, Minami and Kita Hirano-*machi*, Higashi Takatsu, Nakamichi, Honjō, Ono, Imamiya, Kitsu, Namba, Sankenya, Nambajima Nishikawa-*machi*, Kyūjō, Kami and Shimo Fukushima, Sonezaki, and Kawasaki. Merchants from other villages which participated in the 1007-village dispute of 1823 are not required to have *wataya nakama* licenses, whether or not they trade in processed cotton goods. Hereafter, we understand that a distinction exists between Ōsaka, including the seventeen villages mentioned above, and villages more distant from the city. In accord with this the 1823 settlement is still in effect and has not been altered. Consequently, if in the future village merchants are accused of interrupting the cotton trade, their cases will be treated in accord with the above understanding.

(5) When the Ōsaka *wataya nakama* attempted to eliminate the distinction between urban and rural merchants and force membership in the *nakama* on rural cotton traders, they did so for the following reason. They wished to exploit the reestablishment of *nakama kumiai* to expand their control over rural seed and ginned cotton sales. This violates the settlement of 1823 and is a mistaken addition to the order reconstructing merchant associations. Hereafter, because of this, the distinctions between urban and rural merchants will continue in force.

(6) The regulations of 1772 and 1837, together with the recent order of 1854 relating to the *wataya nakama*, as well as the order abolishing the *kabu nakama* in 1842 – which completed the objectives of the 1823 dispute – can all be kept in force without violating the spirit of the 1823 decision. They mean a return to the former status of the *wataya nakama*. Hereafter, orders regarding the rural cotton trade should be submitted for discussion prior to issuance so that the government may discover the attitude of village merchants to their trade policies. As suggested above, any regulations which will interfere with trade in seed cotton, ginned cotton, or processed cotton should be submitted for discussion prior to their circulation for approval.

(7) If rural traders fail because of selfish trading methods, those already active in the trade may continue their involvement. Those who wish to enter the cotton trade will be authorized to do so after they have first notified their village officials and promised to adhere to the regulations for the cotton trade.[72]

As is obvious from this document from Shimokosaka village, the village cotton traders interpreted the 1854 regulations for the cotton trade in their own favor. They carefully stated the trade rights which they had won as the result of the 1823 dispute, illustrated the limitations of the revised trade associations relative to this settlement, and then clearly stated their intention to protect their rights in the Kinai cotton trade.

This document is a remarkable example of the shrewdness of the rural cotton traders in the 1850s. Not only could they take a clear stand in defense of their rights in the Kinai cotton trade, but they were able to use sophisticated claims to legal precedent to justify and support their position. They clearly stated their independence from the Ōsaka *wataya nakama* and their determination to protect this independence. From the perspective of the village cotton merchants, the reestablishment of the Ōsaka *wataya nakama* in no way restricted their rights in the Kinai cotton trade. The jurisdiction of the *wataya nakama* was limited to Ōsaka and seventeen associated villages. Any attempt to expand this area to include other villages was both illegal and unacceptable. The restoration of *nakama kumiai* in 1851 would in no way interfere with the marketing rights which they had won in a struggle which had begun in the late eighteenth century and culminated in the 1007-village dispute of 1823.

Similar efforts to preserve rural trading rights can be seen in the opposition to efforts by the Sakai cotton cloth *tonya nakama* to impose restraints on the Izumi cloth trade in the 1860s. Although some restrictions on white cotton cloth sales appear to have been imposed, village opposition was vigorous and succeeded in preserving an unrestricted trade in striped cloth, as well as undermining the restrictions on trading white cotton cloth in Izumi.[73]

Likewise, in Kuboji village near Yao, in 1867 there were four houses of cotton *nakagai*, two yarn dyers, and twenty-three seed and ginned cotton merchants, all independent of ties with *nakama* in the cotton trade. Each of these village traders was able to participate freely in the cotton trade in the off-season and spend half his time as a cotton merchant and the other half as a farmer in Kuboji.[74]

SUMMARY

It is clear that despite the reestablishment of the urban *nakama* in the cotton trade, urban merchant domination had been replaced by a more open and flexible marketing system in which rural merchants played an independent role. The domination of licensed merchants from Ōsaka and Sakai had been broken and replaced by a proliferation of small-scale rural trading groups and independent cotton traders. The focus of trade was no longer in the cities. Direct sales and shipment by rural traders were commonplace and the government no longer attempted to protect the interests of the urban merchant associations with any conviction. While efforts to reassert urban merchant control continued, as in the example of the Ōsaka *wataya nakama*, they were met with organized rural opposition. In the face of organized opposition from rural merchants and cotton growers the government was unwilling to force the issue. The combination of increased sophistication on the part of rural organizers and increased involvement in commercial agriculture and marketing by cultivators nullified the efforts of urban merchants in the Kinai region to reimpose controls on the cotton trade. While they continued their involvement into the Meiji period, it was not as a dominating force but rather as one of the systems for marketing cotton in the Kinai region.

In retrospect, the last hundred years of the Tokugawa period can be viewed as an interval in which cotton processing technology spread from the cities and towns of Kinai into the villages, and rural cotton traders and cotton growers united to assert their interests and enhance their role in the Kinai cotton trade. While a rearguard effort to protect the interests and trade rights of the urban merchant associations was continued in cooperation with the government, significant changes had occurred in the Kinai cotton trade and the government was increasingly aware of their implications. It was no longer realistic to support the interests of urban merchants in the face of widespread discontent among cotton cultivators and rural traders. New trade patterns, new kinds of rural merchant associations, and new aspirations on the part of the cultivators had dramatically transformed the Kinai cotton trade. While older groups were displaced, rather than dissolved, by these changes, there is no question that the role of the urban cotton merchants in the 1860s was a far cry from their position in the 1770s. This is but one aspect of the kinds of social changes which were taking place in Tokugawa Japan as the distinctions between occupational classes and between the aspirations of urban and rural residents were questioned and subjected to increased pressure for modifications. Many of these changes have been touched on in our discussion of the Kinai cotton trade.

8   Conclusions

ŌSAKA AND THE KINAI COTTON TRADE

Our examination of the Ōsaka and Kinai cotton trade has revealed a series of changes in the marketing structure and in the organization of trade during the course of the Tokugawa period. These changes reflected shifts in the functional position occupied by the various institutions engaged in the cotton trade, as well as a modification of the interaction between them and the Ōsaka city government, the regional representative of the Tokugawa *bakufu*. The process of change reflected in the cotton trade illustrates the increase in functional differentiation within the commercial sector of Tokugawa Japan. As trade proliferated, local marketing activities were increasingly integrated into a national network of commercial enterprise. Included in this process was the development of specialized institutions, defined by the specific role they played in the productive or marketing process. Associated with this development was the appearance of foci of commercial activity in the castle towns of the daimyo, in the major cities controlled by the Tokugawa *bakufu*, and gradually in rural towns and villages as well.

Ōsaka and Edo, which together with Kyōto were the largest cities in Tokugawa Japan, were points of concentration and, hence, of change in the commercial sector. Ōsaka in particular, located in the most advanced productive region of the country, tended to take the lead in adapting to pressures toward economic change. Developments in Ōsaka in many instances were mirrored in Edo at a somewhat later date as conditions in the commercial sector of the Edo region attained levels of differentiation which had been reached earlier in Ōsaka and the Kinai region.

The last half of the seventeenth century in Ōsaka saw the first governmental authorization of merchant institutions in the cotton trade. During the 1660s and 1670s, the Ōsaka city government gave official sanction to the cotton *tonya nakama*, the cotton shipping *nakama*, and the *wataya nakama*. Each of these associations was a functioning merchant group at the time of authorization. Official sanction added legitimacy to the *nakama* and also brought commercial prerogatives and boundaries of authority backed by political as well as economic supports. Authorization reflected a complementary desire on the part of the *bakufu* to limit the proliferation of commercial institutions, to regulate those already formed, and to facilitate the

174

channeling of agricultural products to the cities where the ruling samurai class was concentrated.

Sanctions granted to commercial institutions during this period worked to institutionalize the relationship between the cotton trade and the Ōsaka city government. While this represented a shift in *bakufu* policy towards trade, it was an effort to utilize established forms of commercial organization – the cotton *nakama* – for the realization of government objectives not associated with these institutions prior to their reception of official status.

Interaction between the Ōsaka cotton *nakama* and the *bakufu* at the time of the Kyōhō reforms in the 1720s and 1730s was an extension of this process. The established Ōsaka *nakama* performed a new function and became the source of statistical information used for new price control policies by the shogunate. From the governmental perspective, commercial institutions could be utilized for implementing economic policy as well as for protecting merchant interests. Thus the functional position of the Ōsaka *nakama* shifted to incorporate needs from the political as well as the commercial sector of Tokugawa society.

The late eighteenth century authorization of *kabu nakama* in the cotton trade reflected changes which were occurring in the commercial life of the Kinai region. Institutionalized patterns of commercial activity were altered in an effort to reinforce the associations' position in the Ōsaka cotton trade. This can be viewed as a regressive development in economic terms as it reinforced institutions which had begun to lose their predominant position as the result of economic change. From the governmental perspective, however, *kabu nakama* authorization in the late eighteenth century illustrated the ability of the *kabu nakama* to be used for new ends. They were reinforced to serve as a bulwark against economic changes in the countryside and to protect the functional position of the urban merchants. Their relationship with the government was altered so that they became a regular source of supplementary revenues. The *kabu nakama* were transformed so that they would better accommodate both government and urban merchant objectives in the late eighteenth century.

The conflicts which appeared during this period between the cotton *tonya nakama* and the *wataya nakama* indicate both the hardening of institutional boundaries and the reluctance of *nakama* members to abide by the limitations imposed on them by institutional association. Further exacerbating these conflicts was the breakdown of supply routes from the producers to the Ōsaka cotton merchants. As involvement in both cotton processing and cotton marketing increased in cotton production areas of Settsu, Kawachi, and Izumi, the producers and rural merchants were less and less willing to conform to the subordinate role assigned to them under the institutionalized structure of the officially sanctioned Ōsaka merchants.

This placed new burdens on the Ōsaka cotton *nakama*, as they were forced to contend with competitive pressures from rural areas which supplied the raw materials for the trade as well as within the city of Ōsaka.

Faced with the necessity of arbitrating between groups within the cotton trade which had overlapping trade rights, the *bakufu* was placed in a difficult position. *Kabu nakama* status was the basis of the special prerogatives claimed by the cotton merchant associations. Each group had been granted government protection. Arbitration of disputes between groups necessitated a careful delineation of the functional role assigned to each.

Confirmation of monopoly privileges placed the political authority of the *bakufu* behind the reinforced *kabu nakama*. The new status acquired by the members of the *kabu nakama* required rigid adherence to the very institutional norms which were proving inadequate to the challenge of increased rural commercialization. The inability of the cotton *nakama* to adjust to changing conditions in the cotton trade in the 1770s and 1780s led them to seek enhanced *kabu nakama* status and accept the consequent hardening of their operational procedures.

In effect, the potential for change by the *nakama* was institutionalized out of existence – or eliminated from the associations and transferred for all practical purposes to the government. Technically, after they accepted *kabu nakama* status, all changes in regulations or procedures had to be cleared by the Ōsaka city government prior to adoption. As institutions, the *kabu nakama* were petrified. However, as is evident in some regulations, individual members, while technically restricted in their patterns of operation, were able to modify their activities so that they conformed more closely to their own needs. Institutionalized rigidity was effective only as long as individual members were willing – or could be induced – to abide by it.

Government efforts to solidify the institutional structure of the cotton trade are revealed in a number of incidents, particularly in the abolition of the cotton futures markets in 1787 and the action of the Ōsaka authorities to limit the operation of the Wakayama *han* cotton buying office. Both actions were consistent with the official policy of regularizing the activities of the *kabu nakama*. Elimination of the futures markets removed a variant form of operation within the cotton trade and worked to channel all activity through the authorized mechanism of the *kabu nakama* system. The case of the Wakayama *han* cotton buying office illustrates how far *bakufu* support could go in reinforcing the monopoly position of the Ōsaka cotton *nakama*. Here was a direct challenge to the authorized pattern of operation of the cotton trade backed by a competing political authority, a Tokugawa collateral *han*. By protecting the established position of the Ōsaka *kabu nakama*, the government demonstrated the benefits of officially backed institutionalized authority. But the question remained as to how effective this authority would prove when faced with a more diffuse, less easily contained threat to the Ōsaka cotton trade in the early nineteenth century.

The reaffirmation of *bakufu* support for the *kabu nakama* during the Kansei reforms of 1787 to 1793 revealed a shift in the capacities which the government emphasized in the approved commercial associations. The existing structure of the cotton trade received the full support of the government, but the rationale for this support changed. During the 1770s and early 1780s, the *kabu nakama* were looked upon both to give stability to the commercial order and as sources of revenue. Under the Kansei reforms, protectionism was combined with an effort to use the *kabu nakama* to implement price controls, although licensing fees were not eliminated. Despite the change in rationale, the net effect of government policy was a more rigid adherence to institutionalized forms of operation. The edicts against wetting ginned cotton and the emphasis on *nakama* regulations during the reform illustrate the attention paid to the maintenance of institutional boundaries and norms. The result was further to reduce the flexibility of the *kabu nakama*, making them less able to deal with changes in production and marketing in the early nineteenth century.

The case of Edoya Yahei illustrates the rigidity of the Ōsaka cotton trade in the face of new economic pressures. Initially, Yahei tried to institutionalize an aspect of the ginned cotton trade which was outside the control of the *kabu nakama* system. Opposition to his proposal within the established trade structure was severe. Consequently, the government denied him permission to construct a ginned cotton market. Shifting his interest to the marketing of seed cotton, in 1810 Yahei was able to secure permission to establish a seed cotton market in Ōsaka. While outside of the *kabu nakama* system, his proposed operation was consistent with institutionalized marketing patterns.

Constrained to operate within the city of Ōsaka and required to conform to established commercial practices, Edoya Yahei's market failed to prosper. Yahei therefore asked the government for permission to open a market in one of the cotton production areas outside the city. Opposition was immediate from the producers, who feared that an authorized market would be given new monopoly rights and would consequently limit their access to the growing number of itinerant cotton buyers. Failing in his attempt to alter his operation better to conform with economic conditions, Yahei in 1820 defaulted on his licensing payments to the *bakufu* and closed his market.

Adherence to established but uneconomic practices resulted in the failure of the Ōsaka seed cotton market. Efforts to introduce new methods were repulsed by the political authority, by the established merchants, and finally by the cotton producers. Yahei's example demonstrates the rigidity of the Ōsaka cotton trade in the early nineteenth century. Innovation within the *kabu nakama* system proved extremely difficult. Years of patient supplication were in vain.

Yet while Yahei was experiencing frustration and failure, the commercial sector was on the threshold of new institutional change. This was brought about not by *kabu nakama* merchants, but rather by a shift in government economic policy. The decision taken in the 1007-village dispute of 1823 was evidence of a new outlook on the part of the *bakufu*. Faced with expanded marketing and processing activities in the villages, *bakufu* policy shifted away from protection of the *kabu nakama* system. The institutionalized structure remained intact, but government enforcement powers no longer stood behind it. The resulting imbalance led to a further weakening of the Ōsaka *kabu nakama* system and increased independence for the Kinai cotton trade. Thus, by the 1830s the Ōsaka cotton *nakama* had lost their preferred position within the commercial order and were forced to compete with new patterns of trade outside of their control. Protectionism had been replaced by a policy of official noninterference. Faced with the loss of legal support outside the city, the Ōsaka cotton *nakama* were required to rely on economic power to preserve their position in the cotton trade in the Kinai region. The result was an increase in rural cotton trading and a decline in the volume of cotton marketed through Ōsaka.

The cotton *nakama* proved unable to maintain their position in the Ōsaka cotton trade after the loss of government protection. Competition came not only from cotton cultivators and merchants outside the city, but also from some of the cotton producing *han*, for example Himeji *han*. New trade routes which by-passed Ōsaka had already developed. New patterns of distribution which failed to include the *kabu nakama* merchants were thriving. This failure of the *kabu nakama* had a further effect on government thinking, for it brought into question the desirability of their continued existence. As the *kabu nakama* lost their dominant position in the cotton trade, they also lost their utility to the *bakufu* as a mechanism for implementing government economic policies, particularly price controls. Given the weakened position occupied by these authorized merchants, it was obvious that reliance on them to control inflated prices would be of little value.

By the 1840s, the government came to the conclusion that the *kabu nakama* system could profitably be abolished. New patterns of operation were shown to be more viable. Institutionalization of eighteenth century forms had proven ineffective in the face of nineteenth century conditions. The intent of the Tempō reforms of 1841 and 1842 was to eliminate the outmoded structure so that new patterns of trade would develop which would be more efficient and which would result in a reduction of prices.

The *bakufu* order abolishing the Ōsaka *kabu nakama* caused considerable initial disruption in the Ōsaka cotton trade. Official status was a major factor in the links between Ōsaka cotton merchants and their shippers, creditors, and colleagues in Edo. Loss of *kabu nakama* status interrupted their relations with all of these groups. However, once the initial impact of the reforms was dissipated, the Ōsaka cotton traders utilized traditional forms of commercial organization to reconstruct their marketing facilities, shipping systems, and sources of credit. Abolition of the *kabu nakama* as legal entities did not result in the abolition of established forms of commercial organization. The cotton *nakama* were active in the Ōsaka cotton trade prior to their reception of official status, and they continued to engage in trade after their loss of government authorization in the Tempō reforms.

The seventeenth and eighteenth century experience of the Ōsaka cotton merchants must be kept in mind for any analysis of the impact of the Tempō reforms. Before and after the receipt of official status, the primary support of the Ōsaka cotton *nakama* was their ability to function effectively in the marketplace. Even after their loss of government support following the decision in the 1823 dispute, the Ōsaka cotton *nakama* continued to occupy an important position in the Kinai cotton trade. They no longer held monopoly powers or dominated the marketing of cotton in the Kinai region, but they maintained a major role in trade nevertheless. Cotton marketed via Ōsaka declined in volume, but it was by no means an insignificant portion of the Kinai cotton trade. The cotton trade was distributed throughout the Kinai region, but Ōsaka merchants preserved a share for themselves.

Consequently, the abolition of *kabu nakama* was an official act which failed to alter the form of the Ōsaka cotton trade. As is clear from the ease with which the *nakama* were reconstructed after 1851, they had not disappeared and had continued to function as private, unauthorized trade associations. The experience of the Ōsaka cotton *nakama* was different from that of other groups, particularly those in Edo. Having lost a major portion of their monopoly power in 1823, they suffered less than many other groups by the abolition order. Rural competition was more advanced in the Kinai region than elsewhere, so the loss of official status meant less in terms of increased competition than was the case in Edo and the Kantō region. The loss of status for the Ōsaka cotton *nakama* was a continuous process which began in the first quarter of the nineteenth century. While the decision in the 1823 dispute and the abolition of *kabu nakama* in 1841–2 accelerated this process, they did not alter its direction.

The reconstruction of the *nakama* as *nakama kumiai* after 1851 was a regressive attempt to reassert urban merchant control over commercial activity. The government and the urban merchants joined in an effort to stretch the institutionalized commercial system in the cities to incorporate rural merchants and rural processors. As is evident in the opposition to this process in the Kinai cotton trade, the effort was unsuccessful. Efforts to reestablish the dominance of the Ōsaka cotton merchants in the Kinai region went against tendencies which had been in operation since the late eighteenth century. Government policy objectives notwithstanding, the Kinai cotton traders and cotton processors were unwilling to be subjected to outside controls. Their successful opposition to the government effort illustrates the difficulties faced by the *bakufu* and the effectiveness of new forms of social and economic organization in the countryside.

In the Kinai region surrounding Ōsaka, the diffusion of cotton cultivation and cotton processing during the Tokugawa period were major factors in the transition to commercial agricultural production. Demand for cotton increased in the early Tokugawa period and, as output expanded and cotton became the primary fiber utilized in Japanese textile production, the incentives for cotton cultivation multiplied. Land utilization patterns in Settsu, Kawachi, and Izumi were transformed and cotton became a major crop in areas with sandy soils and limited water resources. High output and high profit rates for cotton encouraged the replacement of less profitable crops, even though the risks of cotton cultivation were extreme and the labor and fertilizer inputs more costly than those for rice and other crops. Many cultivators, once involved in cotton cultivation, were caught in a cycle of indebtedness to fertilizer merchants or to large-scale cotton buyers which made continued cotton cultivation imperative. Years of low cotton yields resulted in debts which could best be paid off by the profits promised by higher yields in subsequent years. Small-scale cultivators, with little margin for experimentation, could not afford to diversify their crops and were at the mercy of the weather, the fertilizer merchants, and the cotton buyers.

Cotton processing offered a source of supplementary income to many farm families. As processing technology diffused into Kinai villages cotton ginning, carding, spinning, and weaving became regular means for enhancing farm family income. This enabled many cultivators to increase the returns from cotton cultivation and offered others a source of non-agricultural employment in the towns and villages of the Kinai region. Specialization in some villages resulted in the development of specific processing techniques, for example ginning or weaving. This led to rural demand for unprocessed and partially processed goods, and inter-village trade in seed cotton, ginned cotton, and yarn increased as a consequence. The expansion of village-level processing brought the villagers into conflict with the Ōsaka *wataya nakama*, which objected to the growth of competitive sources of processed cotton in the villages of Settsu, Kawachi, and Izumi. Efforts to expand *nakama* control over processing were only partially effective, however, and rural output of processed cotton increased well into the nineteenth century.

The diffusion of processing technology was complemented by the expansion of rural trade. Inter-village trade in both seed cotton and processed cotton goods was conducted by village traders. Gradually they expanded their involvement from the local to the regional level and began to compete actively with the Ōsaka cotton *nakama*. Many of the traders were farmers who engaged in trade as a form of seasonal by-employment. Others were increasingly drawn into full-time commercial activity as a form of non-agricultural rural employment. Both groups offered significant competition to the institutionalized marketing system controlled by the Ōsaka *kabu nakama*. The expansion of rural trade in the late eighteenth century led to the reinforcement of the Ōsaka cotton *nakama*. New forms of government support were sought by the urban merchants in the face of competitive marketing systems for cotton which were developing throughout the Kinai region. While temporarily effective in retarding the expansion of rural trade, the invigorated *kabu nakama* were incapable of eliminating it entirely.

Organized rural opposition to the monopoly rights of the Ōsaka merchants was evident in the latter half of the eighteenth century in the reaction against futures markets and the expansion of *kabu nakama* jurisdiction into Settsu and Kawachi. Both developments threatened local marketing patterns and attempted to limit the role of village merchants and cotton cultivators in the Kinai cotton trade. This opposition continued into the nineteenth century and increased in scale and intensity. The successful pursuit of the 1823 suit against the Ōsaka cotton *tonya nakama* illustrates the organizational capacities of the rural complainants and their ability to conduct a successful class-action suit against the restrictive monopoly powers of the Ōsaka merchants. Village leaders, in the form of village officials, large land holders, and rural merchants, coordinated the effort in which 1007 villages united to present their case to the Tokugawa *bakufu*. The scale of the complaint and the intensity of the reaction against urban merchant controls was sufficient to make the government back away from its protection of the Ōsaka cotton *nakama* and authorize the continued expansion of the rural cotton trade in Settsu and Kawachi.

The 1823 dispute was a milestone in the transition from an urban-dominated marketing system to a multi-faceted distribution and processing network for cotton in the Kinai region. Following the 1823 decision, shipments of cotton to the Ōsaka market declined, rural merchant groups asserted themselves with new confidence, and the dominant role of the Ōsaka cotton *nakama* was further undermined. By 1841 and the abolition of the *kabu nakama* in the Tempō reforms, the Ōsaka cotton *nakama* were sufficiently reduced in authority that the elimination of official status merely accelerated the process of decline. The loss of official authorization did not result in their dismemberment or disappearance, but rather completed the process by which the government withdrew its support of the institutionalized marketing system in the Ōsaka cotton trade.

From the rural perspective the abolition of *kabu nakama* continued the tendencies in operation since the decision in the 1823 dispute. Rural trade continued as before. Efforts to lower prices, commission rates, and shipping costs may have had a short-term impact, but they failed to transform the operation of the Kinai cotton trade. While they had a far more severe impact in Edo and the Kantō region, the impact of the Tempō reforms on the Kinai cotton trade was marginal at best. The effort to reconstruct the *kabu nakama* system in slightly modified form after 1851 also failed to alter the nature of rural trade significantly. Rural opposition to expansion of the *kabu nakama* into Settsu, Kawachi, and Izumi served to restrict their jurisdiction to Ōsaka and specific nearby villages. The gains won in 1823 and emphasized in the abolition of the *kabu nakama* in 1841 and 1842 were not lost to the rural merchants after 1851. Neither the rural marketing system for cotton, nor the *han* monopolies, were suppressed by the reform effort. Both continued to be major elements in the commercial life of the Kinai region until the end of the Tokugawa period. The efforts of the *bakufu* and the Ōsaka *kabu nakama* notwithstanding, the Kinai cotton trade was transformed from an urban-dominated restrictive marketing network into a complex of local patterns of distribution integrated into a national system of commodity marketing.

GOVERNMENT POLICY AND INSTITUTIONAL CHANGE

One aspect of the process of institutional change explored in this study deserves further treatment. This is the relationship between government policy and changes in the commercial sector. Most interpretations of the relationship between government and merchants during the Tokugawa period have placed the emphasis on the *bakufu* as creating the environment for commercial activity.[1] Yet this study has demonstrated that more than a one-sided relationship existed. On closer examination it appears that the relationship between the government and the merchants was more of a symbiosis in which cycles of mutual concordance of interest, moving at different speeds, worked to support or inhibit the growth of institutional norms. Government interest in commercial regulation was not always the primary motive force in institutionalization. Government interest often differed from that of the merchants, even when it was expressed in the same institutional structure.

This is evident from the first official recognition of the Ōsaka cotton traders in the late seventeenth century. The impetus for institutional formation came from the cotton traders, not the government. The addition of official status was a means of utilizing extant merchant groups for government objectives. The initiative for this shift in the cotton trade came from the government. While at variance with overall Tokugawa economic policies, specific merchant institutions were singled out for special recognition and monopoly privileges. In this sense, institutional change was promoted by government action, but the institutions themselves had preceded the appearance of official interest.

What brought about this change in official policy? To begin with, it was apparent that the development of commerce was an essential requirement for satisfying the consumption and service needs of the castle towns. In the case of the cotton trade, government recognition introduced a means of government control. It kept deliveries of cotton goods to the cities at a maximum and restricted the circulation of these goods in the countryside. The *kabu nakama* system thus became the backbone of *bakufu* policy for supplying the cities and the samurai class.

The Kyōhō reforms of the 1720s resulted in a further shift in government expectations from the *kabu nakama* system. The merchant associations were required to collect price statistics and import and export data for the Ōsaka market. Government price control policies required that the *kabu nakama* system be modified to provide the *bakufu* with statistical data. Government initiative strengthened the ties with the Ōsaka merchant associations and altered the nature of their institutional status. In Edo, a *kabu nakama* system was institutionalized as a means of controlling trade and regulating prices. Here as well, the initiative came from the government, but even in Edo many of the authorized merchant associations existed prior to the change in *bakufu* commercial policy. Government recognition enhanced their status and confirmed their position in the commercial community.

The authorization of *kabu nakama* in Ōsaka during the 1770s and early 1780s illustrates a change in the nature of the relationship between the *bakufu* and the merchants. Here the initiative for augmented institutional status came from the merchants, rather than the *bakufu*. The merchants requested *kabu nakama* designation as a means of reinforcing their economic position. In this case, the strengthening of ties between the government and the merchant associations was requested by the merchant community, rather than imposed from without by the *bakufu*.

There remain a number of questions about this new round of *kabu nakama* authorizations, however. First of all, since many of the groups authorized in the 1770s had received *kabu nakama* status in the late seventeenth century, why was it necessary to make a further request to the government? What in fact was the difference between the *kabu nakama* status granted in the 1660s and that granted in the 1770s? Regularization of commercial activities was still emphasized, but a new element of using the merchants as a source of regular revenue was introduced. Prior to the 1770s there is no record of regular licensing payments by merchant associations to the *bakufu*. There were a variety of service payments which may have been commuted for cash, but there does not appear to have been anything comparable to the licensing fees paid in the 1770s. In this period, then, the government added the motive of profit.

But this does not answer the question why the merchants desired the reaffirmation of their commercial prerogatives and were willing to pay licensing fees for government support. This desire resulted from the expansion of rural trade and processing activities as well as disputes which had arisen between groups within the Ōsaka merchant community. The new *kabu nakama* included a commitment from the *bakufu* to use its authority to protect their monopoly rights from outside sources of competition. From the merchant point of view, two new elements were introduced by the receipt of *kabu nakama* status in this period. First of all, *nakama* regulations clarified the rights of the merchant groups operating within the cotton trade. Trade rights and jurisdictions were clearly defined in the charters granting *kabu nakama* status. Second, a new mechanism for the adjudication of disputes between merchants groups was established by *kabu nakama* confirmation. Disputes referred to the Ōsaka city government could now be settled on the basis of the rights specifically granted in the new articles of incorporation, and the government assumed the responsibility of upholding the commercial prerogatives it authorized.

The result of the second round of *kabu nakama* authorization in the 1770s was to intensify the contact between the *bakufu* and the merchant associations. While merchant initiative appears to have brought about this broadening of government involvement, it is likely that interest was expressed on both sides. 'Requesting' *kabu nakama* status may well have been a convenient means of satisfying the interests of both parties. In its late eighteenth century format, then, the *kabu nakama* structure took on new characteristics suited to satisfy the needs of both the *bakufu* and the Ōsaka merchants. For the merchants this included increased policing of the cotton trade to prevent incursions by outsiders. From the government perspective the development of new revenue sources in the form of licensing fees paid by the *nakama* was of primary concern. Each side stood to improve its position by the bargain.

If the actions of the 1770s demonstrated a dynamic relationship between the government and the merchant community, the *bakufu*'s action during the Kansei reform showed the growing rigidity of this relationship. The emphasis on merchant monopolies as a source of revenue was largely replaced by a concern with proper behavior and adherence to the established monopoly system. Government action, as illustrated in the abolition of the cotton futures markets, came out more on the regressive side. Tradition, in the form of policies implemented in the 1720s, was used in the late eighteenth century to justify actions which turned away from innovation and toward a hardening of the official conception of economic activity.

Protection and support for authorized merchant institutions became a major element in Tokugawa economic policy in the late eighteenth century. Protectionism induced the government to involve itself in disputes which erupted within the established merchant order. Government decisions, as in the case of the cotton shipping *nakama* dispute, reveal a concern for rigid adherence to established conventions. In cases where violations of conventions occurred, the government was willing to apply official pressure to ensure conformity. At this stage of activity, then, the government was taking the initiative – but largely in a negative manner.

This is evident in the government response to the market proposals of Edoya Yahei. Innovations, efforts to accommodate developing pressures for institutional variants outside the *kabu nakama* system, were an unwelcome incursion into commercial activity. The official reaction indicated that there was no room within the institutionalized structure for new approaches to cotton marketing. Only by modifying his proposals, so that they conformed to the established system within the Ōsaka cotton trade, was Yahei able to win acceptance for his market.

Despite the reluctance of the government to sanction economic change in the cotton trade, pressures from the cotton cultivators and rural merchants were becoming increasingly ebullient. The 1007-village dispute of 1823 resulted in a major shift in government policy toward the cotton trade, and the issues involved went to the very heart of Tokugawa economic policy. By sanctioning the marketing and shipping activities of the cultivators and rural merchants, the government pulled back from its protectionist stance. Official support of the *kabu nakama* system was replaced by a policy of official nonintervention in the cotton trade.

Once again the ability of the government to react directly to economic pressures was demonstrated. Recognizing the difficulty of continued protection for the *kabu nakama* system in the cotton trade, the government absolved itself of further responsibility. The pressures for change came from outside the institutionalized marketing system. By removing its support, the government was able to cut its losses and leave the *kabu nakama* to fend for themselves.

Official recognition of the declining influence of the Ōsaka cotton merchants is evident in the Abe report of 1842. The weakness of the *kabu nakama* system was amply demonstrated. Some new approach to the problems of commercial expansion was required. The question was where to begin. Two precedents were readily available. One was a further modification of the *kabu nakama* system. The other was a return to the trade policies which had characterized the first years of Tokugawa rule. The only other possibility was to attempt a radically new approach to the problems of commercial expansion. There is little evidence that this last possibility was contemplated or that *bakufu* policy makers were sufficiently aware of the magnitude of the problem or technically able to deal with it effectively. The abolition of the *kabu nakama* during the Tempō reforms was an ineffective attempt to eliminate an outmoded institutional structure and replace it with a poorly defined system of unrestricted trade.

The failure of the economic polices included in the Tempō reforms illustrated the inapplicability of seventeenth century economic concepts to nineteenth century economic problems. The failure of the reform policies only led to a reassertion of traditional institutional forms. The effort to reconstruct the *kabu nakama* in the 1850s illustrated their continued vitality as well as the inability of the government to come up with a viable alternative.

The failure of the Tokugawa *bakufu* to deal with economic change in the nineteenth century points out the limited nature of Tokugawa authority. Trade was no longer the preserve of the urban merchants in Ōsaka and Edo. Awareness of this fact did not enable the government to deal with it effectively. The localization of Tokugawa authority to directly administered *bakufu* territory severely restricted the ability of the shogunate to deal with economic problems of national magnitude. The best intentions of the government notwithstanding, it was doomed to failure until the establishment of a central political authority with the ability to make national policies.

As suggested above, in most cases it was commercial activity itself which was the leading force in policy shifts made by the *bakufu*. Previous studies suggest that *bakufu* policy was the source of modifications in the institutional structure of the Ōsaka commercial community. This study of Ōsaka and the Kinai cotton trade indicates that the opposite was generally the case. Functionally, the *bakufu* was in a position to change the uses to which merchant groups were put, but in general it was the commercial community and the economic forces generated by it, not the government, which were the deciding factors in the structure of these associations.

The timing for policy changes was dictated by the shogunate, but in almost all cases they utilized existing merchant organizations. Changing the orientation of merchant groups so that they conformed better with government expectations did not constitute government direction of change within the commercial community. It was the merchants who determined the groupings which were to their advantage, not the government. It was the merchants who through their own initiative established clusters within the commercial community, who joined together for the protection of mutual interests, and who by the late eighteenth century were turning to the government for additional protection for their monopoly rights. Innovations which influenced the nature of the relationship between the merchant community and the Tokugawa shogunate did at times emanate from the *bakufu*, but in general the majority of the institutional changes which occurred in the Ōsaka cotton trade were the result of merchant initiative or economic pressures, not government encouragement.

Yet despite the source of institutional change in the Ōsaka cotton trade, the merchants were constrained by their existence in the political framework of the Tokugawa *bakuhan* order. The degree of constraint has, however, been grossly overemphasized. The total power which could potentially be exercised by the shogunate cannot be questioned. Until the very end of the Tokugawa period there was little indication that the *bakufu* was in less than an unassailable position of political superiority. There is, however, considerable evidence that this authority was applied sparingly, and that the possession of authority did not translate into an effective means of control.

The Ōsaka cotton trade was molded more by internal developments and economic forces than by government action. The government, to be sure, retained an active interest in the commercial sector. But dependence on merchants to supply consumer goods to the major cities reduced the ability of the shogunate to regulate their activities. There is considerable question as to how much control the government felt was desirable. As long as the system worked efficiently, there was little need for government interference. When necessary, the *bakufu* was able to utilize the merchant associations for its own purposes. Political power was applied only when specific policy objectives required its employment. Otherwise, the merchants were left largely to their own devices.

Unchallenged authority was possessed by the Tokugawa shogunate. The extent to which this authority was exercised was, however, extremely limited. As is evident in the process of institutional change in Ōsaka and the Kinai cotton trade, the shogunate was generally placed in a secondary position. The notion of the all-inclusive, repressive authority of the Tokugawa *bakufu* has been stressed excessively by many historians of Japan, not only in the analysis of Tokugawa political history, but in economic and social history as well. At moments of crisis, the shogunate was capable of exercising preponderant power, but this should not be taken as evidence that the threat of such power was at all times hanging over Tokugawa society. The existence of power did not necessarily result in an ability to use it or an interest in its application.

The Kinai cotton trade offers a case study of the process of economic institutional change in Tokugawa Japan. The results of this study provide a new interpretation of the nature of commercial activity during the Tokugawa period. Institutional innovation is shown to have generally originated in the merchant sector. Subsequent shifts in government economic policy tended to utilize merchant institutions for the realization of official policy objectives. The assumed dominance of the shogunate in economic activity is challenged, as the government is shown to have been dependent upon the realities of the commercial sector for the direction of its policies. Emerging from this analysis is a more comprehensive and viable picture of commercial activity and economic change in early modern Japan.

IMPLICATIONS FOR THE FUTURE

The opening of Japan to foreign trade after 1858 resulted in the importation of foreign textiles and foreign yarns and a decline in the demand for domestic cotton yarns and handwoven cotton textiles. The growth of the machine textile industry during the Meiji period was dependent on the availability of low-cost, high quality cotton and cotton yarns, and domestic production was inferior to and more costly than imported goods. As a consequence, cotton cultivation in Settsu, Kawachi, and Izumi declined rapidly in the Meiji period and many cotton cultivators shifted to rapeseed and vegetable production to satisfy the increase in demand from major urban centers. Their experience in commercial agricultural production during the Tokugawa period enabled them to make the transition from cotton to other commercial crops and oriented them to the demand cycle of a market economy.

The expansion of processing and rural trade as forms of farm family by-employment was not restricted to the Kinai region, but was characteristic of all major regions of Japan.[2] The result was the development of a rural labor force which was skilled in processing and marketing techniques as well as those required for agricultural production. Tokugawa period by-employment and rural trade provided a backlog of cottage industrial and organizational experience which could be translated into skills necessary for a modern industrial labor force and modern economic growth. The national marketing mechanism for commodities which developed in the Tokugawa period became the backbone of the traditional sector of the modern Japanese economy. With experience in long distance trade, credit systems, and commercial organization, merchants in the Meiji period were able to adapt readily to modern systems of transportation, banking, and commodity marketing.

The organizational experience of participants in the Kinai cotton trade prepared them for involvement in new forms of social organization during the Meiji period. All cultivators were integrated into village groups and experienced in various forms of government regulation, taxation, and service requirements. When they were integrated into a nation in the Meiji period and taxation and service requirements were administered by a national government, it was not an abrupt or unprecedented transition. Many of the administrators were Tokugawa period carry-overs, and their identification with a national rather than a local governing authority made little difference. Similarly, a precedent existed for government regulation of commerce and industry, making this aspect of the Meiji experience more easily accepted by the Japanese. Rural involvement in organized opposition to the Ōsaka merchant monopolies prepared the Kinai cotton cultivators and rural merchants for political participation in the Meiji period. Their capacity to be mobilized and the availability of local leadership skills had been demonstrated by the scale of the disputes in the cotton trade. To characterize them as 'docile peasantry' who had no skills in organized opposition is to overlook this aspect of the expansion of commercial agricultural production and rural trade.

The growth of major urban centers and the associated demand for consumer goods during the Tokugawa period simulated the expansion of commercial agricultural production and handicraft industry. This served to orient cultivators to market demands, to acquaint them with the benefits of specialized cropping patterns, and to involve them in the marketing and processing of their crops. The particition of cultivators and rural merchants in a national system of commodity distribution integrated them into a national market. While for many this was limited to contact with local merchants and never visualized in a broader context, for others the expansion of rural trade offered a sense of participation in a regional or national environment. The growth of a monetized economy and of demands for fertilizers and tools which were not locally produced forced an awareness of integration into a larger geographical unit. As rural income increased and standards of living improved – and there are indications that both occurred for many households in the Kinai region – farm families were exposed to goods from other regions, various forms of urban culture, and other manifestations of the broader society as a whole.

The indications of social and economic change evident in this study of Ōsaka and the Kinai cotton trade illustrate the institutional dynamics of Tokugawa society. Although viewed by many as a repressive, feudalistic period, we find in the years from 1600 to 1868 indications of a broad-based social transformation. The diffusion of commercial agriculture, processing techniques, and marketing involvement into Kinai villages dramatically altered the life style of the cotton cultivators. Similar changes are evident in other regions where variant forms of commercial agriculture and processing developed. For some, participation in commercial agriculture led to downward mobility, loss of family landholdings, lowered standards of living, and dependence on non-agricultural forms of employment for survival. For others, agricultural income was supplemented by new sources of revenue from by-employment and standards of living improved. As a consequence, status within the village became increasingly dependent on economic rather than social factors and the distinctions between rich and poor were defined in new, more dramatic fashion. The increase in tenancy which resulted in many villages continued into the Meiji period and was characteristic of Japanese agriculture until the land reform following Japan's defeat in the Pacific War.

The process of economic and social change discussed above contributed to the Japanese potential for modern economic growth. When combined with education and literacy skills, it incorporated many of the elements which coalesced as the foundation for industrial development and the establishment of modern forms of social organization. To describe the modern experience of Japan as 'miraculous' – a description which is still current in popular accounts – is to overlook the realities of the Japanese case.

Notes

I. INTRODUCTION

1. *Journal of Economic History*, XXXI, 1 (March 1971), pp. 199–207.

2. Locust Valley, N.Y., 1958.

3. See for example E. Sydney Crawcour, 'Changes in Japanese Commerce in the Tokugawa Period,' *Journal of Asian Studies*, XXII, 4 (August 1963), pp. 387–400, and 'The Development of a Credit System in Seventeenth-Century Japan,' *Journal of Economic History*, XXI, 3 (September 1961), pp. 342–60. Crawcour and Kozo Yamamura, 'The Tokugawa Monetary System: 1787–1868,' *Economic Development and Cultural Change*, vol. 18, no. 4, part 1 (July 1970), pp. 489–518. Yamamura, 'The Increasing Poverty of the Samurai in Tokugawa Japan, 1600–1868,' *Journal of Economic History*, XXXI, 2 (June 1971), pp. 378–406.

4. 'A Quiet Transformation in Tokugawa Economic History,' *Journal of Asian Studies*, XXX, 2 (February 1971), pp. 373–84.

5. Stanford, Cal., 1959.

6. Thomas C. Smith, 'The Japanese Village in the Seventeenth Century' and 'The Land Tax in the Tokugawa Period' in John Whitney Hall and Marius B. Jansen (eds.), *Studies in the Institutional History of Early Modern Japan* (Princeton, 1968), pp. 263–82, 283–99; 'Farm Family By-employments in Preindustrial Japan,' *Journal of Economic History*, XXIX, 4 (December 1969), pp. 687–715.

7. William Jones Chambliss, *Chiaraijima Village: Land Tenure, Taxation, and Local Trade*, 1818–1884 (Tucson, Ariz., 1965); Chie Nakane, *Kinship and Economic Organization in Rural Japan* (New York, 1967); Harumi Befu, 'Village Autonomy and Articulation with the State' in Hall and Jansen (eds.), pp. 169–88; and Susan B. Hanley, 'Toward an Analysis of Demographic and Economic Change in Tokugawa Japan: A Village Study,' *Journal of Asian Studies*, XXXI, 3 (May 1972), pp. 515–37.

8. (Glencoe, Ill., 1961), pp. 58–79.

9. (Cambridge, Mass., 1964), chapters 1–3.

10. In William W. Lockwood (ed.), *The State and Economic Enterprise in Japan* (Princeton, 1965), pp. 17–44.

11. For background on institutional and social change see S. N. Eisenstadt, 'Institutionalization and Change,' *American Sociological Review*, 29, 2 (April 1964), pp. 235–47, and his *Essays on Comparative Institutions* (New York, 1965); and Robert Nisbet, *Social Change and History* (New York, 1969).

12. See Paul Yachita Tsuchihashi, *Japanese Chronological Tables* (Tōkyō: Sophia University Press, 1952).

2. TOKUGAWA COMMERCE: 1600–1720

1. For a more detailed discussion see Hall, 'The Nature of Traditional Society: Japan' in Robert E. Ward and Dankwart A. Rustow (eds.), *Political Modernization in Japan and Turkey* (Princeton, 1964), pp. 14–41.

2. For the most complete discussion of this system in English see Toshio G. Tsukahira, *Feudal Control in Tokugawa Japan: The Sankin Kōtai System* (Cambridge, Mass., 1966).

3. Miyamoto Mataji, *Ōsaka* [Ōsaka] (Tōkyō, 1957), pp. 1–2.

4. Royal Jules Wald, 'The Development of Ōsaka during the Sixteenth Century' (unpublished M.A. thesis, University of California at Berkeley, 1947), pp. 11–25.

5. Hall, *Government and Local Power in Japan, 500 to 1700: A Study Based on Bizen Province* (Princeton, 1966), p. 293. Miyamoto, *Ōsaka*, p. 3.

6. One *koku* equals approximately five bushels.

7. Yasuoka Shigeaki, 'Edo chūki no Ōsaka ni okeru torihiki soshiki' [The trade structure of Ōsaka during the mid-Edo period], part 1, *Dōshisha shōgaku*, 16, 3 (November 1964), p. 294. (Cited hereafter as 'Torihiki soshiki,' 1.)

8. Wakita Osamu, *Kinsei hōken shakai no keizai kōzō* [The economic structure of feudal society in the early modern period] (Tōkyō, 1963), pp. 44–51.

9. Miyamoto, *Ōsaka*, p. 5.

10. Yasuoka, 'Torihiki soshiki,' 1, pp. 294–6.

11. Yasuoka, 'Torihiki soshiki,' 1, pp. 297–8.

12. Kōda Shigetomo, *Edo to Ōsaka* [Edo and Ōsaka], revised edition (Tōkyō, 1942), p. 26.

13. Yasuoka, 'Torihiki soshiki,' 1, p. 298.

14. Yasuoka, 'Torihiki soshiki,' 1, pp. 298–9.

15. Miyamoto, *Ōsaka*, pp. 13–18.

16. Nakai Nobuhiko, *Bakuhan shakai to shōhin ryūtsū* [*Bakuhan* society and commodity marketing] (Tōkyō, 1961), pp. 82–3. (Cited hereafter as *Shōhin ryūtsū*.)

17. Toyoda Takeshi, *Nihon no hōken toshi* [Japanese feudal cities] (Tōkyō, 1952, 1964), pp. 131–2.

18. Nakai, *Shōhin ryūtsū*, p. 90.

19. Nakai 'Kinsei toshi no hatten' [The development of cities in the early modern period], *Iwanami kōza Nihon rekishi* [Iwanami series on Japanese history], vol. 11 or *Kinsei* 3 (Tōkyō, 1963), p. 39. (Cited hereafter as 'Toshi.') Hall, 'The Castle Town and Japan's Modern Urbanization' in Hall and Jansen (eds.), pp. 176–9.

20. Crawcour, 'The Development of a Credit System in Seventeenth-Century Japan,' pp. 342–3. (Cited hereafter as 'Credit.') Nakai, 'Toshi,' p. 42.

21. Nakai, 'Toshi,' p. 39.

22. Hall, 'Castle Town,' pp. 179–80.

23. Wakita, pp. 44, 51–2.

24. Wakita, p. 34.

25. Hall, *Government and Local Power in Japan*, p. 285.

26. *Tokugawa jidai shōgyō sōsho* [Tokugawa period commercial series] (Tōkyō, 1965), II, p. 9. Crawcour, 'Credit,' p. 344.

27. See for example Sheldon, *Rise of the Merchant Class*, pp. 126, 181.

28. Yasuoka, 'Torihiki soshiki,' I, p. 300.

29. Yasuoka, 'Torihiki soshiki,' I, pp. 300–1.

30. *Ōsaka shishi* [History of the city of Ōsaka], ed. Ōsaka-shi (Ōsaka, 1911–15, 1965), V, p. 386.

31. Hayashi Reiko, 'Edo jimawari keizaiken no seiritsu katei – Kuriwata-abura o chūshin to shite' [The formation of the Edo economic region – With emphasis on ginned cotton and oil] in Ōtsuka Hisao, Andō Yoshio, Matsuda Tomoo, and Sekiguchi Hisashi (eds.), *Shihon shugi no keisei to hatten* [The formation and development of capitalism] (Tōkyō, 1968), p. 257.

32. Takeuchi Makoto, 'Kinsei zenki no shōgyō' [Commerce in the beginning of the early modern period] in Toyoda Takeshi and Kodama Kōta (eds.), *Ryūtsūshi* [History of marketing], I (*Taikei Nihonshi sōsho* [Outline library of Japanese history], 13) (Tōkyō: Yamakawa Shuppansha, 1969), p. 128.

33. Takeuchi, 'Kinsei zenki no shōgyō,' p. 154.

34. Crawcour, 'Kawamura Zuiken: A Seventeenth-Century Entrepreneur,' *Transactions of the Asiatic Society of Japan*, third series, IX (1966), pp. 8–15.

35. Ono Masao, 'Kambun-Empōki no ryūtsū kikō' [Marketing structure in the Kambun-Empō period (1661–81)] in Furushima Toshio (ed.), *Nihon keizaishi taikei* [Outline of Japanese economic history], 3 (Tōkyō, 1965), p. 369. Crawcour, 'Kawamura Zuiken,' pp. 12–13.

36. For additional materials on seagoing transport see Robert G. Flershem, 'Some Aspects of Japan Sea Trade in the Tokugawa Period,' *Journal of Asian Studies*, XXIII, 3 (May 1964), pp. 405–16, and 'Some Aspects of Japan Sea Shipping and Trade in the Tokugawa Period, 1603–1867,' *Proceedings of the American Philosophical Society*, 110, 3 (1966), pp. 182–226; and Ryoichi Furuta and Yoshikazu Hirai, *A Short History of Japanese Merchant Shipping* (Tōkyō, 1967).

37. Takeuchi, 'Kinsei zenki no shōgyō,' pp. 154–8. For a complete map of Tokugawa provinces, see T. C. Smith, *Agrarian Origins of Modern Japan*, map facing p. 1.

38. Wakita, pp. 320–1.

39. Takeuchi, 'Kinsei zenki no shōgyō,' p. 159.

40. Yasuoka, 'Ōsaka no hattatsu to kinsei shōgyō' [The development of Ōsaka and early modern commerce] in *Nihon sangyōshi taikei* [Outline of Japanese industrial history], vol. 6, *Kinki chihō* [Kinki region] (Tōkyō, 1960), p. 111.

41. Yasuoka, 'Torihiki soshiki,' I, p. 302.

42. Crawcour, 'Credit,' pp. 345–7.

43. Crawcour, 'Credit,' pp. 348–53. For a discussion of the Tokugawa monetary system see Crawcour and Yamamura, 'The Tokugawa Monetary System.'

44. Yasuoka, 'Torihiki soshiki,' I, pp. 302–3.

45. Yasuoka, 'Torihiki soshiki,' I, p. 304. Takeuchi, 'Kinsei zenki no shōgyō,' pp. 166–9.

46. Miyamoto, *Ōsaka*, p. 70.

47. Miyamoto, *Kabu nakama no kenkyū* [Studies of the *kabu nakama*] (Tōkyō, 1938, 1958), p. 30.

48. Miyamoto, *Kabu nakama no kenkyū*, pp. 37–8.

49. Miyamoto, *Kabu nakama no kenkyū*, pp. 38–41.

50. Miyamoto, *Kabu nakama no kenkyū*, pp. 44–60.

51. Miyamoto, *Kabu nakama no kenkyū*, pp. 65–81.

52. Miyamoto, *Kabu nakama no kenkyū*, pp. 87–100.

53. Miyamoto, *Kabu nakama no kenkyū*, pp. 107–15.

54. Yasuoka, 'Kinai ni okeru shōgyō tōsei' [Commercial control in the Kinai region] in his *Nihon hōken keizai seisaku shiron – Keizai tōsei to bakuhan taisei* [A historical analysis of Japanese feudal economic policy – The *bakuhan* system and economic control] (Ōsaka, 1959), p. 162. (Cited hereafter as 'Shōgyō tōsei.')

55. Miyamoto, *Kabu nakama no kenkyū*, pp. 26–8.

56. Yasuoka, 'Shōgyō tōsei,' p. 162.

57. Yasuoka, 'Torihiki soshiki,' I, pp. 306–7.

58. For a discussion of this point see Crawcour, 'Money and Finance in Tokugawa Japan: A Review of Problems' (mimeographed, 1967–8), pp. 5–7.

59. Ono M., 'Kambun-Empōki no ryūtsū kikō,' p. 362.

60. Shimbō Hiroshi, 'Kinai mensaku ni okeru shōhin seisan no hatten ni kansuru ikkōsatsu' [Examination of the development of commodity production with respect to Kinai cotton cultivation] in *Kōbe Keizai Daigaku sōritsu gojū shūnen kinen rombunshū* [Essays commemorating the fiftieth anniversary of the founding of Kōbe Economic University] (Kōbe, 1953), pp. 493–4.

61. Yasuoka, 'Shōgyō tōsei,' p. 161.

62. Yasuoka, 'Shōgyō tōsei,' pp. 157–9.

63. Yagi Akihiro, *Kinsei no shōhin ryūtsū* [Commodity marketing during the early modern period] (Tōkyō, 1962), pp. 47–9.

64. George B. Sansom, *The Western World and Japan* (New York, 1958), p. 197. Sheldon, *Rise of the Merchant Class*, pp. 85, 88.

65. Ihara Saikaku, *The Japanese Family Storehouse* (*Nippon eitai-gura*), tr. with introduction and commentary by G. W. Sargent (Cambridge: University Press, 1959).

66. Crawcour, 'Some observations on merchants, A translation of Mitsui Takafusa's *Chōnin Kōken Roku*,' *The Transactions of the Asiatic Society of Japan*, third series, VIII (1961), pp. 1–139.

67. Mori Yasuhiro, *Daimyō kinyū shiron* [Historical analysis of daimyo finances] (Tōkyō: Ōhara Shinseisha, 1970) offers an excellent discussion of the dependence of daimyo on merchant loans.

68. Nakai, *Shōhin ryūtsū*, p. 102.

69. Yasuoka, 'Edo chūki no Ōsaka ni okeru torihiki soshiki' [The trade structure of Ōsaka during the mid-Edo period], part II, *Dōshisha shōgaku*, 16, 5 (February 1965), pp. 590–2. (Cited hereafter as 'Torihiki soshiki,' II.) Yasuoka's totals are adjusted to reflect the *tonya* listed in his Table.

70. Yasuoka, 'Torihiki soshiki,' II, pp. 593–7.

71. Yasuoka, 'Torihiki soshiki,' II, pp. 596–7.

72. Yasuoka, 'Torihiki soshiki,' II, pp. 599–601.

73. Nakai, 'Toshi,' pp. 45–6.

74. See Nakai, 'Toshi,' p. 47, and *Ōsaka shishi*, I, pp. 769–79, for the 1736 data on origin of Ōsaka imports.

75. Nakai, 'Toshi,' p. 47, lists Settsu with 8, Yamashiro and Izumi with 6, and Yamato with 5 and omits Kawachi altogether. *Ōsaka shishi*, I, pp. 769–79, lists all five provinces with over 10 commodities, suggesting that Nakai's commodity types are more general than those in the *Ōsaka shishi*. The omission of Kawachi appears to be an oversight by Nakai.

76. Nakai, 'Toshi,' p. 47.

77. Nakai, 'Toshi,' pp. 47–8.

78. Hayashi R., 'Kinsei chūkōki no shōgyō' [Commerce in the mid and late early modern period] in Toyoda Takeshi and Kodama Kōta (eds.), *Ryūtsūshi* [History of marketing], I (*Taikei Nihonshi sōsho* [Outline library of Japanese history], 13) (Tōkyō, 1969), p. 195.

79. Yasuoka, 'Torihiki soshiki,' II, p. 601.

80. For the more traditional view see Sheldon, *Rise of the Merchant Class*, p. 10, and *Nihon keizaishi jiten* [Dictionary of Japanese economic history], ed. Honjō Eijirō (Tōkyō, 1940, 1954), vol. I, p. 141.

81. Yasuoka, 'Torihiki soshiki,' II, pp. 598–9.

82. Nakai, 'Toshi,' pp. 80–1.

83. Nakai, 'Toshi,' pp. 82–3.

84. Nakai, 'Toshi,' pp. 83–7.

85. For a discussion of Tokugawa periodization see Hall, 'The New Look of Tokugawa History' in Hall and Jansen (eds.), pp. 55–64. For a discussion of the increasing economic problems of the samurai class see Yamamura, 'The Increasing Poverty of the Samurai in Tokugawa Japan, 1600–1868,' *Journal of Economic History*, XXXI, 2 (June 1971), pp. 378–406.

3. TOKUGAWA COMMERCE: 1720–1868

1. Ōishi Shinsaburō, 'Kyōhō kaikaku' [Kyōhō reforms] in *Iwanami kōza Nihon rekishi* [Iwanami series on Japanese history] (Tōkyō, 1963), vol. 11 or *Kinsei 3*, p. 271.

2. Hayashi R., 'Genroku-Kyōhōki ni okeru Edo tonya nakama no dōtai' [The dynamics of Edo *tonya nakama* during the Genroku through Kyōhō periods (1688–1736)], *Shakai keizai shigaku*, 28, 3 (1963), pp. 38–40. Miyamoto, *Kabu nakama no kenkyū*, p. 23. Yasuoka, 'Torihiki soshiki,' II, p. 607.

3. Hayashi R., 'Genroku-Kyōhōki Edo tonya nakama,' pp. 40–1.

4. Ōishi, 'Kyōhō kaikaku,' pp. 272–5.

5. Hayashi R., 'Genroku-Kyōhōki Edo tonya nakama,' pp. 41–2. Ōishi, 'Kyōhō kaikaku,' pp. 299–304.

6. Ōishi, 'Kyōhō kaikaku,' p. 303.

7. Yasuoka, 'Torihiki soshiki,' II, p. 608.

8. Ōishi, 'Kyōhō kaikaku,' pp. 306–8. For additional studies of the Tokugawa rice market see Miyamoto Matao, 'Kinsei shoki no Ōsaka ni okeru beikoku ryūtsū – Kurayashiki kenkyū no yobi sagyō to shite' [Rice marketing in Ōsaka during the beginning of the early modern period – A preliminary inquiry into research on *kurayashiki* (daimyo warehouses)] in Miyamoto Mataji (ed.), *Ōsaka no kenkyū* [Studies of Ōsaka], 4 (Ōsaka: Seibundō, 1970), pp. 1–46; Miyamoto Matao, 'Kuramoto henshitsu katei ni tsuite no ichi shiron – Jūshichi seiki kōhan ni okeru Ōsaka shijō no seiritsu to kanren shite' [A preliminary essay on the transformation of the *kuramoto* – With reference to the development of the Ōsaka market in the latter half of the seventeenth century], *Shakai keizai shigaku*, 35, 5–6 (1970), pp. 475–94; Shimamoto Tokuichi, *Kuramai kitte no kisoteki kenkyū* [Basic research on the warehouse-rice stamps] (Ōsaka: Sangyō Keizaisha, 1960); Suzuki Naoji, *Edo ni okeru kome torihiki no kenkyū* [A study of rice transactions in Edo] (Tōkyō: Kashiwa Shobō, 1965).

9. Ōishi, 'Kyōhō kaikaku ni okeru Edo keizai ni tai suru Ōsaka no chii' [The position of Ōsaka relative to the economy of Edo during the Kyōhō reforms], *Nihon rekishi*, no. 191 (April 1964), pp. 10–11. (Cited hereafter as 'Kyōhō-Ōsaka.')

10. *Ōsaka shishi*, III, p. 230. Yasuoka, 'Torihiki soshiki,' II, pp. 607–8.

11. Hayashi R., 'Genroku-Kyōhōki Edo tonya nakama,' p. 44; *Ōsaka shishi*, III, p. 250; Ōishi, 'Kyōhō kaikaku,' p. 305; Yasuoka, 'Torihiki soshiki,' II, p. 608.

12. Yasuoka, 'Torihiki soshiki,' II, pp. 609–10. The challenges to the Ōsaka cotton merchants will be discussed in detail in Chapter 7.

13. A modified statement of this can be found in Sheldon, *Rise of the Merchant Class*, especially Chapter 6.

14. See for example Ōishi, 'Kyōhō-Ōsaka'; Hayashi R., *Edo tonya nakama no kenkyū – Bakuhan taiseika no toshi shōgyō shihon* [Studies of the Edo *tonya nakama* – Urban commercial capital under the Tokugawa shogunate] (Tōkyō, 1967); Hayashi R., 'Bakuhan seiteki shijō to santo shōgyō shihon' [The market structure of the *bakuhan* system and commercial capital in the three major cities], *Rekishigaku kenkyū*, 324 (May 1967), pp. 35–9; Hayashi R., 'Kinsei chūkōki no shōgyō.'

15. Ōishi, 'Kyōhō-Ōsaka,' table 3, p. 12.

16. See Hayashi R., 'Edo jimawari keizaiken,' p. 257, for discussion of this point. For an attempt to analyze the relative value of Edo imports see Hayashi R., 'Jūshichi seiki kōhan ni okeru enkakuchi shōgyō no tenkai – Kantō momen hattatsu zenshi' [The development of trade in remote regions during the latter half of the seventeenth century – The origins of the growth of the Kantō cotton cloth industry] in *Ryūtsū Keizai Daigaku kinen rombunshū* [Articles commemorating the opening of Ryūtsū Keizai University] (Ryūgasaki, 1966), pp. 366–8.

17. Takeuchi, 'Kinsei zenki no shōgyō,' pp. 161–3.

18. Ōishi, 'Kyōhō-Ōsaka,' pp. 14–21.

19. Hayashi R., 'Edo momen tonya nakama to Kantō momen' [Edo cotton cloth *tonya nakama* and Kantō cotton cloth], *Rekishigaku kenkyū*, 274 (March 1963), pp. 30–42, and *Edo tonya nakama no kenkyū*, pp. 120–2. See also Kitajima Masamoto (ed.), *Edo shōgyō to Ise dana* [Edo commerce and Ise-based stores] (Tōkyō, 1962, 1963), and Hayashi Hideo, *Zaikata momen tonya no shiteki tenkai* [The historical development of rural cotton cloth *tonya*] (Tōkyō, 1965).

20. For a comprehensive study of the oil trade see Tsuda Hideo, *Hōken keizai*

seisaku no tenkai to shijō kōzō [The evolution of feudal economic policy and market formation] (Tōkyō: Ocha No Mizu Shobō, 1961).

21. Hayashi R., 'Kinsei chūkōki no shōgyō,' pp. 193–4, 223–5.

22. Miyamoto, *Kabu nakama no kenkyū*, p. 28.

23. Yasuoka, 'Torihiki soshiki,' ii, p. 614.

24. Nakai Nobuhiko, *Tenkanki bakuhansei no kenkyū – Hōreki-Temmeiki no keizai seisaku to shōhin ryūtsū* [Studies of the *bakuhan* system in a period of transition – Hōreki-Temmei period (1751–88) economic policy and commodity marketing] (Tōkyō, 1971), pp. 31–7.

25. Hayashi R., 'Kinsei chūkōki no shōgyō,' pp. 242–3. One *ryō* is usually equated to around 60 *momme* silver, the approximate cost of one *koku* of rice. One *kan* silver equals 1000 *momme* silver. In the 1780s, one *ryō* was valued at 65–6 *momme* silver. Silver was often circulated in units called *mai* which were wrapped and sealed packets containing 43 *momme* by weight.

26. Miyamoto, *Nihon shōgyōshi gairon* [An introduction to Japanese commercial history] (Tōkyō, 1954), p. 235; Yamaguchi Kazuo, *Nihon keizaishi kōgi* [Lectures on Japanese economic history] (Tōkyō, 1960), pp. 69, 106.

27. Nakai, *Tenkanki bakuhansei no kenkyū*, pp. 113–20.

28. Yagi, *Kinsei no shōhin ryūtsū*, pp. 78–81.

29. Yagi, *Kinsei no shōhin ryūtsū*, pp. 104–25.

30. Yasuoka, 'Torihiki soshiki,' ii, p. 614.

31. Hayashi R., 'Kinsei chūkōki no shōgyō,' p. 228.

32. Matsumoto Shirō, 'Shōhin ryūtsū no hatten to ryūtsū kikō no saihensei' [The development of commodity marketing and the reorganization of the marketing system] in Furushima Toshio (ed.), *Nihon keizaishi taikei* [Outline of Japanese economic history], 4 (Tōkyō, 1965), pp. 90–3.

33. Nakai, *Tenkanki bakuhansei no kenkyū*, pp. 118–23.

34. Nakai, *Tenkanki bakuhansei no kenkyū*, pp. 124–9.

35. Matsumoto, 'Shōhin ryūtsū no hatten,' pp. 106–7; Yagi, *Kinsei no shōhin ryūtsū*, pp. 128–31, 150–1; Yasuoka, 'Torihiki soshiki,' ii, p. 614. The impact of these policies on the Kinai cotton trade will be discussed in detail in Chapter 7.

36. Yasuoka, 'Edo chūki ni okeru Ōsaka shijō no kōzō – maki tonya no funsō o tsūjite,' [The structure of the Ōsaka market in the mid-Edo period – concerning disputes among the firewood *tonya*] in his *Nihon hōken keizai seisaku shiron* [A historical analysis of Japanese feudal economic policy] (Ōsaka, 1959), pp. 45–78. See also Matsumoto, 'Shōhin ryūtsū no hatten,' pp. 112–13.

37. Yasuoka, 'Torihiki soshiki,' ii, p. 620.

38. Hayashi R., 'Kinsei chūkōki no shōgyō,' pp. 218–19.

39. Matsumoto, 'Shōhin ryūtsū no hatten,' p. 113.

40. Fujino Tamotsu, *Daimyō : Sono ryōkoku keiei* [Daimyo: The economic administration of their domains] (Tōkyō, 1964), pp. 229–30.

41. Fujino, *Daimyō*, pp. 230–2.

42. Fujino, *Daimyō*, pp. 232–4.

43. Fujino, *Daimyō*, pp. 235–7.

44. Yasuoka, 'Torihiki soshiki,' II, pp. 611–13.

45. Yasuoka, 'Torihiki soshiki,' II, p. 617. The increase in processing as a form of rural by-employment will be discussed in Chapter 6.

46. Yasuoka, 'Torihiki soshiki,' II, p. 618; Hall, *Tanuma Okitsugu, 1719–1788: Forerunner of Modern Japan* (Cambridge, Mass.: Harvard University Press, 1955), pp. 75–7.

47. Yasuoka, 'Torihiki soshiki,' II, p. 618; Hayashi R., 'Kinsei chūkōki no shōgyō,' p. 219.

48. Matsumoto, 'Shōhin ryūtsū no hatten,' pp. 113–16, 123. See Chapter 7 for a discussion of this process in the cotton trade.

49. Hall, *Tanuma*, p. 141.

50. Harold Bolitho, *The Fudai Daimyo in the Tokugawa Settlement* (Ph.D. dissertation, Yale University, 1969) (Ann Arbor, Mich.: University Microfilms, 1970, no. 70–2699), pp. 229–31.

51. Tsuda Hideo, 'Kansei kaikaku' [Kansei reforms] in *Iwanami kōza Nihon rekishi* [Iwanami series on Japanese history], vol. 12 or *Kinsei* 4 (Tōkyō, 1963), p. 236.

52. Yasuoka, 'Shōgyō tōsei,' p. 165.

53. Yasuoka, 'Shōgyō tōsei,' pp. 165–6; Tsuda, 'Kansei kaikaku,' p. 255.

54. Nakai, *Tenkanki bakuhansei no kenkyū*, pp. 235–47.

55. Tsuda, 'Kansei kaikaku,' p. 263.

56. For a more detailed discussion of this group see Takeuchi Makoto, 'Edo jidai toshi shōnin no dōkō' [Tendencies of urban merchants during the Edo period], *Rekishi kyōiku*, VII, 11 (1959), pp. 19–26.

57. Hayashi R., 'Kinsei chūkōki no shōgyō,' pp. 225–6; Yamazaki Ryūzō, 'Edo kōki ni okeru nōson keizai no hatten to nōminsō bunkai,' [The economic development of agricultural villages and the decomposition of the peasant class in the late Edo period] in *Iwanami kōza Nihon rekishi* [Iwanami series on Japanese history], vol. 12 or *Kinsei* 4 (Tōkyō, 1963), pp. 347–8.

58. Yamazaki, 'Edo kōki ni okeru nōson keizai no hatten,' pp. 349–50.

59. Slightly different data are available in Yamazaki, 'Edo kōki ni okeru nōson keizai no hatten,' table 8.6, p. 347. I have chosen to use the data in table 8 because they were published more recently and use index numbers.

60. Fujino, *Daimyō*, pp. 251–5.

61. Hayashi R., 'Kinsei chūkōki no shōgyō,' pp. 225–6.

62. Yasuoka, 'Shōgyō tōsei,' pp. 170–1.

63. For the complete report see *Ōsaka shishi*, V, pp. 639–86.

64. Hayashi R., 'Kaseiki ni okeru shōhin ryūtsū' [Commodity marketing in the Kasei (1804–29) period], *Rekishi kyōiku*, 12, 12 (1964), p. 10.

65. Yasuoka, 'Shōgyō tōsei,' pp. 178–84.

66. Yasuoka, 'Shōgyō tōsei,' pp. 191–5. For a presentation of the other side of this issue see E. Herbert Norman, *Japan's Emergence as a Modern State: Political and Economic Problems of the Meiji Period* (New York, 1940), pp. 49–61.

67. Yagi, *Kinsei no shōhin ryūtsū*, pp. 137–9.

68. Tsuda, 'Kansei kaikaku,' pp. 273–4.

69. Hayashi R., 'Kaseiki ni okeru shōhin ryūtsū,' pp. 12–13.

70. Hayashi R., 'Kaseiki ni okeru shōhin ryūtsū,' pp. 13–15.

71. Hayashi R., 'Edo momen tonya nakama to Kantō momen,' pp. 33–5.

72. Okamoto Ryōichi, 'Tempō kaikaku' [Tempō reforms] in *Iwanami kōza Nihon rekishi* [Iwanami series on Japanese history], vol. 13 or *Kinsei 5* (Tōkyō, 1964), pp. 220–2; Ōishi Shinsaburō, Tsuda Hideo, Sakai Kōjin, and Yamamoto Hirobumi, *Nihon keizai shiron* [Discussion of Japanese economic history] (Tōkyō, 1967), pp. 234–6; Arai Eiji, *Bakuhansei shakai no tenkai katei* [The process of social development under the *bakuhan* system] (Tōkyō, 1965), pp. 597–600; Bolitho, *The Fudai Daimyo*, pp. 236–42.

73. Okamoto, 'Tempō kaikaku,' pp. 229–36; Ōishi et al., *Nihon keizai shiron*, pp. 238–9; Tsuda Hideo, 'Tempō kaikaku no keizaishiteki igi' [The economic-historical significance of the Tempō reforms] in Furushima Toshio (ed.), *Nihon keizaishi taikei* [Outline of Japanese economic history], 4 (Tōkyō, 1965), p. 347; Bolitho, *The Fudai Daimyo*, pp. 239–40.

74. Ōishi et al., *Nihon keizai shiron*, p. 239; Arai, *Bakuhansei shakai no tenkai katei*, pp. 601–2.

75. Okamoto, 'Tempō kaikaku,' pp. 224–6; Ōishi et al., *Nihon keizai shiron*, p. 237; Miyamoto, *Kabu nakama no kenkyū*, pp. 288–300.

76. Miyamoto, *Kabu nakama no kenkyū*, p. 291.

77. Ōishi et al., *Nihon keizai shiron*, p. 238; Okamoto, 'Tempō kaikaku,' p. 226.

78. Okamoto, 'Tempō kaikaku,' pp. 237–8; Miyamoto, *Kabu nakama no kenkyū*, pp. 320–3.

79. Okamoto, 'Tempō kaikaku,' p. 240; Hayashi R., 'Kinsei chūkōki no shōgyō,' p. 223; Miyamoto, *Kabu nakama no kenkyū*, pp. 324–45.

80. Okamoto, 'Tempō kaikaku,' pp. 240–1.

81. See Chapter 7 for a discussion of the Kinai cotton trade after 1851.

82. For this 'plot theory' see Tsuda, 'Tempō kaikaku no keizaishiteki igi.' Okamoto, 'Tempō kaikaku,' pp. 241–2, questions this interpretation.

4. THE ŌSAKA COTTON TRADE: ESTABLISHMENT AND CONSOLIDATION

1. The following is from *Nihon keizaishi jiten*, II, pp. 1615, 1725; *Sekai rekishi jiten* [Dictionary of world history], 18 (Tokyo, 1953), p. 285; and *Nihon rekishi daijiten* [Encyclopedia of Japanese history], 18 (Tōkyō, 1956–60), p. 123.

2. Takao Kazuhiko, 'Settsu Hirano-gō ni okeru mensaku no hatten' [The growth of cotton cultivation in Settsu Hirano-gō], *Shirin*, 34, 1–2 (January-February 1951), p. 714.

3. Conversations with Ingrid Cole, a weaver interested in Japanese hand woven textiles, and examination of traditional Japanese pattern books in her possession. See also Tsujiai Zenyotarō, *Kawachi momenfu* [Notes on Kawachi cotton cloth] (Tōkyō, 1965).

4. Takao, 'Settsu Hirano-gō,' p. 722.

5. Yamaguchi Yukio, 'Hōken hōkaiki ni okeru Settsu Hirano-gō no henshitsu

katei – kuriwata no ryūtsū yori mitaru' [The process of change in Settsu Hirano-*gō* as related to feudal decline – viewed from the marketing of ginned cotton], *Historia*, no. 20 (1957), p. 45.

6. This and the following from *Ōsaka shishi*, I, 350–1. My study of the Ōsaka cotton trade is largely drawn from materials contained in *Ōsaka shishi*. Much of this documentation is also contained in *Ōsaka shōgyōshi shiryō* [Historical documents for the commercial history of Ōsaka], 31–2, ed. Ōsaka Shōkō Kaigisho [Osaka Chamber of Commerce and Industry] (Ōsaka, 1964), *Watashō kyūki* [Old records of the cotton trade], contained in vol. 31, pp. 178–267, includes copies of many of the documents used from the *Ōsaka shishi*. However, these were all hand-copied in the late nineteenth century and contain many copyists' errors, making them less reliable than the carefully corrected *Ōsaka shishi*. I have consequently utilized the *Ōsaka shishi* as the primary source of the materials on the cotton trade. Documents on the Ōsaka cotton trade are also included in *Ōsaka hennenshi* [Yearly history of Ōsaka] which is being edited and published by the Ōsaka Shiritsu Chūō Toshokan Shishi Henshū Shitsu [City History Editorial Section of the Central Ōsaka Municipal Library]. The manuscript from which this is being published was the source of the materials included in the *Ōsaka shishi*. Thus far (1972), 12 volumes have been published out of a projected total of 23 and they include material through 1787. Although I made some use of the manuscript edition, time constraints have made it impossible to effectively utilize the published edition of *Ōsaka hennenshi*. While material not included in *Ōsaka shishi* may be available in *Ōsaka hennenshi*, it is extremely unlikely that it would alter the interpretations advanced in the current study. In the future, I hope to make use of this valuable new source for further research on the economic and social history of Ōsaka.

7. For a brief biography of Ishimaru Sadatsugu see *Nihon keizaishi jiten*, I, pp. 42–3; and Miyamoto, *Ōsaka jimbutsushi* [History of famous Ōsakans] (Tōkyō, 1960), pp. 53–71.

8. The following is from *Ōsaka shishi*, I, pp. 409–10.

9. To ease readers' comprehension of the following an effort will be made to simplify the names of the various merchant associations which are discussed. Hereafter, the *sansho wata-ichi tonya nakama* will be referred to as the cotton *tonya nakama*.

10. Hereafter, the *wata kaitsugi tsumi tonya nakama* will be referred to as the cotton shipping *nakama*.

11. The difficulty of distinguishing between the special rights of the *wataya nakama* and the cotton *tonya nakama* is noted by Yagi in *Kinsei no shōhin ryūtsū*, pp. 226–7. The most obvious distinction is that the *wataya nakama* also engaged in cotton processing.

12. Because the Japanese name is short and no comprehensive translation would be practical given the divergent activities of the *wataya nakama*, I have chosen to use the transliterated title of this group.

13. Yasuoka, 'Torihiki soshiki,' I, p. 304.

14. *Ōsaka shishi*, III, pp. 75, 84, 93.

15. Crawcour, 'Money and Finance in Tokugawa Japan,' pp. 5–7.

16. See Chapter 3, table 7, p. 39.

17. *Ōsaka shishi*, II, p. 230.

18. *Ōsaka shishi*, III, p. 265.

19. *Ōsaka shishi*, III, pp. 288–9.

20. *Ōsaka shishi*, III, p. 289. 1 *koku* equals 44.8 gallons or 4.96 bushels. 1 *kamme* equals 8.72 lb. The omission of 1691 is presumably a copyist's error.

21. *Ōsaka shishi*, III, pp. 421–2.

22. *Ōsaka shishi*, III, pp. 478, 555, 557.

23. This and the following from *Ōsaka shishi*, I, p. 1084.

24. Yagi, *Kinsei no shōhin ryūtsū*, pp. 228–9. This is discussed in detail in Chapters 6 and 7.

25. *Ōsaka shishi*, III, pp. 803–4.

26. A *mai* equals 43 *momme* silver wrapped in a sealed packet. Conversations with Professor Sakudō Yōtarō of Ōsaka University, Faculty of Economics.

27. *Ōsaka shishi*, I, p. 1084.

28. There is some question as to whether or not the *wataya nakama* had been authorized to deal in both seed and ginned cotton in the 1660s. This is not clear in the sources, but the combination of the change in name and the government's subsequent request for an increase in license fee payments from ten to fifteen *mai* annually suggests that the *nakama* sphere of influence had been extended. See *Ōsaka shishi*, I, pp. 1084–5, and Yagi, *Kinsei no shōhin ryūtsū*, p. 227.

29. The following is from *Ōsaka shishi*, I, pp. 1085–6.

30. *Ōsaka shishi*, V, p. 713.

31. This and the following from *Ōsaka shishi*, I, pp. 1086–7.

32. Yagi, *Kinsei no shōhin ryūtsū*, pp. 224–50; Yamaguchi Y., 'Hōken hōkaiki ni okeru Settsu Hirano-gō,' pp. 43–56.

33. Yagi, *Kinsei no shōhin ryūtsū*, p. 243; Yamaguchi Y., 'Hōken hōkaiki Settsu Hirano-gō,' p. 45.

34. *Nihon keizaishi jiten*, I, p. 663.

35. Hereafter this association will be referred to as the cotton shipping *nakama*. The following is from *Ōsaka shishi*, I, pp. 1088–9.

36. Hereafter the *momen tonya nakama* will be referred to as the cloth *tonya nakama* and the *nana kumi momenya nakama* will be referred to as the seven *kumi nakama*.

37. *Ōsaka shishi*, V, p. 714. See also *Ōsaka momengyō shi* [History of the Ōsaka cotton cloth trade], (Ōsaka, 1936), pp. 48–9.

38. *Ōsaka shishi*, I, pp. 1091–2. With the exception of the Edo *kumi*, all of the *kumi* names came from neighborhoods in Ōsaka and designated the area of the city where the membership was concentrated.

39. This and the following from *Ōsaka shishi*, I, pp. 1092–3.

40. See *Ōsaka shishi*, V, pp. 717–18.

41. *Ōsaka shishi*, I, pp. 1093–4, for material above and following. See *Ōsaka shishi*, V, p. 713, for the *nakama* register preamble; also *Ōsaka momengyō shi*, pp. 50–1.

42. For a discussion of merchant ethics see Robert N. Bellah, *Tokugawa Religion: The Values of Pre-Industrial Japan* (Glencoe, Ill., 1957), in particular Chapters 5 and 6.

43. See Miyamoto, *Kabu nakama no kenkyū*, pp. 112–16, and Sheldon, *Rise of the Merchant Class*, pp. 111–12.

44. Preambles for all seven *kumi* of the seven *kumi nakama* are in *Ōsaka shishi*, v, pp. 713–20.

45. *Ōsaka shishi*, v, p. 713.

46. See *Ōsaka shishi*, I, pp. 1094–5, for more specific information on the establishment of these groups of cotton cloth merchants.

47. Hayashi R., *Edo tonya nakama no kenkyū*, pp. 175–6, 190–1.

48. For a listing of disputes relating to the cotton trade which were brought to the *bakufu* see Yagi, *Kinsei no shōhin ryūtsū*, pp. 171–3.

49. Yagi, *Kinsei no shōhin ryūtsū*, pp. 233–5. See Chapter 7 for a more detailed discussion of the opposition to the *wataya nakama*.

50. Yagi, *Kinsei no shōhin ryūtsū*, pp. 235–6.

51. Yagi, *Kinsei no shōhin ryūtsū*, pp. 231–7.

52. *Ōsaka shishi*, I, p. 1089; v, p. 115. See also Yagi, *Kinsei no shōhin ryūtsū*, p. 237.

53. *Ōsaka shishi*, III, p. 638.

54. *Ōsaka shishi*, III, p. 784.

55. *Ōsaka shishi*, I, p. 1089. See Yamaguchi Y., 'Hōken hōkaiki Settsu Hirano-gō,' p. 47, for Hirano-*gō* market petitions.

56. *Ōsaka shishi*, I, pp. 1089–90; v, p. 115. See Yagi, *Kinsei no shōhin ryūtsū*, p. 233, for other rejected examples.

57. *Ōsaka shishi*, I, p. 1090; III, pp. 1233–4.

58. Yagi, *Kinsei no shōhin ryūtsū*, table 36, pp. 171–3.

59. *Ōsaka shishi*, I, p. 1090.

60. *Ōsaka shishi*, I, p. 1090; Nakai, *Tenkanki bakuhansei no kenkyū*, pp. 270–2.

5. THE ŌSAKA COTTON TRADE: INSTITUTIONAL DECLINE

1. See Conrad D. Totman, *Politics in the Tokugawa Bakufu, 1600–1843* (Cambridge, Mass., 1967), pp. 223–7; George B. Sansom, *A History of Japan, 1615–1867* (Stanford, 1963), pp. 193–206; Hall, *Tanuma Okitsugu*, pp. 135–42.

2. For related documents for the years 1787–92 see *Ōsaka shishi*, III, pp. 1198, 1266; IV, pp. 31, 99, 132.

3. Much of the material available on the Kansei reforms is of an impressionistic nature and not well documented. This, unfortunately, is also the case with respect to the Ōsaka cotton trade. *Ōsaka shishi* has very little of interest on this point and further illumination will have to wait until publication of *Ōsaka hennenshi* is completed.

4. *Ōsaka shishi*, II, pp. 357–8.

5. *Ōsaka shishi*, II, p. 358.

6. *Ōsaka shishi*, II, pp. 358–9. At the time of the dispute the cotton shipping *nakama* had *kabu* for 12 houses, paid license fees of around 32 *mai* silver annually,

and had less than 12 active members. With the settlement of the 1797 dispute in its favor membership began to increase. In 1806 a petition was sent to the city government requesting 20 additional *kabu*. This was authorized in 1807 when total *kabu* were increased to 32 and the license fee was fixed at 36 *mai* silver per year.

7. The following from *Ōsaka shishi*, II, pp. 359–61.

8. *Ōsaka shishi*, II, p. 361. See Hayashi R., *Edo tonya nakama no kenkyū*, for a study of the Edo cotton trade.

9. Yagi, *Kinsei no shōhin ryūtsū*, p. 237.

10. Yamaguchi Y., 'Hōken hōkaiki Settsu Hirano-gō,' p. 47.

11. Yagi, *Kinsei no shōhin ryūtsū*, pp. 171–2, 237–8.

12. *Ōsaka shishi*, II, p. 120.

13. *Ōsaka shishi*, II, p. 120.

14. *Ōsaka shishi*, II, p. 351.

15. *Ōsaka shishi*, II, pp. 351–2.

16. The value of this payment relative to the silver standard current in the Ōsaka region would vary with fluctuations in the gold/silver price. Assuming that this ranged from 55 to 65 *momme* silver per *ryō* gold, the silver value of the license fee might range from 11 000 to 13 000 *momme* silver. Calculated in terms of *mai* silver this would range from 258 *mai* to around 302 *mai* silver, sums considerably in excess of that being paid by the various Ōsaka cotton *nakama*.

17. *Ōsaka shishi*, II, p. 352.

18. *Ōsaka shishi*, II, p. 362. Calculated in terms of silver this would become something between 130 and 150 *mai* silver as the annual licensing fee.

19. *Ōsaka shishi*, II, pp. 352–3; Yagi, *Kinsei no shōhin ryūtsū*, p. 238.

20. *Ōsaka shishi*, II, p. 353.

21. Yagi, *Kinsei no shōhin ryūtsū*, pp. 239–40.

22. *Ōsaka shishi*, IV, p. 514; *Hiraoka shishi* [History of the city of Hiraoka], IV (Hiraoka, 1966), pp. 514–15.

23. Yagi, *Kinsei no shōhin ryūtsū*, p. 240.

24. *Ōsaka shishi*, II, p. 354.

25. *Ōsaka shishi*, IV, p. 783.

26. *Ōsaka shishi*, IV, pp. 842–3.

27. *Ōsaka shishi*, II, p. 354.

28. *Ōsaka shishi*, IV, p. 918.

29. *Ōsaka shishi*, II, p. 354.

30. *Ōsaka shishi*, II, p. 354, and Yamaguchi Y., 'Hōken hōkaiki Settsu Hirano-gō,' p. 47.

31. *Ōsaka shishi*, II, p. 355.

32. Yagi, *Kinsei no shōhin ryūtsū*, pp. 241–2.

33. Yagi, *Kinsei no shōhin ryūtsū*, p. 244.

34. The following is from *Ōsaka shishi*, II, pp. 355–7, and Yagi, *Kinsei no shōhin*

ryūtsū, pp. 245–8. See also Asao Naohiro, 'Bunsei rokunen senshichi kason kokuso ni kansuru oboegaki' [Note on the 1007-village dispute of 1823], *Kinseishi kenkyū*, no. 9 (May 1955), pp. 1–12; Irimajiri Yoshinaga, 'Bakumatsu Kinai nōson ni okeru "kokuso" no seikaku – Bunsei 6–7 nen no kokuso o chūshin to shite (On the nature of legal proceedings in court as found in villages of the five home provinces)' in *Kindaika to kōgyōka* [Modernization and industrialization] (Tōkyō, 1968), pp. 53–82.

35. *Ōsaka shishi*, II, pp. 356–7.

36. Asao, 'Bunsei rokunen senshichi kason kokuso ni kansuru oboegaki,' pp. 5–12.

37. *Ōsaka shishi*, II, pp. 681–2.

38. See *Ōsaka shishi*, V, pp. 639–86, for the complete report.

39. The following excerpts are from *Ōsaka shishi*, V, pp. 652–4.

40. It appears that Abe has included both the *wataya nakama* and the cotton shipping *nakama* in his 'cotton *nakama*' category.

41. Abe regards this price as relatively low, but the dates for the statistics are not given and suggest that they were considerably before 1841. Prices for 1841 are given as 1 *kin* seed cotton at 1 *momme* 1 *fun* and 1 *kamme* ginned cotton at 25 *momme* silver. *Ōsaka shishi*, II, p. 682; V, p. 652.

42. It would appear that the significance of the *bakufu* decision in 1823 was understood in government circles.

43. This and the following is from Horie Yasuzō, *Waga kuni kinsei no sembai seido* [The Japanese monopoly system in the early modern period] (Tōkyō, 1933), pp. 17–19, and *Nihon keizaishi jiten*, II, p. 1379. For more detailed coverage see Hozumi Katsujirō, *Himeji han kokusan momen to Edo no momen tonya* [Himeji *han* domestic cotton cloth and Edo cotton cloth *tonya*] (Himeji, 1971).

44. Horie, *Waga kuni kinsei no sembai seido*, p. 19.

45. *Ōsaka shishi*, V, pp. 650–1.

46. *Ōsaka shishi*, V, p. 651.

47. *Ōsaka shishi*, IV, p. 1504.

48. *Ōsaka shishi*, IV, p. 1513.

49. *Ōsaka shishi*, IV, p. 1533.

50. *Ōsaka shishi*, II, p. 684.

51. Fujino, *Daimyō*, pp. 256–8.

52. See Miyamoto Mataji (ed.), *Kinsei Ōsaka no bukka to rishi* [Prices and interest in Ōsaka during the early modern period] (Ōsaka, 1963), pp. 200–21.

53. The data presented in the Miyamoto book cited above are presented in monthly intervals. In an effort to simplify the analysis and compensate for price fluctuations which occur throughout the year normally, a yearly average has been computed for each year of the period under discussion. While this may tend to obscure some of the short-run fluctuations, it should not negate any long-term effects towards which the reforms might have contributed.

54. *Osaka shishi*, II, p. 723.

55. *Ōsaka shishi*, II, p. 725.

56. *Ōsaka shishi*, II, pp. 723–5.

6. COTTON CULTIVATING AND PROCESSING IN THE KINAI REGION

1. Ōkura Nagatsune, *Menpo yōmu* [The important points of cotton farming] in Saigusa Hiroto (ed.), *Nihon kagaku koten zensho* [Complete set of Japanese scientific classics], 11 (Tōkyō, 1942), p. 251.

2. Shimbō, 'Kinai mensaku ni okeru shōhin seisan,' pp. 491–2.

3. Shimbō, 'Kinai mensaku ni okeru shōhin seisan,' pp. 492, 517.

4. Shimbō, 'Kinai mensaku ni okeru shōhin seisan,' pp. 492–3; 494, note 5. For a discussion of river shipping networks in the Ōsaka region see *Fuse shishi* [History of the city of Fuse], 11 (Fuse, 1967), pp. 349–84.

5. *Yao shishi* [History of the city of Yao], 1 (Ōsaka-fu Yao-shi, 1958), p. 276.

6. *Izumi-sano shishi* [*History of Izumi-sano city*] (Izumi-sano-shi, 1958), pp. 251–2. Takebe Yoshito, 'Sekkasen no mengyō' [The cotton industry in Settsu, Kawachi, and Izumi] in *Nihon sangyōshi taikei* [*Systematic history of Japanese industry*], vol. 6 (*Kinki chihō*) (Tōkyō, 1960), p. 127.

7. *Fuse shishi*, 11, pp. 61–2. *Sayama chōshi* [History of the town of Sayama], 1 (Ōsaka-fu Sayama-chō, 1967), p. 249. *Nishinomiya shishi* [History of the city of Nishinomiya], 11 (Nishinomiya, 1960), p. 176. Takao Kazuhiko, 'Kan'eiki Kawachi no mensaku nōson ni tsuite' [Concerning cotton cultivating villages in Kawachi during the Kan'ei period (1624–43)], *Kenkyū* (Kōbe Daigaku), no. 25 (March 1961), pp. 4–9.

8. *Sakai shishi zokuhen* [History of the city of Sakai – Continuation], 1 (Sakai, 1971), p. 691.

9. Takebe, 'Sekkasen no mengyō,' pp. 129–31.

10. Shimbō, 'Tokugawaki ni okeru mensaku no hatten ni tsuite' [Concerning the development of cotton cultivation in the Tokugawa period], *Kokumin keizai zasshi*, 86, 2 (August 1952), pp. 36–8.

11. Takebe, 'Kinki nōgyō no tenkai – Kawachi momen no hōkai to kinkō nōgyō no seiritsu' [The development of agriculture in the Kinki region – The decline of Kawachi cotton cloth and the realization of suburban agriculture], *Keizai kenkyū* (Ōsaka Furitsu Daigaku), no. 2 (March 1957), p. 37.

12. Kojima Shōji, 'Kawachi mensaku shirabe oboegaki' [Examination memo on Kawachi cotton cultivation], *Kamigata*, no. 86 (1938), pp. 64–5.

13. *Sakai shishi zokuhen*, 1, pp. 979–82.

14. For studies of Yamato cotton, the following are of interest: Okuda Shūzō, 'Kinsei Yamato no mensaku ni tsuite – Kinai mensaku ni okeru sono chii' [Concerning cotton cultivation in Yamato in early modern times – Its status with respect to cotton cultivation in the Kinai region], *Historia*, no. 11 (February 1955), pp. 47–65. Nakamura Nobuji, *Kinsei Yamato no shōhin ryūtsū* [Commodity marketing in Yamato in early modern times] (Nara, 1967).

15. Ōkura, *Menpo yōmu*, pp. 293–8. *Kashihara chōshi* [History of the town of Kashihara] (Ōsaka-fu Naka Kawachi-gun, Kashihara-chō, 1955), pp. 670–1. Takebe, *Kawachi momen no kenkyū* [*Studies of Kawachi cotton cloth*] (Yao, 1957), pp. 11–12.

16. *Fuse chōshi* [History of the town of Fuse] (Ōsaka-fu Naka Kawachi-gun Fuse-chō, 1929), p. 15.

17. Takebe, 'Sekkasen no mengyō,' p. 131. For a table of labor inputs for cotton cultivation and cotton processing, see *Fuse shishi*, II, p. 529.

18. *Sayama chōshi*, I, p. 252.

19. *Yao shishi*, I, p. 278.

20. *Hikishō chōshi* [History of the town of Hikishō] (Ōsaka-fu Hikishō-chō, 1954), pp. 161–2.

21. Ihara Saikaku, The Japanese family storehouse, *(Nippon eitai-gura)*, pp. 115–20.

22. *Fuse shishi*, II, pp. 556–7.

23. *Nishinari gunshi* [History of Nishinari-*gun*] (Ōsaka, 1915), p. 426. Output has been computed from bales (*hon*), which weighed 12 *kan*, to *kin* at the rate of 220 *momme* per *kin*.

24. Takebe, 'Sekkasen no mengyō,' p. 129. This is computed at 220 *momme* per *kin*.

25. *Nishinomiya shishi*, II, pp. 152–3, 157.

26. A recent annotated edition is included in Furushima Toshio and Aki Kōchi (eds.), *Kinsei kagaku shisō* [Scientific thought in the early modern period], I (vol. 62 of *Nihon shisō taikei* [Outline of Japanese thought]) (Tōkyō, 1972), of which pp. 142–51 are on cotton cultivation. *Nishinomiya shishi*, II, p. 227.

27. *Amagasaki shishi*, II, p. 569.

28. *Hikishō chōshi*, pp. 432–5.

29. *Moriguchi shishi*, IV, pp. 31–2. Ten *to* equal one *koku*.

30. *Fuse shishi*, II, p. 521.

31. *Yao shishi*, I, p. 278.

32. *Fuse shishi*, II, p. 522.

33. Shimbō, 'Kinai mensaku ni okeru shōhin seisan,' pp. 517–18.

34. Shimbō, 'Kinai mensaku ni okeru shōhin seisan,' note 16, p. 521.

35. *Amagasaki shishi*, II, pp. 727–34.

36. *Amagasaki shishi*, II, pp. 727–8.

37. *Amagasaki shishi*, II, pp. 728–9.

38. *Itami shishi* [History of the city of Itami], II (Itami, 1969), p. 233.

39. *Amagasaki shishi*, II, pp. 730–1.

40. *Amagasaki shishi*, II, pp. 732–3.

41. *Amagasaki shishi*, II, p. 734. For a discussion of disputes in the Itami region see *Itami shishi*, II, pp. 222–6.

42. For additional data on late Tokugawa fertilizer prices see *Nishinomiya shishi*, IV, pp. 801–3, and Miyamoto (ed.), *Kinsei Ōsaka no bukka to rishi*, table 36, pp. 302–12.

43. For an analysis of the relation between fertilizer costs and agricultural commodity sales see Yamazaki, 'Edo kōki ni okeru nōson keizai no hatten to nōminsō bunkai,' pp. 355–8.

44. *Amagasaki shishi*, II, pp. 644–5.

45. *Amagasaki shishi*, II, p. 626.

46. *Fuse shishi*, II, pp. 64–6.

47. *Yao shishi*, I, pp. 231–40.

48. *Yao shishi*, I, pp. 240–3.

49. *Fuse shishi*, II, pp. 63, 70.

50. *Fuse shishi*, II, pp. 70–1.

51. *Fuse shishi*, II, table 24, p. 535; table 28, p. 539. See tables 21–3, pp. 534–5, for cotton cultivation rates in Kowakae and Arakawa villages in the mid-eighteenth century.

52. *Fuse shishi*, II, tables 25, 30, 32, pp. 536, 541.

53. *Sakai shishi zokuhen*, I, pp. 691, 949.

54. *Sakai shishi zokuhen*, I, pp. 949–52.

55. *Sayama chōshi*, I, p. 250.

56. *Yao shishi*, I, pp. 276–7.

57. *Izumi shishi* [History of the city of Izumi], II (Ōsaka-fu Izumi-shi, 1968), p. 250.

58. *Kashihara chōshi*, p. 668.

59. *Kami sonshi*, p. 154.

60. *Itami shishi*, II, pp. 212–14.

61. *Amagasaki shishi*, II, pp. 655–6.

62. Takao, 'Settsu Hirano-gō ni okeru mensaku no hatten,' p. 714; Yamaguchi Y., 'Hōken hōkaiki Settsu Hirano-gō,' p. 45; Hayashi R., 'Kinsei chūkōki no shōgyō,' p. 244.

63. *Amagasaki shishi*, II, p. 656; Yagi, *Kinsei no shōhin ryūtsū*, pp. 22–30.

64. *Fuse shishi*, II, pp. 543–5; Tsujiai, *Kawachi momenfu*, pp. 19–29; Takebe, 'Sekkasen no mengyō,' pp. 136–7.

65. Takebe, 'Sekkasen no mengyō,' pp. 148–9.

66. Takebe, 'Sekkasen no mengyō,' pp. 142–3.

67. Yagi, *Kinsei no shōhin ryūtsū*, pp. 89–93.

68. *Nishinari gunshi*, pp. 448–9.

69. *Fuse shishi*, II, p. 73.

70. *Sakai shishi zokuhen*, I, p. 947.

71. *Sakai shishi zokuhen*, I, p. 960.

72. *Sayama chōshi*, I, pp. 262–4.

73. *Yao shishi*, I, p. 282.

74. *Yao shishi*, II, pp. 284, 306.

75. *Higashi Tottori sonshi* [History of the village of Higashi Tottori] (Ōsaka-fu Higashi Tottori-mura, 1958), p. 341. *Hikishō chōshi*, pp. 167, 437, 460. *Kashihara chōshi*, pp. 670, 681. *Hiraoka shishi*, IV, p. 514. *Izumi shishi*, II, pp. 250–1. *Izumi-sano shishi*, pp. 265–6. *Moriguchi shishi*, IV, pp. 45, 53, 59.

76. Yamazaki, 'Kinsei kōki Settsu nōson ni okeru shōhin ryūtsū,' p. 62.

77. Yamazaki, 'Kinsei kōki Settsu nōson ni okeru shōhin ryūtsū,' table 10, p. 77.

7. CHANGES IN COTTON MARKETING IN THE KINAI REGION

1. See for example *Yao shishi*, I, p. 280

2. *Amagasaki shishi*, II, pp. 679–80.

3. *Kanan chōshi* [History of the town of Kanan] (Ōsaka-fu Minami Kawachi-gun Kanan-chō, 1968), p. 201.

4. *Sakai shishi zokuhen*, I, p. 690.

5. *Kanan chōshi*, p. 201.

6. *Amagasaki shishi*, II, p. 679.

7. *Hirano-gō chōshi*, p. 301.

8. *Kaizuka shishi* [History of the city of Kaizuka], I (Ōsaka-fu Kaizuka-shi, 1955), p. 602.

9. *Kaizuka shishi*, I, p. 586.

10. *Itami shishi*, II, pp. 214–15.

11. *Itami shishi*, II, pp. 215–16.

12. *Itami shishi*, II, p. 216.

13. *Itami shishi*, II, p. 217.

14. *Itami shishi*, II, p. 218.

15. *Itami shishi*, II, pp. 218–19.

16. *Itami shishi*, II, p. 219.

17. *Itami shishi*, II, pp. 219–20.

18. *Itami shishi*, II, p. 220.

19. *Sakai shishi* [History of the city of Sakai], III, VI (Sakai, 1930, 1929), III, pp. 438–9; VI, p. 124. *Sakai shishi zokuhen*, I, p. 962.

20. *Sakai shishi*, III, pp. 450–1; *Sakai shishi zokuhen*, I, p. 978.

21. *Sakai shishi zokuhen*, I, pp. 979–82. Takebe, 'Sekkasen no mengyō,' pp. 144–5.

22. *Sakai shishi zokuhen*, I, p. 983.

23. *Yao shishi*, I, p. 286.

24. *Yao shishi*, II, pp. 662–3; *Hiraoka shishi*, IV, pp. 512–13; Takebe, *Kawachi momen no kenkyū*, pp. 14–16.

25. *Yao shishi*, II, pp. 665–6.

26. Takebe, *Kawachi momen no kenkyū*, pp. 17–21; 'Sekkasen no mengyō,' p. 143.

27. Takebe, 'Sekkasen no mengyō,' table 3, p. 143.

28. Takebe, *Kawachi momen no kenkyū*, pp. 21–2.

29. *Hiraoka shishi*, IV, p. 513. Trading licenses in the petition were called *nakagai kabu* and the traders referred to as *nakagai*. Nakai, *Tenkanki bakuhansei no kenkyū*, pp. 119–22.

30. *Hiraoka shishi*, IV, p. 514.

31. *Nishinomiya shishi*, IV, pp. 823–4.

32. *Yao shishi*, II, p. 632.

33. *Yao shishi*, I, p. 285.

34. *Yao shishi*, I, pp. 283–4.

35. Furushima and Nagahara, pp. 94–5.

36. *Yao shishi*, I, pp. 284–5.

37. *Yao shishi*, II, p. 667.

38. *Izumi-sano shishi*, pp. 305–6; Takebe, 'Sekkasen no mengyō,' p. 146.

39. *Sakai shishi*, III, pp. 439–40; *Izumi-sano shishi*, p. 306; *Sakai shishi zokuhen*, I, p. 987; Takebe, 'Sekkasen no mengyō,' p. 146.

40. *Sakai shishi*, III, p. 440; *Izumi-sano shishi*, p. 306; *Sakai shishi zokuhen*, I, p. 962; Takebe, 'Sekkasen no mengyō,' p. 146.

41. *Izumi-sano shishi*, p. 306.

42. *Kaizuka shishi*, III, p. 205; *Sakai shishi zokuhen*, I, p. 962.

43. *Izumi shishi*, II, pp. 253–4.

44. *Izumi shishi*, II, pp. 254–7.

45. *Sakai shishi zokuhen*, I, pp. 983–6.

46. *Sakai shishi*, III, p. 452.

47. *Kaizuka shishi*, III, pp. 233–4, 238.

48. Furushima and Nagahara, p. 112.

49. *Yao shishi*, II, p. 665.

50. *Nishinomiya shishi*, V, p. 617.

51. *Nishinomiya shishi*, V, pp. 617–18.

52. *Nishinomiya shishi*, IV, p. 830.

53. Furushima and Nagahara, pp. 107–9.

54. *Fuse shishi*, II, p. 830.

55. *Fuse shishi*, II, p. 832. Furushima and Nagahara, pp. 107–9.

56. *Hirano-gō chōshi*, p. 302.

57. *Fuse shishi*, II, p. 846.

58. *Fuse shishi*, II, pp. 848–9.

59. *Nishinomiya shishi*, IV, pp. 829–30.

60. Yamazaki, 'Kinsei kōki Settsu nōson ni okeru shōhin ryūtsū,' p. 82. *Nishinomiya shishi*, II, p. 239.

61. All data for Ujita house seed cotton are computed at 1 bale = 40 *kin* of seed cotton. This is approximately equivalent to 5 *kan* of ginned cotton. Data from Nishikoya and Tsunematsu villages have 1 *kin* = 300 *momme* by weight. See Yamazaki, 'Kinsei kōki Settsu nōson ni okeru shōhin ryūtsū,' note to table 12, p. 82, and note 22, p. 116.

62. Yamazaki, 'Kinsei kōki Settsu nōson ni okeru shōhin ryūtsū,' p. 82.

63. Yamazaki, 'Kinsei kōki Settsu nōson ni okeru shōhin ryūtsū,' pp. 90–3.

64. *Fuse shishi*, II, table 23, p. 832.

65. Furushima and Nagahara, p. 84.

66. *Yao shishi*, I, p. 287.
67. *Yao shishi*, II, pp. 663–5; Takebe, *Kawachi momen no kenkyū*, pp. 24–6.
68. *Yao shishi*, I, pp. 285–6.
69. *Nishinomiya shishi*, IV, p. 830.
70. *Fuse shishi*, II, p. 834.
71. *Fuse shishi*, II, p. 834.
72. *Fuse shishi*, II, pp. 835–8.
73. *Sakai shishi*, III, pp. 440–1; VI, p. 125; *Sakai shishi zokuhen*, I, pp. 962–4.
74. *Yao shishi*, I, p. 285.

8. CONCLUSIONS

1. For example see Sheldon, *Rise of the Merchant Class*; Miyamoto, *Nihon shōgyō-shi* [A commercial history of Japan] (Tōkyō, 1943); and Honjō, *Economic Theory and History of Japan in the Tokugawa Period* (New York, 1965).
2. Thomas C. Smith, 'Farm Family By-employments in Preindustrial Japan,' pp. 705–9.

Bibliography

A. JAPANESE LOCAL HISTORIES AND DOCUMENT COLLECTIONS

Amagasaki shishi [History of the city of Amagasaki], II, ed. Okamoto Seishin. Amagasaki: Amagasaki Shiyakusho, 1968.

Fuse chōshi [History of the town of Fuse], ed. Fuse Chōyakuba. Ōsaka-fu Naka Kawachi-gun Fuse-chō: Fuse Chōyakuba, 1929.

Fuse shishi [History of the city of Fuse], II, ed. Fuse Shishi Hensan Iinkai. Fuse: Fuse Shiyakusho, 1967.

Higashi Tottori sonshi [History of the village of Higashi Tottori], ed. Shimizu Tomotoshi. Ōsaka-fu Higashi Tottori-mura: Higashi Tottori Murayakuba, 1958.

Hikishō chōshi [History of the town of Hikishō], ed. Takao Kazuhiko. Ōsaka-fu Hikishō-chō: Hikishō Chōyakuba, 1954.

Hirano-gō chōshi [History of the town of Hirano-*gō*], ed. Hirano-gō Kōekikai Ōsaka-fu Sumiyoshi-gun Hirano-*gō*: Hirano-*gō* Kōekikai, 1931.

Hiraoka shishi [History of the city of Hiraoka], I, IV, ed. Hiraoka Shishi Hensan Iinkai. Hiraoka: Hiraoka Shiyakusho, 1967, 1966.

Itami shishi [History of the city of Itami], II, ed. Itami Shishi Hensan Semmon Iinkai. Itami: Itami Shiyakusho, 1969.

Izumi shishi [History of the city of Izumi], II, ed. Izumi Shishi Hensan Iinkai. Ōsaka-fu Izumi-shi: Izumi Shiyakusho, 1968.

Izumi-sano shishi [History of the city of Izumi-sano], ed. Shibata Minoru. Izumi-sano-shi: Izumi-sano Shiyakusho, 1958.

Kami sonshi [History of the village of Kami], ed. Ōsaka Shiyakusho. Ōsaka: Ōsaka Shiyakusho, 1957.

Kaizuka shishi [History of the city of Kaizuka], I, III, ed. Kaizuka Shiyakusho. Ōsaka-fu Kaizuka-shi: Kaizuka Shiyakusho, 1955, 1958.

Kanan chōshi [History of the town of Kanan], ed. Kanan Chōshi Hensan Iinkai. Ōsaka-fu Minami Kawachi-gun Kanan-chō: Kanan Chōyakuba, 1968.

Kashihara chōshi [History of the town of Kashihara], ed. Kashihara Chōshi Kankōkai. Ōsaka-fu Naka Kawachi-gun Kashihara-chō: Kashihara Chōshi Kankōkai, 1955.

Kōbe shishi [History of the city of Kōbe], III, ed. Kōbe Shiyakusho. Kōbe: Kōbe Shiyakusho, 1922.

Miyazaki Antei. *Nōgyō zensho* [Complete treatise on agriculture] in Furushima Toshio and Aki Kōichi (eds.), *Kinsei kagaku shishō* [Scientific thought in the early modern period], I (vol. 62 of *Nihon shishō taikei* [Outline of Japanese thought]) (Tōkyō: Iwanami Shoten, 1972), pp. 67–167.

Moriguchi shishi [History of the city of Moriguchi], III, IV, V, ed. Moriguchi Shishi Hensan Iinkai. Moriguchi: Moriguchi Shiyakusho, 1966, 1962, 1966.

Nakatsu chōshi [History of the town of Nakatsu], ed. Nakatsu Kyōreikai. Ōsaka: Nakatsu Kyōreikai, 1939.

Nishinari gunshi [History of Nishinari *gun*], ed. Ōsaka-fu Nishinari Gunyakusho. Ōsaka: Ōsaka-fu Nishinari Gunyakusho, 1915.

Nishinomiya shishi [History of the city of Nishinomiya], II, IV, V, ed. Uozumi Sōgorō. Nishinomiya: Nishinomiya Shiyakusho, 1960, 1962, 1963.

Ōkura Nagatsune. *Menpo yōmu* [The important points of cotton farming] in Saigusa Hiroto (ed.), *Nihon kagaku koten zensho* [Complete set of Japanese scientific classics], II (Tōkyō: Asahi Shimbunsha, 1942), pp. 241–303. An annotated edition is in Furushima Toshio and Aki Kōichi (eds), *Kinsei kagaku shishō* [Scientific thought in the early modern period], I (vol. 62 of *Nihon shisō taikei* [Outline of Japanese thought]) (Tōkyō: Iwanami Shoten, 1972), pp. 169–217.

Ōsaka fushi [History of Ōsaka prefecture], I, ed. Ōsaka-fu. Ōsaka: Sobunkaku, 1970 (reprinted).

Ōsaka shishi [History of the city of Ōsaka], 8 vols., ed. Ōsaka-shi. Ōsaka: Ōsaka Shisanjikai, 1911–15 (reprinted Ōsaka: Seibundō, 1965).

Ōsaka shōgyōshi shiryō [Historical documents for the commercial history of Ōsaka], 31–2, ed. Ōsaka Shōkō Kaigisho. Ōsaka: Ōsaka Shōkō Kaigisho, 1964.

Ōsaka shōgyō shiryō [Collected historical documents on Ōsaka commerce], 6 vols., ed. Kuroha Hyōjirō. Ōsaka: Ōsaka Shōka Daigaku Keizai Kenkyūsho, 1934–40.

Sakai shishi [History of the city of Sakai], III, VI, ed. Sakai Shiyakusho. Sakai: Sakai Shiyakusho, 1930, 1929.

Sakai shishi zokuhen [History of the city of Sakai – continuation], I, ed. Obata Jun. Sakai: Sakai Shiyakusho, 1971.

Sayama chōshi [History of the town of Sayama], I, II, ed. Sayama Chōshi Hensan Iinkai. Ōsaka-fu Sayama-chō: Sayama Chōyakuba, 1967, 1966

Tokugawa jidai shōgyō sōsho [Tokugawa period commercial series], 3 vols., ed. Kokusho Kankōkai. Tōkyō: Kokusho Kankōkai, 1913–14 (reprinted 1965).

Tondabayashi shishi [History of the city of Tondabayashi], ed. Fujita Norikazu. Tondabayashi: Tondabayashi Shiyakusho, 1955.

Yao shishi [History of the city of Yao], 2 vols., ed. Yao Shishi Hensan Iinkai. Ōsaka-fu Yao-shi: Yao Shiyakusho, 1958, 1960.

B. JAPANESE SECONDARY SOURCES

Andō Sei-ichi. *Kinsei zaikata shōgyō no kenkyū* [Studies of rural commerce during the early modern period]. Tōkyō: Yoshikawa Kōbunkan, 1958.

——'Wakayama no wataneru' [Wakayama cotton flannel] in *Nihon sangyōshi taikei* [Systematic history of Japanese industry], 6 (*Kinki chihō*) (Tōkyō: Tōkyō Daigaku Shuppankai, 1960), pp. 347–50.

Arai Eiji. *Bakuhansei shakai no tenkai katei* [The process of social development under the *bakuhan* system]. Tōkyō: Shinseisha, 1965.

Asao Naohiro. 'Bunsei rokunen senshichi kason kokuso ni kansuru oboegaki' [Note on the 1007-village dispute of 1823], *Kinseishi kenkyū*, no. 9 (May 1955): 1–12.

Fujino Tamotsu. *Daimyō: Sono ryōkoku keiei* [Daimyo: The economic administration of their domains]. Tōkyō: Jimbutsu Ōraisha, 1964.

Fukushima Miyakura. 'Kinai watasaku no hensen to tame-ike kangai' [Changes in Kinai region cotton production and reservoir irrigation], *Historia*, 47 (March 1967): 25–42.

Furushima Toshio. *Nihon nōgyō gijutsushi* [History of Japanese agricultural technology]. Tōkyō: Taikaidō, 1949.

Furushima Toshio and Nagahara Keiji. *Shōhin seisan to kisei jinushisei – Kinsei*

Kinai nōgyō ni okeru [Commodity production and the parasitic landlord system – Concerning Kinai agriculture in early modern times]. Tōkyō: Tōkyō Daigaku Shuppankai, 1954.

Hatanaka Seiji. 'Kaseiki Naikai chi-iki ni okeru zaikata shōgyō shihon to han kenryoku' [Rural commercial capitalism along the Inland Sea and *han* political power in the first quarter of the nineteenth century], *Rekishigaku kenkyū*, 264 (April-May 1962): 78–82.

Hayashi Hideo. 'Bisai to Sainō no orimonogyō' [The weaving industry in western Owari and Minō] in *Nihon sangyōshi taikei* [Systematic history of Japanese industry], 5 (Chūbu chihō) (Tōkyō: Tōkyō Daigaku Shuppankai, 1960), pp. 26–53.

——*Zaikata momen tonya no shiteki tenkai* [The historical development of rural cotton cloth *tonya*]. Tōkyō: Hanawa Shobō, 1965.

Hayashi Reiko. 'Bakuhan seiteki shijō to santo shōgyō shihon' [The market structure of the *bakuhan* system and commercial capital in the three major cities], *Rekishigaku kenkyū*, 324 (May 1967): 35–9.

——'Edo jimawari keizaiken no seiritsu katei – Kuriwata-abura o chūshin to shite' [The formation of the Edo economic region – with emphasis on ginned cotton and oil] in Ōtsuka Hisao, Andō Yoshio, Matsuda Tomoo, and Sekiguchi Hisashi (eds.), *Shihon shugi no keisei to hatten* [The formation and development of capitalism] (Tōkyō: Tōkyō Daigaku Shuppankai, 1968), pp. 255–71.

——'Edo momen tonya nakama to Kantō momen' [Edo cotton cloth *tonya nakama* and Kantō cotton cloth], *Rekishigaku kenkyū*, 274 (March 1963): 30–42.

——*Edo tonya nakama no kenkyū – Bakuhan taiseika no toshi shōgyō shihon* [Studies of the Edo *tonya nakama* – Urban commercial capital under the Tokugawa shogunate]. Tōkyō: Ocha No Mizu Shobō, 1967.

——'Genroku-Kyōhōki ni okeru Edo tonya nakama no dōtai – Sanjūken kumi soshiki tonya o chūshin to shite' [The dynamics of Edo *tonya nakama* during the Genroku through Kyōhō periods (1688–1736) – Focusing on the thirty-house association of sundry goods *tonya*], *Shakai keizai shigaku*, 28, 3 (1963): 28–45.

——'Jūshichi seiki kōhan ni okeru enkakuchi shōgyō no tenkai – Kantō momen hattatsu zenshi' [The development of trade in remote regions during the latter half of the seventeenth century – The origins of the growth of the Kantō cotton cloth industry] in *Ryūtsū Keizai Daigaku kinen rombunshū* [Articles commemorating the opening of Ryūtsū Keizai University] (Ryūgasaki: Ryūtsū Keizai Daigaku, 1966), pp. 365–402.

——'Kaseiki ni okeru shōhin ryūtsū' [Commodity marketing in the Kasei (1804–29) period], *Rekishi kyōiku*, 12, 12 (1964): 10–15.

——'Kinsei chūkōki no shōgyō' [Commerce in the mid and late early modern period] in Toyoda Takeshi and Kodama Kōta (eds.), *Ryūtsūshi* [History of marketing), 1 (*Taikei Nihonshi sōsho* [Outline library of Japanese history], 13) (Tōkyō: Yamakawa Shuppansha, 1969), pp. 187–250.

——'Review of *Kinsei momen tonya no shiteki tenkai,* by Hayashi Hideo,' *Shigaku zasshi*, 74, 12 (1965): 73–81.

Honjō Eijirō. 'Tokugawa jidai no shio tonya' [The Tokugawa period salt *tonya*] in *Keizaishi kenkyū* (Kyōto: Kōbundō Shoten, 1920), pp. 250–80.

Honjō Eijirō (ed.). *Nihon keizaishi jiten* [Dictionary of Japanese economic history], 3 vols. Tōkyō: Nihon Hyōron Shinsha, 1940, 1954.

Horie Yasuzō. *Kinsei Nihon no keizai seisaku* [Japanese economic policy during the early modern period]. Tōkyō: Yūikaku, 1942.

Economic Institutional Change in Tokugawa Japan

——*Waga kuni kinsei no sembai seido* [The Japanese monopoly system in the early modern period). Tōkyō: Nihon Hyōronsha, 1933.

Hozumi Katsujirō. *Himeji han kokusan momen to Edo no momen tonya* [Himeji *han* domestic cotton cloth and Edo cotton cloth *tonya*]. Himeji, Hozumi Katsujirō, 1971.

——*Himeji han mengyō keizaishi* – *Himeji han no mengyō to Kawai Sunō* [Economic history of the Himeji *han* cotton industry – The Himeji *han* cotton industry and Kawai Sunō]. Himeji: Hozumi Katsujirō, 1962.

——*Himeji han mengyō keizaishi no kenkyū* [Studies in the economic history of the Himeji *han* cotton industry]. Himeji: Hozumi Katsujirō, 1970.

Inoue Kōji and Irimajiri Yoshinaga. *Keizai shigaku nyūmon* [Introduction to the study of economic history]. Tōkyō: Kōbunsha, 1966.

Inui Hiromi. 'Kinsei shokunin nakama no hatten katei – Ruikeiteki bunseki ni tsuite' [The development process for early modern artisan *nakama* – An analysis of similar types], *Chihōshi kenkyū*, 16, 3 (or no. 81) (June 1966): 43–57.

Irimajiri Yoshinaga. 'Bakumatsu Kinai nōson ni okeru "kokuso" no seikaku – Bunsei 6–7 nen no kokuso o chūshin to shite' (On the nature of legal proceedings in court as found in villages in the five home provinces) in *Kindaika to kōgyōka : Komatsu Yoshitaka kyōju kanreki kinen ronbunshū* [Modernization and industrialization: Essays commemorating the sixty-first birthday of Professor Yoshitaka Komatsu] (Tōkyō: Ichijō Shoten, 1968), pp. 53–82.

——*Tokugawa bakuhansei no kōzō to kaitai* [Structure and dissection of the Tokugawa *bakuhan* system]. Tōkyō: Yūshōdō Shoten, 1963.

Irimoto Masuo. 'Kantō no zaigō shōnin' [Rural merchants of Kantō], *Rekishigaku kenkyū*, 275 (April 1963): 16–25.

Itō Kōichi. 'Edo jidai no shijō no hattsu' [The growth of the market in the Edo period], *Rekishi kyōiku*, 7, 11 (1959): 27–33.

Kawakami Tadashi. 'Bakumatsuki Ōsaka momen tonya no keiei soshiki – Bunsei gannen eizairoku no shōkai' [The organization of Ōsaka cotton *tonya* financial management during the Bakumatsu period – Introduction of account books from 1818], *Chihōshi kenkyū*, 16, 6 (or no. 84) (December 1966): 15–28.

Kimura Motoi. 'Sandai kaikaku' [The three great reforms], *Nihon rekishi*, no. 200 (January 1965): 126–35.

Kitajima Masamoto. *Edo jidai* [The Edo period], Tōkyō: Iwanami Shoten, 1958, 1964.

——'Kaseiki o dō hyōka shitaru yoi ka?' [How should we best evaluate the first quarter of the nineteenth century?], *Rekishigaku kenkyū*, 264 (April-May 1962): 76–8.

——(ed.) *Edo shōgyō to Ise dana* [Edo commerce and Ise-based stores]. Tōkyō: Yoshikawa Kōbunkan, 1962, 1963.

Kōda Shigetomo. *Edo to Ōsaka* [Edo and Ōsaka], revised edition. Tōkyō: Fuzambō, 1942.

——*Nihon keizaishi kenkyū* [Studies of Japanese economic history]. Tōkyō: Ōokayama Shoten, 1928.

Kodama Shōzaburō. 'Kinsei kōki ni okeru shōhin ryūtsū to zaikata shōnin' [Commodity marketing and rural merchants in the late Tokugawa period], *Rekishigaku kenkyū*, 273 (February 1963): 9–14.

Kojima Shōji. 'Kawachi mensaku shirabe oboegaki' [Examination memo on Kawachi cotton cultivation], *Kamigata*, no. 86 (1938): 64–70.

Matsumoto Shirō. 'Edo no shokunin' [The artisans of Edo], *Nihon sangyōshi taikei*

[Systematic history of Japanese industry], 4 (*Kantō chihō*) (Tōkyō: Tōkyō Daigaku Shuppankai, 1959), pp. 43–53.

——'Edo no tonya nakama oyobi tonya shōnin ni tsuite' [Concerning the Edo *tonya nakama* and *tonya* merchants], *Rekishigaku kenkyū*, 264 (April-May 1962): 70–5.

——'Shōhin ryūtsū no hatten to ryūtsū kikō no saihensei' [The development of commodity marketing and the reorganization of the marketing system] in Furushima Toshio (ed.), *Nihon keizaishi taikei* [Outline of Japanese economic history], 4 (Tōkyō: Tōkyō Daigaku Shuppankai, 1965), pp. 87–130.

Mitsui Takafusa. See Crawcour, 'Some Observations on Merchants.'

Mitsuwa Katsuhiko. 'Kawachi no orimono to Kawachi momen ni tsuite' [Concerning Kawachi textiles and Kawachi cotton cloth], *Kamigata*, no. 86 (1938): 71–3.

Miyamoto Mataji. 'Bakuhan taiseika no shōgyō kikō to kari kumi no mondai' [The problem of temporary *kumi* in commercial systems under the *bakuhan* order], *Ōsaka Daigaku keizaigaku*, 7, 2 (July 1957): 1–32.

——'Bunsei rokunen Settsu-Kawachi 1007 mura no soshō no shiryō' [Documents on the 1823 lawsuit by 1007 villages in Settsu and Kawachi] in Miyamoto Mataji (ed.), *Nōson kōzō no shiteki bunseki* [Historical analysis of the structure of agricultural villages] (Tōkyō: Nihon Hyōron Shinsha, 1955), pp. 453–9.

——*Gaisetsu Nihon keizaishi* [Outline of Japanese economic history]. Tōkyō: Nihon Hyōron Shinsha, 1956, 1960,

——*Kabu nakama no kenkyū* [Studies of the *kabu nakama*]. Tōkyō: Yūikaku, 1938, 1958.

——*Kinsei shōnin ishiki no kenkyū* [Studies of merchant ideology in the early modern period]. Tōkyō: Yūikaku, 1941.

——*Nihon girudo no kaihō* [The emancipation of the Japanese guilds]. Ōsaka: Ōsaka Daigaku Keizai Gakubu Shakai Keizai Kenkyūshitsu, 1957.

——*Nihon kinsei tonyasei no kenkyū* [Studies of the Japanese *tonya* system during the early modern period]. Tōkyō: Tōe Shoin, 1951.

——*Nihon shōgyōshi* [A commercial history of Japan]. Tōkyō: Ryūginsha, 1943.

——*Nihon shōgyōshi gairon* [An introduction to Japanese commercial history]. Tōkyō: Sekai Shisōsha, 1954.

——*Ōsaka* [Ōsaka]. Tōkyō: Ibundō, 1957.

——*Ōsaka chōnin* [Merchants of Ōsaka]. Tōkyō: Kōbundō, 1957.

——*Ōsaka jimbutsūshi – Ōsaka o kizuita hito* [History of famous Ōsakans – Men who built Ōsaka]. Tōkyō: Kōbundō, 1960.

——(ed.). *Kinsei Ōsaka no bukka to rishi* [Prices and interest in Ōsaka during the early modern period]. Ōsaka: Miyamoto Mataji, 1963.

Miyazaki Antei. See section A.

Mori Sugio. 'Kawachi mensaku nōson no dōkō' [Trends in cotton cultivating villages in Kawachi], *Fuse shishi kenkyū kiyo*, no. 3 (July 1960). (The same article appeared in *Kinseishi kenkyū*, no. 29 (June 1960): 1–31).

——'Kinsei Kawachi no mensaku' [Cotton cultivation in Kawachi in the early modern period], *Fuse shishi kenkyū kiyo*, no. 24 (March 1963).

Nagano Susumu. 'Bakuhan taisei chūki no shijō kōzō ni tsuite no oboegaki' [Notes on market structure during the middle of the Tokugawa period] in Miyamoto Mataji (ed.), *Ōsaka no kenkyū : Kinsei Ōsaka no shōgyōshi – keieishiteki kenkyū* [Studies of Ōsaka: Studies of commercial and business management history in Ōsaka during the early modern period], 3 (Ōsaka: Seibundō, 1969), pp. 359–92.

——'Bakumatsuki ni okeru shijō kōzō ni tsuite' [Concerning market structure during the *bakumatsu* period], *Rekishigaku kenkyū*, 324 (May 1967): 39–42.

Economic Institutional Change in Tokugawa Japan

Nakabe Yoshiko. *Kinsei toshi no seiritsu to kōzō* [The establishment and structure of cities during the early modern period]. Tōkyō: Shinseisha, 1967.

——'Ōsaka shūhen zaigō machi no keisei' [The formation of rural towns in the Ōsaka region], part 1, *Historia*, no. 20 (1957): 34–42; part 2, *Historia*, no. 21 (1957): 46–48.

Nakai Nobuhiko. *Bakuhan shakai to shōhin ryūtsū* [*Bakuhan* society and commodity marketing]. Tōkyō: Hanawa Shobō, 1961. Cited as *Shōhin ryūtsū*.

——'Chōnin ukeoi shinden no seikaku to kinō – Kyū-kawasuji mensaku shinden no baai' [The character and function of *chōnin* contract reclaimed lands – The case of the Old Yamato river channel reclaimed lands in cotton cultivation], *Shigaku*, 24, 4 (1951): 494–547.

——'Kinsei toshi no hatten' [The development of cities in the early modern period] in *Iwanami kōza Nihon rekishi* [Iwanami series on Japanese history], vol. 11 or *Kinsei* 3 (Tōkyō: Iwanami Shoten, 1963), pp. 37–100. Cited as 'Toshi.'

——*Tenkanki bakuhansei no kenkyū – Hōreki-Temmeiki no keizai seisaku to shōhin ryūtsū* [Studies of the *bakuhan* system in a period of transition – Hōreki-Temmei period (1751–88) economic policy and commodity marketing]. Tōkyō: Hanawa Shobō, 1971.

Nakamura Nobuji. *Kinsei Yamato no shōhin ryūtsū* [Commodity marketing in Yamato in the early modern period]. Nara: Nakamura Nobuji, 1967.

Nihon Keizaishi jiten [Dictionary of Japanese economic history], 3 vols., ed. Honjō Eijirō. Tōkyō: Nihon Hyōron Shinsha, 1940, 1954.

Nihon rekishi daijiten [Encyclopedia of Japanese history], 22 vols., ed. Nihon Rekishi Daijiten Henshu Iinkai. Tōkyō: Kawade Shobō, 1956–60.

Ōishi Shinsaburō. 'Genroku-Kyōhō ki no keizai dankai' [The economic stages of the Genroku and Kyōhō periods] in Furushima Toshio (ed.), *Nihon keizaishi taikei* [Outline of Japanese economic history], 4 (Tōkyō: Tōkyō Daigaku Shuppankai, 1965), pp. 45–83.

——'Kyōhō kaikaku' [Kyōhō reforms] in *Iwanami kōza Nihon rekishi* [Iwanami series on Japanese history] (Tōkyō: Iwanami Shoten, 1963), vol. 11 or *Kinsei* 3, pp. 265–310.

——'Kyōhō kaikaku ni okeru Edo keizai ni tai suru Ōsaka no chii – Kyōhō kaikaku ni okeru shijō kōzō ni tsuite' [The position of Ōsaka relative to the economy of Edo during the Kyōhō reforms – Concerning the structure of the market during the Kyōhō reforms], *Nihon rekishi*, no. 191 (April 1964): 2–31. Cited as 'Kyōhō-Ōsaka.'

Ōishi Shinsaburō, Tsuda Hideo, Sakai Kōjin, and Yamamoto Hirobumi. *Nihon keizai shiron* [Discussion of Japanese economic history]. Tōkyō: Ocha No Mizu Shobō, 1967.

Oka Mitsuo. 'Banshū momen' [Harima cotton cloth] in *Nihon sangyōshi taikei* [Systematic history of Japanese industry], 6 (*Kinki chihō*) (Tōkyō: Tōkyō Daigaku Shuppankai, 1960), pp. 166–73.

——*Kinsei nōgyō keiei no tenkai – Jisaku keiei no shokeitai* [The evolution of agricultural management in early modern times – Various forms of self-cultivating management]. Kyōto: Minerva Shobō, 1966.

Okamoto Ryōichi. 'Tempō kaikaku' [Tempō reforms] in *Iwanami kōza Nihon rekishi* [Iwanami series on Japanese history], vol. 13 or *Kinsei* 5 (Tōkyō: Iwanami Shoten, 1964), pp. 209–50.

Okuda Shūzō. 'Kinsei Yamato no mensaku ni tsuite – Kinai mensaku in okeru sono chii' [Concerning cotton cultivation in Yamato in early modern times –

Its status with respect to cotton cultivation in the Kinai region], *Historia*, no. 11 (February 1955): 47–65.

Ōkura Nagatsune. See section A.

Ono Hitoshi. *Kinsei jōkamachi no kenkyū* [Research into castle towns in the early modern period]. Tōkyō: Ibundō, 1928.

Ono Masao. 'Kambun-Empōki no ryūtsū kikō' [Marketing structure in the Kambun-Empō period (1661–81)] in Furushima Toshio (ed.), *Nihon keizaishi taikei* [Outline of Japanese economic history], 3 (Tōkyō: Tōkyō Daigaku Shuppankai, 1965), pp. 351–81.

——'Kambunki ni okeru chūkei Shōgyō toshi no kōzō – Echizen Tsuruga-kō ni kansuru ikkōsatsu' [The structure of an intermediary commercial city during the Kambun period (1661–72) – Concerning the port of Tsuruga in Echizen], *Rekishigaku kenkyū*, no. 248 (December 1960): 17–27.

——'Okayama han ni okeru Kokura orimono ni tsuite no ikkōsatsu – Kaei-Anseiki o chūshin to shite' [An inquiry into Kokura textiles in Okayama *han* – Focusing on the period from 1848 to 1859] in Hōgetsu Keigo Sensei Kanreki Kinenkaihen, *Nihon shakai keizaishi kenkyū – Kinseihen* [Studies of Japanese social and economic history – Early modern period] (Tōkyō: Yoshikawa Kōbunkan, 1967), pp. 437–67.

——'Tempō ki o kaki to shita shijō kōzō no henka' [Change in market structure during the Tempō period], *Rekishigaku kenkyū*, no. 329 (October 1967): 1–2.

Ōsaka momengyō shi [History of the Ōsaka cotton cloth trade], ed. Ōsaka Momensho Kumiai. Ōsaka: Ōsaka Orimono Dōgyō Kumiai, 1936.

Ōta Kenichi. 'Bakumatsu ni okeru nōson kōgyō no tenkai katei – Okayama han Kojima chihō no baai' [The process of development for agricultural village industry in the Bakumatsu period – The case of the Kojima region of Okayama *han*], *Tochi seido shigaku*, no. 6 (vol. II, no. 2) (January 1960): 24–34.

Sakai Hitoshi. 'Kinai mensaku no shomondai' [Various problems of cotton cultivation in the Kinai region], *Historia*, no. 31 (1961): 27–38.

Sakata Yoshio. 'Meiji ishin to Tempō kaikaku' [The Meiji restoration and the Tempō reforms], *Jimbun gakuhō*, II (1952): 1–26.

Sakudō Yōtarō. 'Tokugawa chūki ni okeru shinyō seido no tenkai – Tokuni kinyū to zaisei no kansen o chūshin to shite' [The development of the credit system in the mid-Tokugawa period – With special reference to main routes of monetary circulation and finance], *Rekishigaku kenkyū*, 264 (April-May 1962): 66–70.

Sasaki Junnosuke. 'Bakuhan taisei ni okeru Kinai no chii ni tsuite' [Concerning the position of the Kinai region in the *bakuhan* system), *Hitotsubashi ronsō*, 47, 3 (1962): 325–39.

——'Bakuhan taisei no ichi dankai no shogakki ni tsuite' [Periodization of the first stage of the *bakuhan* system], *Rekishigaku kenkyū*, no. 260 (December 1961): 2–13.

Sekai rekishi jiten [Dictionary of world history], 18. Tōkyō: Heibonsha, 1953.

Shimbō Hiroshi. 'Kinai mensaku ni okeru shōhin seisan no hatten ni kansuru ikkōsatsu' [Examination of the development of commodity production with respect to Kinai cotton cultivation] in *Kōbe Keizai Daigaku sōritsu gojū shūnen kinen rombunshū* [Essays commemorating the fiftieth anniversary of the founding of Kōbe Economic University] (Kōbe: Kōbe Keizai Daigaku, 1953), pp. 491–531.

——'Tokugawaki ni okeru mensaku no hatten ni tsuite' [Concerning the development of cotton cultivation in the Tokugawa period], *Kokumin keizai zasshi*, 86, 2 (August 1952): 34–50.

Takahashi Kamekichi. *Tokugawa hōken keizai no kenkyū* [Studies of Tokugawa feudal economics]. Tōkyō: Senshinsha, 1932.

Takao Kazuhiko. 'Kan'eiki Kawachi no mensaku nōson ni tsuite' [Concerning cotton cultivating villages in Kawachi during the Kan'ei period (1624–43)]', *Kenkyū* (Kōbe Daigaku) no. 25 (March 1961): 1–68.

——'Ōsaka shūhen ni okeru mensaku no hatten to jinushisei no keisei' [The development of cotton cultivation and the formation of the landlord system in the Ōsaka region] in Rekishigaku kenkyūkai (ed.), *Meiji ishin to jinushisei* [The Meiji restoration and the landlord system] (Tōkyō: Iwanami Shoten, 1956), pp. 31–70.

——'Settsu Hirano-*gō* ni okeru mensaku no hatten' [The growth of cotton cultivation in Settsu Hirano-*gō*], *Shirin*, 34, 1–2 (January–February 1951): 713–33.

Takebe Yoshito. *Kawachi momen no kenkyū* [Studies of Kawachi cotton cloth]. Yao: Yao Shiritsu Kōminkannai Kyōdo Shiryō Kankōkai, 1957.

——'Kinki nōgyō no tenkai – Kawachi momen no hōkai to kinkō nōgyō no seiritsu' [The development of agriculture in the Kinki region – The decline of Kawachi cotton cloth and the realization of suburban agriculture], *Keizai kenkyū* (Ōsaka Furitsu Daigaku), no. 2 (March 1957): 27–54.

——'Sekkasen no mengyō' [The cotton industry in Settsu, Kawachi, and Izumi] in *Nihon sangyōshi taikei* [Systematic history of Japanese industry], 6 (*Kinki chihō*) (Tōkyō: Tōkyō Daigaku Shuppankai, 1960), pp. 127–65.

Takenaka Yasukazu and Kawakami Tadashi. *Nihon shōgyōshi* [History of Japanese commerce]. Kyōto: Minerva Shoten, 1965.

Takeuchi Makoto. 'Edo jidai toshi shōnin no dōkō – tokumi tonya no hensen' [Tendencies of urban merchants during the Edo period – Change in the *tōkumi tonya*], *Rekishi kyōiku*, 7, no. 11 (1959): 19–26.

——'Kinsei zenki no shōgyō' [Commerce in the beginning of the early modern period] in Toyoda Takeshi and Kodama Kōta (eds.), *Ryūtsūshi* [History of marketing], 1 (*Taikei Nihonshi sōsho* [Outline library of Japanese history], 13 (Tōkyō: Yamakawa Shuppansha, 1969), pp. 123–86.

Toyoda Takeshi. *Nihon no hōken toshi* [Japanese feudal cities]. Tōkyō: Iwanami Shoten, 1952, 1964.

Tsuchiya Takao. *Nihon keizaishi (Japanese Economic History)*. Tōkyō: Kōbundō, 1955, 1965.

Tsuda Hideo, 'Kansei kaikaku' [Kansei reforms] in *Iwanami kōza Nihon rekishi* [Iwanami series on Japanese history], vol. 12 or *Kinsei* 4 (Tōkyō: Iwanami Shoten, 1963), pp. 233–81.

——'Tempō kaikaku no keizaishiteki igi' [The economic-historical significance of the Tempō reforms] in Furushima Toshio (ed.), *Nihon keizaishi taikei* [Outline of Japanese economic history], 4 (Tōkyō: Tōkyō Daigaku Shuppankai, 1965), pp. 303–57.

Tsuji Tatsuya. 'Bakuseishi kara mita Kyōhō yori Tanuma e no katei ni tsuite' [Concerning the process of change from the Kyōhō to the Tanuma period as viewed from the political history of the shogunate], *Rekishigaku kenkyū*, 264 (April–May 1962): 63–6.

——'Kyōhō kaikaku ni okeru Edo shōnin nakama settei ni tsuite' [Concerning the establishment of Edo merchant *nakama* during the Kyōhō reforms], *Nihon rekishi*, no. 159 (September 1961): 14–20.

——*Kyōhō kaikaku no kenkyū* [Studies of the Kyōhō reforms]. Tōkyō: Sōbunsha, 1963.

Tsujiai Zenyotarō. *Kawachi momenfu* [Notes on Kawachi cotton cloth]. Tōkyō: Iseikatsu Kenkyūkai, 1965.

Wakita Osamu. *Kinsei hōken shakai no keizai kōzō* [The economic structure of feudal society in the early modern period]. Tōkyō: Ocha No Mizu Shobō, 1963.

Yagi Akihiro. *Kinsei no shōhin ryūtsū* [Commodity marketing during the early modern period]. Tōkyō: Hanawa Shobō, 1962.

Yamaguchi Kazuo. *Nihon keizaishi kōgi* [Lectures on Japanese economic history]. Tokyō: Tōkyō Daigaku Shuppankai, 1960.

Yamaguchi Tetsu. 'Obama, Tsuruga ni okeru kinsei shoki gōshō no sonzai keitai – Bakuhan taisei seiritsu ni kansuru ikkōsatsu' [The condition of wealthy merchants in Obama and Tsuruga in the beginning of the early modern period – A view of the *bakuhan* system during its origins], *Rekishigaku kenkyū*, no. 248 (December 1960): 1–16.

Yamaguchi Yukio. 'Hōken hōkaiki ni okeru Settsu Hirano-gō no henshitsu katei – Kuriwata no ryūtsū yori mitaru' [The process of change in Settsu Hirano-*gō* during the decline of feudalism – Viewed from the marketing of ginned cotton], *Historia*, no. 20 (1957): 43–56.

Yamazaki Ryūzō. 'Edo kōki ni okeru nōson keizai no hatten to nōminsō bunkai' [The economic development of agricultural villages and the decomposition of the peasant class in the late Edo period] in *Iwanami kōza Nihon rekishi* [Iwanami series on Japanese history], vol. 12 or *Kinsei* 4 (Tōkyō: Iwanami Shoten, 1963), pp. 331–74.

——'Kinsei kōki Settsu nōson ni okeru shōhin ryūtsū' [Commodity marketing in Settsu agricultural villages in the late Tokugawa period], (Ōsaka Shiritsu Daigaku) *Keizaigaku Nenpō*, no. 8 (1956): 59–141.

Yasuoka Shigeaki. 'Edo chūki ni okeru Ōsaka shijō no kōzō – maki tonya no funsō o tsūjite' [The structure of the Ōsaka market during the mid-Edo period – concerning disputes among the firewood *tonya*] in Yasuoka Shigeaki, *Nihon hōken keizai seisaku shiron – Keizai tōsei to bakuhan taisei* [A historical analysis of Japanese feudal economic policy – The *bakuhan* system and economic control]. Ōsaka: Ōsaka Daigaku Keizai Gakubu, 1959), pp. 45–78.

——'Edo chūki no Ōsaka ni okeru torihiki soshiki' [The trade structure of Ōsaka during the mid-Edo period], part I, *Dōshisha shōgaku*, vol. 16, no. 3 (November 1964): 290–307; part II, *Dōshisha shōgaku*, 16, 5 (February 1965): 589–625. Cited as 'Torihiki soshiki.'

——'Hiryōkoku ni tsuite' [Concerning private domains], *Dōshisha shōgaku*, 15, 2 (1963): 73–99.

——'Kinai ni okeru shōgyō tōsei' [Commercial control in the Kinai region] in Yasuoka Shigeaki, *Nihon hōken keizai seisaku shiron – Keizai tōsei to bakuhan taisei* [A historical analysis of Japanese feudal economic policy – The *bakuhan* system and economic control] (Ōsaka: Ōsaka Daigaku Keizai Gakubu, 1959), pp. 157–96. Cited as 'Shōgyō tōsei.'

——Ōsaka no hattatsu to kinsei shōgyō' [The development of Ōsaka and early modern commerce] in *Nihon sangyōshi taikei* [Outline of Japanese industrial history], 6, *Kinki chihō* [Kinki region] (Tōkyō: Tōkyō Daigaku Shuppankai, 1960), pp. 109–26.

Yokoi Tokifuyu. 'Tokugawashi jidai ni okeru Ōsaka no shōgyō' [The commercial history of Ōsaka during the Tokugawa family period] in Ōsaka Shōkō Kaigisho (ed.), *Ōsaka shōgyōshi shiryō*, 9 (Ōsaka: Ōsaka Shōkō Kaigishō, 1964), pp. 52–67.

Yoshinaga Akira. 'Tempō kaikaku ni tsuite – santo chūō shijō to han ryōiki, keizai to no kankei o chūshin ni' [Concerning the Tempō reforms – with special reference to the three urban central markets and the *han* domain economies and the effect on them], *Rekishigaku kenkyū*, no. 264 (April–May 1962): 82–6.

C. WESTERN LANGUAGE WORKS

Barbour, Violet. *Capitalism in Amsterdam in the 17th Century*. Ann Arbor: University of Michigan Press, 1963.

Befu, Harumi. 'Village Autonomy and Articulation with the State' in John W. Hall and Marius B. Jansen (eds.), *Studies in the Institutional History of Early Modern Japan* (Princeton: University Press, 1968), pp. 301–14.

Bellah, Robert N. *Tokugawa Religion: The Values of Pre-Industrial Japan*. Glencoe, Ill.: Free Press, 1957.

Bolitho, Harold. *The Fudai daimyo in the Tokugawa Settlement* (Ph.D. dissertation, Yale University, 1969). Ann Arbor, Mich.: University Microfilms, 1970, no. 70–2699.

Chambliss, William Jones. *Chiaraijima Village: Land Tenure, Taxation, and Local Trade, 1818–1884*. Tucson: University of Arizona Press for the Association for Asian Studies, 1965.

Choi, Kee Il, 'Technological Diffusion in Agriculture under the *Bakuhan* System,' *Journal of Asian Studies*, XXX, 4 (August 1971): 749–59.

——'Tokugawa Feudalism and the Emergence of the New Leaders of Early Modern Japan,' *Explorations in Entrepreneurial History*, 9, 2 (December 1956): 72–90.

Craig, Albert M. *Chōshū in the Meiji Restoration*. Cambridge, Mass.: Harvard University Press, 1961.

Crawcour, E. Sydney. 'Changes in Japanese Commerce in the Tokugawa Period.' *Journal of Asian Studies*, XXII, 4 (August 1963): 387–400.

——'The Development of a Credit System in Seventeenth-Century Japan,' *Journal of Economic History*, XXI, 3 (September 1961): 342–60. (Cited as 'Credit.')

——'Documentary Sources of Tokugawa Economic and Social History,' *Journal of Asian History*, XX, 3 (May 1961): 343–51.

——'Kawamura Zuiken: A Seventeenth-Century Entrepreneur,' *Transactions of the Asiatic Society of Japan*, third series, IX (1966): 1–23.

——'Money and Finance in Tokugawa Japan: A Review of Problems.' 1967–8 (mimeographed).

——'Notes on Shipping and Trade in Japan and the Ryukyus,' *Journal of Asian Studies*, XXIII, 3 (May 1964): 377–81.

——'Some Observations on Merchants, A translation of Mitsui Takafusa's *Chōnin Kōken Roku*, with an introduction and notes,' *Transactions of the Asiatic Society of Japan*, third series, VIII (1961): pp. 1–139.

——'The Tokugawa Heritage' in William W. Lockwood (ed.), *The State and Economic Enterprise in Japan* (Princeton: University Press, 1965), pp. 17–44.

—— and Kozo Yamamura. 'The Tokugawa Monetary System: 1787–1868,' *Economic Development and Cultural Change*, vol. 18, no. 4, part 1 (July 1970): 489–518.

Dore, R. P. *Education in Tokugawa Japan.* Berkeley and Los Angeles: University of California Press, 1965.
——'The Legacy of Tokugawa Education' in Marius B. Jansen (ed.), *Changing Japanese Attitudes toward Modernization* (Princeton: University Press, 1965), pp. 99–131.
Dorfman, Joseph. *Institutional Economics: Veblen, Commons, and Mitchell Reconsidered.* Berkeley and Los Angeles: University of California Press, 1963.
Dunn, C. J. *Everyday Life in Traditional Japan.* London: B. T. Batsford, 1969.
Eisenstadt, S. N. *Essays on Comparative Institutions.* New York: John Wiley and Sons, 1965.
——'Institutionalization and Change,' *American Sociological Review*, 29, 2 (April 1964): pp. 235–47.
Firth, Raymond (ed.). *Themes in Economic Anthropology* (A.S.A. monograph, no. 6). London, 1967.
Flershem, Robert G. 'Some Aspects of Japan Sea Shipping and Trade in the Tokugawa Period, 1603–1867,' *Proceedings of the American Philosophical Society*, 110, 3 (1966): 182–226.
——'Some Aspects of Japan Sea Trade in the Tokugawa Period,' *Journal of Asian Studies*, XXIII, 3 (May 1964): 405–16.
Furuta, Ryoichi and Yoshikazu Hirai. *A Short History of Japanese Merchant Shipping*, tr. and annotated Duncan Macfarlane. Tōkyō: Tokyo News Service, 1967.
Geertz, Clifford. *Peddlers and Princes: Social Change and Economic Modernization in Two Indonesian Towns.* Chicago: University of Chicago Press, 1963.
Golden Book Encyclopedia 16 vols. New York: Golden Press, 1959.
Hall, John Whitney. 'The Castle Town and Japan's Modern Urbanization' in John W. Hall and Marius B. Jansen (eds.), *Studies in the Institutional History of Early Modern Japan* (Princeton: University Press, 1968), pp. 169–88.
——'Foundations of the Modern Japanese Daimyo' in John W. Hall and Marius B. Jansen (eds.), *Studies in the Institutional History of Early Modern Japan* (Princeton: University Press, 1968), pp. 65–77.
——*Government and Local Power in Japan, 500 to 1700: A Study Based on Bizen Province.* Princeton: University Press, 1966.
——*Japan: From Prehistory to Modern Times.* New York: Delacorte Press, 1970.
——*Japanese History: A Guide to Japanese Reference and Research Materials.* Ann Arbor: University of Michigan Press, 1954.
——'Materials for the Study of Local History in Japan: Pre-Meiji Daimyo Records' in John W. Hall and Marius B. Jansen (eds.), *Studies in the Institutional History of Early Modern Japan* (Princeton: University Press, 1968), pp. 143–68.
——'The Nature of Traditional Society: Japan' in Robert E. Ward and Dankwart A. Rustow (eds.), *Political Modernization in Japan and Turkey* (Princeton: University Press, 1964), pp. 14–41.
——'The New Look of Tokugawa History' in John W. Hall and Marius B. Jansen (eds.), *Studies in the Institutional History of Early Modern Japan* (Princeton: University Press, 1968), pp. 55–64.
——*Tanuma Okitsugu, 1719–1788: Forerunner of Modern Japan.* Cambridge. Mass.: Harvard University Press, 1955.
——'Tokugawa Bakufu and the Merchant Class' in University of Michigan, Center for Japanese Studies, *Occasional Papers,* no. 1 (1951): 26–33.
——'Tokugawa Japan: 1800–1853' in James B. Crowley (ed.), *Modern East Asia:*

Essays in Interpretation (New York: Harcourt Brace and World, 1970), pp. 62–93.

—— and Marius B. Jansen (eds.), *Studies in the Institutional History of Early Modern Japan*. Princeton: University Press, 1968.

Hanley, Susan B. 'Population Trends and Economic Development in Tokugawa Japan: The Case of Bizen Province in Okayama,' *Daedalus*, 97, 2 (Spring 1968): 622–35.

——'Toward an Analysis of Demographic and Economic Change in Tokugawa Japan: A Village Study,' *Journal of Asian Studies*, XXXI, 3 (May 1972): 515–37.

—— and Kozo Yamamura. 'A Quiet Transformation in Tokugawa Economic History,' *Journal of Asian Studies*, XXX, 2 (February 1971): 373–84.

Henderson, Dan Fenno. *Conciliation and Japanese Law: Tokugawa and Modern*, 2 vols. Tōkyō: University of Tokyo Press, 1964.

——'The Evolution of Tokugawa Law' in John W. Hall and Marius B. Jansen (eds.), *Studies in the Institutional History of Early Modern Japan* (Princeton: University Press, 1968), pp. 203–29.

——'Some Aspects of Tokugawa Law,' *Washington University Law Review*, no. 27 (1952): 85–109.

Hirschmeier, Johannes S. V. D. *The Origins of Entrepreneurship in Meiji Japan*. Cambridge, Mass.: Harvard University Press, 1964.

Honjō, Eijirō. *Economic Theory and History of Japan in the Tokugawa Period*. New York: Russell and Russell, 1965.

——*The Social and Economic History of Japan*. New York: Russell and Russell, 1965.

Horie, Yasuzō. 'The Feudal States and the Commercial Society in the Tokugawa Period,' *Kyoto University Economic Review*, XXVIII, 2 (October 1958): 1–16.

Joy, Leonard. 'One Economist's View of the Relationship between Economics and Anthropology' in Raymond Firth (ed.), *Themes in Economic Anthropology* (London, 1967), pp. 29–46.

Kitano, Seiichi. 'Dozoku and Ie in Japan: The Meaning of Family Geneological Relationships' in Robert J. Smith and Richard K. Beardsley (eds.), *Japanese Culture: Its Development and Characteristics* (Chicago: Aldine Publishing Co., 1962), pp. 42–6.

Marshall, Byron K. *Capitalism and Nationalism in Prewar Japan: The Ideology of the Business Elite, 1868–1941*. Stanford: University Press, 1967.

McEwan, J. R. *The Political Writings of Ogyū Sorai*. Cambridge: University Press, 1962.

Mitsui, Takaharu. 'Chonin's Life under Feudalism,' *Cultural Nippon*, 8, 2 (1940): 65–96.

Miyamoto, Mataji. 'La Decadence et l'abolition des kabunakama,' *Ōsaka Economic Papers*, vol. V (1), no. 10 (August 1956): 9–32.

——'Economic and Social Development of Ōsaka,' *Ōsaka Economic Papers*, III, 1 (December 1954): 11–28.

——'Kabu-nakama, corporations des marchands du temps des Tokugawa, son organisation et ses fonctions,' *Ōsaka Economic Papers*, III, 2 (March 1955), 29–40.

——'The Merchants of Ōsaka,' *Ōsaka Economic Papers*, vol. VII (1), no. 14 (September 1958): 1–13.

Miyamoto Mataji, Sakudō Yōtarō, and Yasuba Yasukichi. 'Economic Development in Preindustrial Japan, 1859–1894,' *Journal of Economic History*, XXV, 4 (December 1965): 541–64.

Najita, Tetsuo. 'Ōshio Heihachirō (1793–1837)' in Albert M. Craig and Donald H.

Shively (eds.), *Personality in Japanese History* (Berkeley: University of California Press, 1970), pp. 155–79.

Nakane, Chie. *Kinship and Economic Organization in Rural Japan.* New York: Humanities Press, 1967.

Nakano, Takashi. 'Merchant *Dozoku* of Japan: Process of their change from the Tokugawa period to pre-war times.' 1966 (mimeographed).

Neville, Edward L. 'The Development of Transportation in Japan: A Case Study of Okayama *Han*, 1600–1868,' Unpublished Ph.D. Thesis, University of Michigan, 1958.

Nisbet, Robert. *Social Change and History.* New York: Oxford University Press, 1969.

Norman, E. Herbert. *Japan's Emergence as a Modern State : Political and Economic Problems of the Meiji Period.* New York: Institute of Pacific Relations, 1940.

Rosovsky, Henry. *Capital Formation in Japan: 1868–1940.* Glencoe, Ill.: Free Press, 1961.

Sahlins, Marshall D. 'On the Sociology of Primitive Exchange' in A.S.A. Monograph no. 1, *The Relevance of Models for Social Anthropology* (London: Tavistock, 1965), pp. 139–236.

Sakai, Robert. 'The Satsuma-Ryukyu Trade and the Tokugawa Seclusion Policy,' *Journal of Asian Studies*, XXIII, 3 (May 1964): 391–403.

Sakudō, Yōtarō. 'Grown of Securities Market in Feudal Japan,' *Ōsaka Economic Papers*, vol. VIII (2), no. 17 (March 1960): 25–40.

Sansom, George B. *A History of Japan, 1334–1615.* Stanford: University Press, 1961.

——*A History of Japan, 1615–1867.* Stanford: University Press, 1963.

——*Japan: A Short Cultural History*, revised edition. New York: Appleton-Century-Crofts, 1943.

——*The Western World and Japan: A Study in the Interaction of European and Asiatic Cultures.* New York: Alfred A. Knopf, 1958.

Service, Elman R. 'The Law of Evolutionary Potential' in Marshall D. Sahlins and Elman R. Service (eds.), *Evolution and Culture* (Ann Arbor: University of Michigan Press, 1960), pp. 93–122.

Sheldon, Charles David. '"Pre-Modern" Merchants and Modernization in Japan,' *Modern Asian Studies*, vol. 5, part 3 (July 1971): 193–206.

——*The Rise of the Merchant Class in Tokugawa Japan, 1600–1868: An Introductory Survey.* Locust Valley, N.Y.: J. J. Augustin for the Association of Asian Studies, 1958.

Shimbō, Hiroshi. 'A Study of the Growth of Cotton Production for the Market in the Tokugawa Era – Especially in the Settsu-Kawachi District,' *Kōbe University Economic Review*, I (1955): 55–70.

Shiraishi, Bon. 'Merchants of Ōsaka,' *Japan Quarterly*, 5 (1958): pp. 169–77.

Shively, Donald H. 'Bakufu versus Kabuki' in John W. Hall and Marius B. Jansen (eds.), *Studies in the Institutional History of Early Modern Japan* (Princeton: University Press, 1968), pp. 231–61.

——'Sumptuary Regulation and Status in Early Tokugawa Japan,' *Harvard Journal of Asiatic Studies*, 25 (1964–5): 123–64.

——'Tokugawa Tsunayoshi, The Genroku Shogun' in Albert M. Craig and Donald H. Shively (eds.), *Personality in Japanese History* (Berkeley: University of California Press, 1970), pp. 85–126.

Sjoberg, Gideon. *The Preindustrial City : Past and Present.* Glencoe, Ill: Free Press, 1960.

Skinner, G. William. 'Marketing and Social Structure in Rural China,' part I, *Journal of Asian Studies*, XXIV, 1 (November 1964): 3–43; part II, *Journal of Asian Studies*, XXIV, 2 (February 1965): 195–228.

Smith, Neil Skene. 'An Introduction to Some Japanese Economic Writings of the 18th Century,' *Transactions of the Asiatic Society of Japan*, second series, 11 (1934): 33–104.

——'Materials on Japanese Social and Economic History: Tokugawa Japan,' *Transactions of the Asiatic Society of Japan*, second series, 14 (1937): 1–176.

Smith, Robert J. 'Pre-Industrial Urbanism in Japan: A Consideration of Multiple Traditions in a Feudal Society,' *Economic Development and Cultural Change*, 9, 1 (October 1960): pp. 241–57.

Smith, Thomas C. *The Agrarian Origins of Modern Japan*. Stanford: University Press, 1959.

——'Farm Family By-employments in Preindustrial Japan,' *Journal of Economic History*, XXIX, 4 (December 1969): 687–715.

——'The Japanese Village in the Seventeenth Century' in John W. Hall and Marius B. Jansen (eds.), *Studies in the Institutional History of Early Modern Japan* (Princeton: University Press, 1968), pp. 263–82.

——'The Land Tax in the Tokugawa Period' in John W. Hall and Marius B. Jansen (eds.), *Studies in the Institutional History of Early Modern Japan* (Princeton: University Press, 1968), pp. 283–99.

——'Ōkura Nagatsune and the Technologists' in Albert M. Craig and Donald H. Shively (eds.), *Personality in Japanese History* (Berkeley: University of California Press, 1970), pp. 127–54.

Takekoshi, Yoshisaburō. *The Economic Aspects of the History of the Civilization of Japan*, 3 vols. London: George Allen and Unwin, 1930.

Totman, Conrad D. *Politics in the Tokugawa Bakufu, 1600–1843*. Cambridge, Mass.: Harvard University Press, 1967.

Toyoda Takeshi. *A History of Pre-Meiji Commerce in Japan*. Tōkyō: Kokusai Bunka Shinkokai, 1969

Tsukahira, Toshio G. *Feudal Control in Tokugawa Japan: The Sankin Kōtai System*. Cambridge, Mass.: East Asian Research Center, 1966.

Wald, Royal Jules. 'The Development of Ōsaka during the Sixteenth Century.' Unpublished M. A. thesis, University of California at Berkeley, 1947.

Yamamura, Kozo. 'Agenda for Asian Economic History,' *Journal of Economic History*, XXXI, 1 (March 1971): 199–207.

——'The Increasing Poverty of the Samurai in Tokugawa Japan, 1600–1868,' *Journal of Economic History*, XXXI, 2 (June 1971): 378–406.

Yazaki, Takeo. *Social Change and the City in Japan: From earliest times through the Industrial Revolution*. Tōkyō: Japan Publications Trading Co., 1968.

Yoshihara, Kunio. 'Foreign Trade during the Tokugawa Period.' Ann Arbor Mich., 1968 (mimeographed).

——'The Tokugawa Monetary and Credit System.' Ann Arbor, Mich., 1968 (mimeographed).

Glossary

Abura-*machi kumi* (*Aburamachi kumi shokoku momen shi-ire shōbainin*): Abura-*machi kumi* of regional cotton cloth warehousing merchants

bakufu: Tokugawa house government or shogunate, presided over by the *shogun* and headquartered in Edo

bu: Unit of land equal to $\frac{1}{30}$ *se* and $\frac{1}{300}$ *tan*

chō: suffix meaning block, neighborhood, or town; unit of land equal to 10 *tan* or 2.45 acres

chōnin: urban residents excluding samurai

cloth *tonya nakama* (*momen tonya nakama*): cotton cloth *tonya nakama*

cotton shipping *nakama* (*wata kaitsugi tsumi tonya nakama*): cotton buying and shipping *tonya nakama*

cotton *tonya nakama* (*sansho wataichi tonya nakama*): seed and ginned cotton *tonya nakama*

daimyo: feudal lord possessing a domain assessed at over 10 000 *koku* productivity in rice

Edo *kumi* (*Edo kumi shi-ire tsumi tonya*): Edo *kumi* of cotton cloth warehousing and shipping *tonya*

fu: suffix meaning prefecture

fun: unit of weight equal to $\frac{1}{10}$ *momme*

furegaki: edict issued by the Tokugawa *bakufu*

gō: suffix meaning district or village

Go-Kinai merchants: association of cotton merchants in Kyōto, Hachiman, Hirano-*gō*, Sakai, and Nishinomiya linked to the Ōsaka cotton shipping *nakama*

gun: suffix meaning district or county

han: the domain of a daimyo

handa: fields with elevated dry sections and lower wet sections in which cotton and rice could be grown simultaneously

hatamoto: retainers of the Tokugawa house enfeoffed with domains assessed at less than 10 000 *koku* productivity

Higashibori *kumi* (*Higashibori kumi momen shi-ire tsumi tonya*): Higashibori *kumi* of cotton cloth warehousing and shipping *tonya*

kabu: membership share or license held by members of *kabu nakama*

kabu nakama: a limited membership craft or trade association, authorized by the *bakufu* or *han*, in which members were issued certificates or licenses called *kabu*

kan or *kamme*: unit of weight equal to 1000 *momme*, 3.75 kg, or 8.72 lb; also used as a unit of silver by weight

Kantō: the region surrounding Edo which included 8 provinces

kin: unit of weight equal to 1.32 lb, but which varied regionally during the Tokugawa period from 220 to 300 *momme*

Kinai: the region around the cities of Ōsaka and Kyōto including the provinces of Settsu, Kawachi, Izumi, Yamato, and Yamashiro

225

Kita *kumi* (*Kita kumi shokoku momen shōbainin*) : Kita *kumi* of regional cotton cloth traders

koku : unit of capacity equal to 180 l, 44.8 gal, or 4.96 bu

kokudaka : productive capacity of a ricefield in *koku* of rice; assessed output of agricultural land converted into *koku* of rice as the base for tax levies

konnyaku : a starch food made from a tuberous root called 'devil's tongue'

Kuboji *kumi :* association of cotton cloth traders in the Yao area

kuri wata : ginned cotton

kumi; group; often used to designate sub-groups of larger *nakama* associations; suffix meaning section as in the sub-divisions of Ōsaka

kumiai : merchant group or association

kuni : province

machi : urban block or neighborhood; suffix used for place names in cities; town

machi bugyō : city magistrate

mai silver: unit of silver currency equal to 43 *momme* silver by weight

momen : cotton cloth

momme or *me :* unit of weight equal to 3.75 g or 0.1325 oz.; also used as a unit of silver by weight

mon : 1/1000 *kan;* unit of copper currency

mura : suffix meaning village

myōga or *myōga kin :* licensing fees paid by merchant groups to the Tokugawa *bakufu*, normally paid annually

nakagai : jobber, broker, or intermediary merchant or processor

nakama : a craft or trade association

ryō : unit of gold currency; one *ryō* gold was equal in value to approximately 60 *momme* silver for most of the Tokugawa period, but fluctuated considerably particularly in the late Tokugawa period when its value relative to silver increased

Sakai-*suji kumi* (*Sakai-suji kumi shokoku momen shi-ire shōbainin*): Sakai-*suji kumi* of regional cotton cloth warehousing merchants

sake : fermented alcoholic beverage made from rice

samurai: member of the hereditary warrior class

sankin kōtai : alternate attendance system under which daimyo spent half their time in Edo and half their time in their domains and were required to leave their immediate families and some major retainers in Edo as hostages to insure their loyalty to the Tokugawa house

se : unit of land equal to $\frac{1}{10}$ *tan*

seven *kumi nakama* (*nanakumi momenya nakama*): seven *kumi* cotton cloth dealers *nakama*

shi : suffix meaning city

shinomaki : carded cotton fibers

shogun : head of the Tokugawa house and leader of the Tokugawa *bakufu*

shogunate: government of the *shogun* or *bakufu*

suji : suffix for north-south streets in Ōsaka

tan : unit of land equal to 0.245 acres; roll of cloth approximately 12 yd in length suitable for making one garment

Temma *kumi* (*Temma kumiai momen shōbainin*): Temma *kumiai* of cotton cloth traders

tōkumi tonya nakama: association of ten *kumi* of Edo *tonya* including merchants active in the cotton trade who held a monopoly on cotton exports from Ōsaka to Edo

tonya: wholesale merchants, processors, or shippers; *tonya*, pronounced *toiya* in Ōsaka, referred to either individual merchants and artisans or to a merchant house

tonya nakama: trade association composed of wholesale merchants, processors, or shippers

Uemachi *kumi* (*Uemachi momen nakagai kumi*): Uemachi *kumi* of cotton cloth *nakagai*

wata: cotton; normally designates seed cotton

wataya nakama: cotton dealers and processors *nakama*

Yamanoneki *kumi*: association of cotton cloth traders from east of Yao

Yao *kumi*: association of cotton cloth traders from around Yao

yoriya: rural cloth buyers associated with *kabu nakama*

Index